A HART LIFE

By Colin Hart & Dick Allix

"For Ronnie, a diminutive figure of a man with a giant heart and an even bigger voice. The world misses you."

A HART LIFE

By Colin Hart & Dick Allix

WP
WYMER
PUBLISHING
Bedford, England

First published in Great Britain in 2011
by Wymer Publishing
PO Box 155, Bedford, MK40 2YX
www.wymerpublishing.co.uk
Tel: 01234 326691

First edition. Copyright © 2011 Colin Hart, Dick Allix / Wymer Publishing.

ISBN 978-0-9557542-7-2

Edited by Jerry Bloom.

Typeset by Wymer UK.
Printed and bound in Great Britain by
MPG Biddles Ltd
King's Lynn, Norfolk

A catalogue record for this book is available from the British Library.

Cover design by Michelle Greenaway.
Front cover photo © Colin Hart.

CONTENTS

" Play me that beat, boys and lose my Soul,
I wanna get lost in that Rock & Roll"

Jim Croce

FOREWORD

I've spent a large portion of my life with Colin and we have shared many an adventure and a laugh, on and off the road. He was present at many pivotal moments in the lives of some strange, eccentric and creative personalities. And he has a lot of tales to tell. It is illuminating to see a different interpretation of events over the last forty years or so, even if sometimes they don't tally with the way things were, or at least the way I recall them. But this is his book and he, quite fairly, is viewing it from his own perspective. He has done well to even attempt, let alone finish, a book recounting his unusual life. So far...

Roger Glover
January 2011

FOREWORD

I remember him coming home at Christmas: My brother and I had to be quiet for the first day or so while our Uncle Colin, only vaguely discernible through the frosted glass door of Grandma Hart's spare bedroom, got over his jetlag. And then he'd come to life and the presents would come out - exotic things from distant places with which we'd impress our school friends after the holidays. (I particularly remember the almost mythical digital watches and electronic calculators he brought us from Japan in the early days.) Steve and I loved all this of course, especially since it wasn't exactly the kind of stuff we could have found at the South Shields branch of Woolworths, but in retrospect there were other reasons why his visits were so special. He completed the family, he was great to have around, and we always wished we could see more of him.

Even more memorable than the Christmases, therefore, were the rare occasions when the Rainbow bandwagon would hitch up at Newcastle City Hall and the whole family would go along. I'll never forget the visceral thrill that first time, sitting in the wings on a flight case, within reaching distance of the keyboards. The blackout, the sudden roar of the crowd, and the voice of Judy Garland: "we must be over the rainbow…" And then that ear splitting, stomach-clenching wall of sound as the band kicked in. I was 12 years old. Although it's true that there's nothing quite like a symphony orchestra in full cry, the sheer adrenaline rush of that night remained unmatched until I conducted Smoke on the Water with the massed forces of the LSO, Deep Purple and guests at the Albert Hall more than twenty years later.

In spite of the tantalizing "go" at his keyboards Don Airey so generously allowed me at a sound check on the 'Difficult To Cure' tour (as documented in this book), my thoughts of following in his footsteps were really just daydreams. Gesturing towards the bank of synthesizers on that occasion, Don had said, "mind, not one of these is as good as a grand piano", and I guess I took that to heart. I certainly knew that Ritchie was just being kind to a precocious kid when he said that if I ever needed a job, I knew where to come. So I stuck to that grand piano, and eventually became a conductor.

But thanks to Colin, I finally succeeded in squaring the childhood dream with grown-up reality at the Royal Albert Hall in September 1999, and on that joyfully insane tour, an incredible feat of logistics which would simply have ground to a halt on about the third day if it hadn't been for Colin, for Charlie Lewis, and the general good will of all concerned. It remains the longest continuous period I have ever been able to spend with Uncle Colin, a belated opportunity to try and make up for the fact that the band and crew knew him so much better than I did. As a child, his lifestyle had seemed so glamorous to me. Now that I got the chance to experience at first hand the rather more complicated truth, my admiration for him went on an exponential curve. It was one of the happiest times of my life - the musical bonds and family ties all coming together with perfect synchronicity.

Over the course of the concerts, I got everyone involved to sign my conducting score of the Concerto. Back at that first Rainbow show, in my autograph book, Ronnie James Dio had written, "you've got an incredible uncle by the way". A couple of decades on, after the second Albert Hall show, I reminded him of this and he wrote: "To Paul, who always knew this would happen - Colin is still the best…"

At the other end of the road, on the last day of the Japanese tour, in March 2001, I asked Colin to sign the score. He took it away, obviously waiting for a suitably quiet moment, and later that night it reappeared in my dressing room with the following message, written in his distinctive hand:

"Once upon a time, there was a small boy named Mann who I used to bounce around on my knee. Before I noticed, this Mann had become a Mann I admire and am extremely proud of. Well done, that Mann!
Yer little uncle, Colin"

Full circle. I'm extremely proud too.

For some of the European concerts, as is also related in this book, we were provided with a fleet of very posh Audi cars in which to drive from place to place. Jon Lord and I usually travelled together, but on one occasion Colin joined us, I suppose having been given a day off from his duties as luggage driver. All the cars were equipped with a state of the art sat nav system, and on an autobahn somewhere, the rather husky feminine voice of the computer informed us that after two hundred yards we should turn left. "Aye', Colin said, "I'll have fucked her by the end of the tour."

Which proves that while you can take the boy out of South Shields, you can't take South Shields out of the boy. I think I'd be right in saying that goes for both of us.

So what this book tells is the absorbing, occasionally outrageous, and ultimately moving story of what 'me little Uncle' was doing all that time I was growing up. It's a unique piece of rock 'n' roll history. I hope you enjoy reading it as much as I did.

Paul Mann
Henley-on-Thames, UK
September 6th 2009

PREFACE

olin Hart devoted over thirty years of his life to one of the greatest bunch of rock musicians in the world - Deep Purple and Ritchie Blackmore's Rainbow. He was their tour manager for most of that time. This is his story and indeed theirs; a tale of excess in terms of greed, petulance, anger and devotion. It is counter balanced by extremes of pure talent, showmanship and, of course musicianship. He was the constant 'man in the middle' through all of the break ups, make-ups and revolving door line-up changes.

Joining them at twenty-four years old and leaving with a curt email dismissal thirty years later, he was there, every step of their rock 'n' roll way. It's not a tale of dishing the dirt by a dismissed aggrieved ex-employee, its rather a story of two of the most innovative, often copied, rock bands; seen through the eyes, ears and emotions of their 'Mother Hen' (as Jon Lord described him). He was their minder, chauffeur, carer, provider, protector, father confessor and confidant. In truth he is the only one who can tell this tale of both bands as he was the only one there on the road throughout the life of, not one, but both gigantic bands. Read on, it was a wild ride.

Dick Allix

CHAPTER ONE
SOUTH SHIELDS

South Shields - its 350 miles or so north of London in the United Kingdom as opposed to The Magic Kingdom which is somewhere else entirely. It's on the North Sea coast at the mouth of the majestic river Tyne; yes that Tyne that Lindisfarne sang about with fog on it. It's where I was born and grew up until I left some thirty-four years ago to journey, well, on the road to rock. I now live in Florida, near the Magic Kingdom, where I pay my taxes and have sunk permanent roots. It's my home. I doubt I will ever return to 'Shields'. It's been quite a trip from there to here.

Back in 1969, I was about to embark on a journey that I could never have envisaged. Perhaps if I had, I'd have turned around and gone back to Warwick Road, back to my mam and dad, cut my shoulder length hair and got a proper job. Mmmmmm, Nah, I wouldn't!

A life in this business of rock music amplifies every emotion that 'ordinary folk' perhaps never experience. Incredible highs, bottomless lows, but as a tour manager they, thankfully for the most part, are other peoples, you are just the observer and most times the individual who has to deal with the aftermath of those emotional roller coasters.

Tour managers; we are a rare breed. We are the glue that keeps most rock stars... no ALL rock stars, together. We are travel agents, father confessors, child minders and dog walkers, keepers of secrets and tellers of lies (for the best possible reasons), bankers, procurers, fixers of every imaginable whim, amateur doctors, chemists, psychiatrists, even gaolers. We get 'em to the show, outta the show, on the stage and off it. To the hotel, airport, recording studio, TV and radio station, just about any place that they or their management ordain, usually to the complete annihilation of any of your own, rapidly diminishing personal life. But that's the job description - you don't like it then there's a rather long queue to take your place, buddy.

So, where to begin? I guess the start would be good. Oh, if your browsing in a book shop wondering whether this book is worth the asking price and as usual, have flicked through the photo's and are now reading this opening page, its about my life with the many manifestations of Deep Purple and, of course, Mr Ritchie Blackmore's Rainbow. A thirty-year 'marriage' to not one, but two of the legendary bands and rock icons of all time. It has been an extraordinary life, one that has nearly killed me, but one I would not have swapped with any one else. It has taken me all over the world many times over, to almost every country and city worthy of the name and some that weren't. I've experienced gob smacking cruelty and heart busting kindness from folk you least expect it from. You see, over those years most bands and stars have met and played with my 'guys', either on the way up, when being on the bill with 'Purple' was a career builder, or on the way down, when it plainly wasn't. Purple and Rainbow were 'musicians bands', they could play, I mean really play and sing too, of course. I'm sure, for a lot of aspiring musicians, watching Purple was like a tutorial. You either went away inspired or you just went away and cursed your ineptitude. The magical, and to most folk, the best line up of Paice, Blackmore, Lord, Gillan and Glover was unequalled, but of course ultimately unsustainable. You'll see why - just buy the damn book! This ain't a library, bro!

It was the spring of 1969; I was a roadie in South Shields driving a rather a nice red transit, full of band instruments for a band called Toby Twirl. They were the house band for the Bailey Organisation, a company that ran over a dozen nightclubs throughout England. It was the height of the sixties pop and rock explosion. They were pretty good and who knew, might go places.

I'd had a good upbringing. My dad, Eddie, worked for the local Government Treasurer's Department as the Rating Officer and my mam, Betty, was, as you were in those days, a housewife, working occasionally for the big department store in town, Binns, in the accounting department. My life as a lad in 'Shields' had been happy, though not spectacular, much the same as millions of other 'Baby Boomers' of The Sixties. My first school, at the age of five, was Horsley Hill Elementary, then onto Mortimer Road Secondary at eleven. That would make it 1958 and popular music, unbeknownst to me, was a-changin'. Buddy Holly had 'Peggy Sue' in the US Charts while Elvis was number 1. In England, Presley dominated with 'Jailhouse Rock' and 'Don't' at No.3 and No.4

respectively. You heard him all the time at South Shields Fair on the sea front. It operated the summer long and was a magnet for every hot-blooded teenager. Whizzing around on the 'Waltzer' to "Paralyzed' is still attractive today, though perhaps now I would lose my lunch.

I often spent my Saturdays at Whitley Bay ice rink which was quite a complicated journey involving a bus from my house to Shields market place, then a ferry across the River Tyne to North Shields followed by another bus to the rink. I had to have been keen, thinking about it now. Years later they built a rink a lot closer in Sunderland where bands like Free cut their teeth on their way to dizzier heights. My abiding musical memory of Whitley Bay rink is skating round to the sounds of Paul Anka's 'Diana' and to Elvis, which, by the nature of the venue acquired a wicked echo. I was a pretty fair skater, even had my own, none of this queuing up to rent 'em, how cool was that! If getting there was a trek, finding the money to fund it was always a task. A combination of pocket money, the proceeds of a Sunday paper round and begging from "me mam" usually got it sorted with some left over for a bag of greasy chips (fries to my American readers) on the way home. Little did I realise that I'd be back to Whitley Bay years later with Rainbow!

It would now be 1960 or thereabouts and our English scene had still not caught up. Our stars of the time were Michael Holliday, Tommy Steele (the first real English rocker who went mainstream, into movies like 'Half A Sixpence' and, as a result, dead boring very quickly), and Petula Clark! I don't think many TV sets did the hotel high dive from that lot. I listened then to Radio Luxembourg at night, beamed from darkest Europe (as mainstream radio in England was appalling). It was the only place really that you could hear all this new stuff from America like Danny And The Juniors, Jerry Lee Lewis and Little Richard. A certain young Richard Blackmore was about 250 miles south in Heston, close to London Airport, about the same time, and pricking his ears up to this exciting music called rock 'n' roll.

At school, I kept tight with two friends, Geoff Tate and Billy Borthwick. We were never a 'gang' as such; any old lady could have taken us all on and kicked our arses. We were mates and had a common interest in pop music and soccer, which I played very badly. I still play now in Florida, forty years on, for a merry bunch of 'Ex Pats'. I kid myself it keeps me fit, but it's for the social life really. Anyway, I digress.

I took my exams and left school to go to the Marine And Technical

College to study architectural drawing for a further two years, while securing a job in The Borough Engineer's Department. Eddie, I'm sure, had a hand in that. Job security and all that, which was fine. He cared, God bless him. You only realise that when it's too late to say thanks. I passed the entry exam and went to work at the Town Hall: A proper civil servant in a proper nice suit. I'd be eighteen, it would be 1965 and the beat boom was in full swing. The Rolling Stones, The Beatles, The Kinks, and Manfred Mann. The Brits had taken over. Mind you, Petula Clark was still having hits.* She sure had staying power. Motown was making headway too, with The Supremes, Temptations, and Marvin Gaye: A veritable musical buffet. For me though, it was The Beatles, first, last and everywhere in between. Had you told me then that I'd spend some time in the company of George Harrison in the years to come, I would have considered you mad.

By this time, my mam Betty had been ill, not that I had realised it at the time. I learned afterwards that she'd been having terrible pains in the back of the neck and to the back of her head for weeks prior to having her first stroke. She was rushed into hospital where dad and I spent most of the night. She then suffered another stroke while she was unconscious with the first. It was a miracle she pulled through and without, mercifully, any paralysis. The upshot was it meant us moving to a small ground floor apartment to avoid her having to work so hard on a big house and climb stairs. It only had one bedroom, a kitchen / diner and a posh front room. There wasn't a lot of room for me, especially as I was now topping out at 6' 3". I remember being upset at the time because I had a big bedroom and a huge attic where I had all my Beatles pictures and assorted posters all over the walls in the old house. Warwick Road was very small by comparison which forced me to get rid of a lot of the memorabilia, but you've only got one mam, so the disappointment I felt I kept to myself. Hey, it could've have been way worse, and was for most people in the North.

Eddie was an amateur entertainer or 'turn' as they called 'em in the North of England. I never understood why though. Perhaps it was because they could 'turn' themselves to most forms of entertainment. Eddie's act was a comedian / singer, playing the ukulele and he went out, on average, twice a week. He didn't rehearse that much, but I would hear

---

* Clark secured three of her biggest hits during the Beatlemainia era, including three top ten singles, of which two achieved silver disc status and 'Downtown' (No. 2, November 1964), achieved Gold.

4

him thrash out a few numbers in his bedroom now and again. I only ever remember going to see him play live once, at The Old Time Music Hall in Newcastle. He was very good although I did feel a bit embarrassed for reasons that are unclear now. I wish that I could have seen him more. Anyway, I guess that's what gave me the entertainment bug. There were always entertainers and amateur dramatic type people calling round our house and they seemed so... well... alive.

By the time we moved to 47 Warwick Road from that nice place nearby at 181 Grosvenor Road, my elder sister Carol by four years, had left our previous home in High Meadows. (That's one before Grosvenor Road, we moved a lot - try to keep up!) She had married David, a solicitors cashier two years earlier in 1963 at Glebe Methodist Church. When she moved out, it gave me the BIG bedroom in the back, which was a real treat; one a lad could get used too. Carol's birthday is on Christmas Eve and I can remember as a kid that it always slightly pissed me off as she appeared to get 'two Christmases', little realising or caring when it was pointed out, that she hadn't had a birthday in the proceeding twelve months. I think she regarded me as a bit of as pest, after all she had been 'top dog' for four years until I had arrived to wind Eddie round my little finger. Much more of Carol and David later as their lives too, interweave directly with the 'Purps' in the years yet to come. Intrigued eh?

Music now filled my life and I'd spend all my spare time going to see local bands and hanging out with them, whilst still being a 'suit' during the day at the Town Hall. I'd had a motorbike licence from the age of sixteen, and then passed my driving test for a car, first time, a year later. I remember nearly killing the driving test examiner during the 'emergency stop' part of the test. He shouted stop and I did, perhaps a tad too forcefully, his seat instantly folded forward at the same time catapulting all the crap on the back seat onto him including a natty umbrella, which gave him a serious whack on the head. I remember gripping the steering wheel so hard it hurt, to stop myself from laughing out loud. Amazingly, he still passed me! Mam and Dad paid for the test and although they had a car, neither of them could drive which on reflection was a bit odd! So, then I used to take dad out while he learned. It's usually the other way round, but us Harts never were conventional. In view of this Eddie would let me use the car to go out on the town, albeit reluctantly. Well, you see there was history, as I'd borrowed his motor scooter once to go to college, the year before, and it got stolen! Bastards! It was recovered however and I had to go to court as a witness. Yet his reticence remained to hand over the keys to his car, go figure!

I then persuaded Eddie to help me buy a van, so I could drive a local bunch of lads who had a band, around to local gigs. The method of persuasion followed a clearly worked out cunning plan, which stood me well through out my childhood. Work on me Mam for a couple of days, she then softened him up nicely and I followed up with whatever I wanted at a suitable and well-timed mellow moment right into the end zone. Touchdown! It rarely failed and looking back now, I doubt if he was fooled for an instant.

For me to be driving bands around was like, hey, if you can't play in 'em, then try the next best thing. Well, I had tried to learn the guitar, but could never get past the standard three-chord bash. What's the matter with that, I hear you say, there are some pretty famous rockers who never did either! I used to borrow my cousins electric guitar for months at a time. I actually played in front of a live audience while on holiday at a summer camp we used to go to. I can't remember now who it was with, but we did a Beatles song which contained a chord unknown to me at the time or even now, so I just sort of drifted past it without hitting the strings. I gripped the neck so tightly that my fingers bled from the rusty strings. The guitar was in tune when I started, but badly out by the time I finished. Never again!

The first van was a Bedford with two wooden bench seats down each side. I can't remember the cost now, but it was an astronomical amount to me then and I could not have done it without Eddie. I agreed to pay him back and did, as I was able to generate more money per night being a roadie than I could get per week working at the Town Hall. (Now either roadies were over paid, or the Town Hall practised slavery - it's worth checking!) Trouble was the van used to leave an oil slick bigger than the Exxon Valdez outside the house, which didn't go down too well with the neighbours. It used to leak terrible exhaust fumes inside too, making it necessary to use the nifty sliding drivers door to breath. That was a bugger on a winter's night, but it did keep the band unnaturally quiet which, at times, was a distinct blessing.

It was great, a huge buzz, going to gigs most weekends and even during the week. It was all I got up for every day. The first band to avail themselves of my services was a school band that featured one Dave Bainbridge and Kenny Mountain on guitars. They were a good little outfit

6

who played school dances, YMCA's and the odd Working Men's Club. I then got a gig with "The Jazz Board", who had their own vehicle, which I then drove. It was a big old ambulance, in which we managed to squeeze everyone, including the gear and any one else who happened to turn up. I actually played drums at one of their rehearsals when the drummer failed to show. That's when I discovered I couldn't play drums either! No rhythm see. Speaking of drummers, Nigel Olsen played with them before he went off with Elton John. Thought I'd drop that in. Why? I haven't a clue. Of course the ambulance was also a big hit with the neighbours, you know, to go with the oil slick. A big white thingy sitting in the road with my red van also up the drive merrily dripping away. Boy, was I Mr Popularity and I bet Eddie and Betty got missed off a few cheese and wine party invites too!

It was about this time that I met Jimi Hendrix for the first time. The Jazz Board would be a regular at the New Cellar Club in South Shields on Fowler Street when Jimi was slated to appear.* I showed up in the afternoon, having 'disappeared' from the Town Hall, to get a look at a 'real' band in action. I met the roadie, whose name I should remember, but can't and offered to give him a hand getting the gear up the stairs. He gladly accepted (funny that!) and was delighted when I provided him with much needed fuses to get Jimi's Marshall rig running from the previous night's beating. (Well, it's the sort of stuff everyone carries in their pockets just in case Jimi Hendrix is in a fix, isn't it? Well, us Geordies do!) I was happy to oblige and nipped out to the van to get some. I offered the use of an amp and did bring one up, but not sure if it was used for the show. I was a bit flustered at the time, to say the least!

So that's how I got to meet THE MAN himself, introduced as "The guy who helped us out today". He was such a polite, quiet, shy, sweet man off stage, but Jesus, what a show! The Cellar Club was really jumping that night and seemed about as full as they used to allow back then. As far as their set, I can't remember what they played, other than it was an incredible show and they played for ages for a band in their league. It was over an hour, easily. I stayed to help them out with the equipment and also to hopefully retrieve my fuses; after all I might have bumped into our Eric the God the next night! I was astonished to see the roadie kicking the 4 x 12's down concrete stairs at the back of the building, saying "no one will

---

* Wednesday 1st February 1967

notice the difference tomorrow night". I made sure that I didn't pick up too many of his habits that night. From what I recall they kept the fuses, so I had to scramble the next day at Darlington to replace all the fuses I'd nicked out of the amps!

It was at one of The Jazz Board shows that I came to the attention of a local band who was better than the average - Toby Twirl, who said they'd heard I was a reliable sort of chap and would I be interested in a permanent professional position (steady at the back), driving their brand new Ford Transit. (Be still my beating heart! Roadie heaven - bite fist in anticipation). I agreed before they finished the sentence showing suitable inscrutability. "Have I been too eager?" I asked myself. It would, I thought, increase my income by about eight times my weekly Town Hall pay and I'd get to take the van home too. Those poor neighbours. Well, at least the ambulance would be history! So there it was - per chance officially a full time, professional roadie!

However, they did work almost every night! (This would be the back end of 1967). The workload of being out every night and working at the Town Hall every day would prove to be too much. Not that the work at the Town Hall was a stretch. It involved answering the phone; dealing with complaints (well, nobody rings to sing your praises, odd that!), sometimes going face to face with the darling general public over streetlights that were out or cracked paving stones that Mrs. Smith has taken a tumble over whilst walking the dog. I then would send a report to the appropriate department. I went to college for that?

The end of each day couldn't come quick enough to dump the suit, jump into the jeans and T-shirt and head off into the night till 2am or 3am, then back at work by 8.30am. Even at 19 years of age, burn out beckoned, so I had to quit to go full time with the band. So now I had to tell my boss, but worse yet, tell Eddie! The boss was the easy part and I did it prior to telling Eddie so there would be no turning back. Well, actually, working to the well-used plan, I told me Mam first and then she'd break it to Eddie. She refused! Help! Abandoned at my hour of need. Nothing for it, I just blurted it out and he took instant physical retribution. Wasn't that bad as dear Eddie wasn't that way inclined, but I'd really pissed him off this time. I could kinda tell. It came as a one slap, one word boogie. You know how it goes, slap "pension", slap "lifetime job", slap "security" each word uttered on the down stroke. None of that, of course, meant anything to me then, but those words have come back to haunt me since.

As Eddie saw it, I was throwing away a steady career, a job for life and for what? Yet I saw it that I was only nineteen going on twenty, single with a long exciting life ahead of me. I had no commitments, so why not, for just a couple of years, have some fun. I really didn't think that 'a couple of years' would be the rest of my life.

CHAPTER TWO
TOBY TWIRL THE NIGHT AWAY

So my new job unfolded. Out most nights, back in the early hours, sleep 'til noon and out again. Toby Twirl's date sheet was handled by Eve Colling at the Bailey Club headquarters in South Shields housed in The Latino Club. That's where I met Diane Butchart, Linda Irving and Carol Cotlarz, the terrific trio who ran the front of house operation. The Latino became the first place to stop after a show, as it stayed open really late and where I'd hang out on nights off. I became quite a permanent fixture there. Di, Carol and Linda were great fun to be around and I felt comfortable there. It was also very handy to be able to walk past the line waiting to get in and piss everyone off, hah!

I met a lot of big names that played at the club. The Casuals were one of my big favourites (you remember 'Jesamine' and 'Adios Amour', no? Please yourself) and I got to help them out doing the 'double'. That's playing an early show in Newcastle with a late show ten miles back at The Latino. I got nothing for it (no change there then) other than to see them play fourteen shows in week. Well, I thought it was cool at the time!

Now and again, I'd also get asked by Eve to take some visiting artistes around the area whilst they fulfilled a contract for Bailey's. One such band was 'The Ivy Benson All Girl Band.' A fifteen piece swing band, I guess is the best description and they were pretty good if you liked that sort of thing. I was warned by the front office not to 'mess' with them, but frankly there wasn't the opportunity. I caused quite a stir though walking into all night cafes followed by fifteen young women! Your speechless now, aren't you? There was also a trio of lovelies called 'The She Trinity' that I ferried around for a week, too. All the good jobs, eh!

As the good vibes of Toby Twirl spread, and their single, 'Back in Time' was getting some serious airplay, we often got to support the big name bands of the time, as well as many cabaret acts and singers. One such top name was Long John Baldry, on a windy night in Middlesbrough.

He was enjoying a certain amount of fame at the time with the single 'When The Heartaches Begin', which was a sizeable hit.* It was the era of the power ballad, you see. John Baldry was called 'Long' for a very good reason. Now I'm tall at 6' 3" and he towered over me, must have been 6' 8", maybe even 6' 10". The single was not representative of his music at all, however. It was a 'sell out' really.

Baldry's music was the blues at which he was a consummate master. His pick up musicians read like a who's who - Rod Stewart (backing vocals) and Elton John (keyboards, what else) to name but two. John Baldry was also unashamedly gay, which probably went a long way in explaining Reg Dwight's presence on keyboards. This was just prior to him transforming himself into Elton John, meeting Bernie Taupin and, well, we all know what happened after that. Baldry's band members certainly all seemed to appreciate their leaders musical influence and his leadership. His mere presence was, to say the least, charismatic. Reg Dwight, at that time, was somewhat plump and very, very, shy with no hint of the worldwide stardom and the outrageous behaviour that was just around the corner. Baldry, I heard, when the fame dissipated, went off to Canada and became a very successful DJ and sadly passed away in 2005.** Who could tell what the future had in store for any of us at that time.

Another big local band around this time was The Influence, fronted by a blonde haired, multi instrumentalist named John Miles. John was unbelievable, could play anything and sang the balls off most of his contemporaries. If you know your music history, you'll know he went on to a career, first as a solo performer and had a huge hit with 'Music'† and later as one of the world's most sought after musical directors. He has fronted and led all Tina Turner's bands throughout her illustrious career (post Ike) and Joe Cocker's too.

I first met him when I was still at school, this would be before he formed The Influence and I would try to get to see him as often as I could. I think I drove him nuts back then requesting the same song every time I saw him. It was called 'Melinda'. I've run into John many times over in the last thirty years, including a memorable 'piss up' in Hamburg in Goldie's Bar. I even put his name forward to replace Ian Gillan (in 1989). I called John to ask the question and he said he would like time to consider

---

* 'When The Heartaches Begin' reached number one on the UK charts on 22nd November 1967.
** Baldry passed away at the Vancouver General Hospital, at 10:30pm on 21st July after fighting a severe chest infection.
† 'Music' reached number 3 in the UK charts in March 1976.

the offer. He had the good taste to subsequently decline, probably appreciating more than me at the time, that his musical style wasn't Purple's. I still think that it would have been an intriguing and successful mix, though! I went to see him when he was leading Joe Cocker's Band in the mid nineties in Connecticut. Like the good guy he is, he got a special box for some friends and I, which really racked me up some valuable Brownie points at the time. If you appreciate good music, played to its best and sung to perfection, check out John Miles, you won't be disappointed. His great work leading Tina Turner's band throughout all its success is legendary.

So, back to the plot. As I said, it was 1969 and it was a Sunday afternoon. I was relaxing after a heavy gig the night before, when the phone rang and it was Di from the club, who by this time was my girlfriend. She said that Stu (Somerville), Toby Twirls bass player, who lived north of the Tyne in Morpeth, had gone out into the North Sea in his kayak and had not returned. His parents were worried. Now Stu was often taken with going out offshore in his kayak, have a bit paddle around, chill out and return, but the North Sea off that coast is not exactly Malibu, it is seriously cold even in the summer with rip tides and current surges, but Stu was local, experienced, so probably would not take risks. I went straight to the club to meet Diane. We were pretty close, confidantes, I guess. I'd often pick her up after she finished work, go to a party or simply drive her home. We'd talk for hours outside her home, shoot the breeze as they say today.

As the afternoon stretched into evening, we, and others searched the shoreline for Stu or his boat, but neither showed up and alas they never would. The police were called, the coastguard too, but poor Stu had gone. Neither he nor his kayak was ever found and it broke the band's spirit. It was a tragedy and even to this day I have not got to grips with it. I just imagine him on some island, somewhere, hanging out.

With Toby Twirl in disarray, I was at a loose end. I hung around the club, doing odd jobs, helping out with other bands, but getting increasingly bored. I had some good drinking mates then, who were the ever-present Geoff Tate, Billy Borthwick and Diane's younger brother, Malcolm who had just started to go to sea as a cabin boy, so was only around when he came back from trips. The days dragged into weeks and then months. My relationship with Diane was at an end, but the friendship has endured to this day. She remains a very close friend, so I guess those days meant a lot to both of us. Soon she had started to date the drummer of Vanity Fare, Dick Allix. They were a tight five-piece harmony band from London, who had three hits from 1968 to 1969, the biggest being probably 'Hitchin' A Ride' which went gold and was a big top five hit in America.* They played the club and Diane and Dick hit it off. I got to know the band socially as well, when they played in the North, either in South Shields or Newcastle, ten miles west. Dick is the co-author of this book, and married to Diane, so he, too, was to play an on going part of my life - the cast assembles!

However all of that was still in the future. One day, Diane phoned and asked me what I was doing right then. Nothing, as she well knew. It seemed Mick Minto; Vanity Fare's head roadie had taken an unscheduled Hammond organ sleigh ride down the back fire escape of a Birmingham club at the wrong end! Mick, son, you should have been on the back, not the front, duh! Any way, he was in hospital (no shit!) and a replacement was sought. Did I want the gig? I didn't need asking twice. I phoned Dick at their hotel in Birmingham. He told me what had happened to the erstwhile Mick and would I like to run things for now and I'd still have a job when Mick returned, as they were one short anyway on the road crew. I do not remember what the wage was and it didn't matter anyway. It was my ticket out of Shields, out of a cramped home and out to an exciting world, I hoped, with a pro band that were in the charts, for God's sake.

I met the band at the hotel, well; actually it was a rather small hotel. Aw shit, back to a cramped bedroom and now I'm sharing! Vanity Fare were much maligned and dismissed as a 'here today, gone tomorrow' pop band. Yet, like so many other bands that were tarred with the same brush, they had real talent, but crap, over bearing, hold all the aces, management. They could sing so well, real goose bump harmonies, but suffered from bad material and bad gigs. In England in the sixties, you either played cabaret clubs of which there were dozens for a week a time, or universities and colleges. The latter were tougher, but way more rewarding. The former, a piece of cake and lots of it, mucho commission for management and the bands not in your hair! Vanity Fare wanted to play colleges, wanted to play more intricate stuff, but that wasn't chart stuff, it was the stuff of albums and frowned upon by their management who wanted quick, three-minute pop ditties that turned a quick buck and required no in-depth thought process.

* Vanity Fare's biggest UK hit was 'Early In The Morning', which reached number 8.
'Hitchin' A Ride' only reached number 16 on the UK charts but was a million seller in America.

The band, drums (Dick), keyboards (Barry Landeman, Ex-Brinsley Schwarz), lead guitar (Eddie Wheeler), bass (Tony Jarrett), and lead vocals (Trevor Brice) were forever disagreeing over direction. Dick and Barry shared a flat in London, Trevor lived close by in Shepherd Bush with his girlfriend, Jackie, whilst the other two guys, who were married, lived in Kent, about thirty miles away. Rehearsals were tough to organise and murder to behold when they did happen. Dick and Barry, being single and in London went to see other bands socially and were into, what can be best described as album bands, such as Yes, Cream, Jimi Hendrix et al who were just emerging on the London club scene. They wanted Vanity Fare to write their own stuff as, hitherto, all the records had been written for them. They believed any long-term future for the band lay in a hit album, not instant pop singles. The management did not agree, nor did the other band members, or perhaps they did, but feared the effort to achieve it. Way easier to hit the cabaret trail, whack out an hour of hits and covers, albeit fantastically well, and then retire with some local lovely for a quick shag and a pizza. Rehearsals, forgeddaboutit!

As for me, it was easy and it was a big change. This was my first intro into the big time where I had the equipment truck to myself (the band travelling in a large American station wagon which weren't exactly two a penny on British streets in the sixties) and I could ride around like a star with all the lipstick-smeared messages of endearment all over it. I just loved my time with them. Cabaret, their main style of gig, didn't take a huge PA rig, lights, sound, and a road crew of twenty or more. That would come a bit later with some other guys! Usually, we'd settle into a city for a week. The band would top the bill at the top club and play Sunday through Saturday for an hour and a bit each night. The bit was the encore, but you guessed that. One load in, one sound check prior to opening night and a load out on the final night. If everyone got really greedy, management and club, the band would do the old 'double' like The Casuals, that is do an early show at one club and a late show at one nearby, maybe twenty miles apart. That took a bit more out of me and the road crew as Barry and Dick always insisted on their own keyboards and drum kit. It wasn't always possible which resulted in Barry, in particular, 'going off on one'. Dick was more easy going, but still disliked playing on a strange kit. Most clubs were city centre with the worst access possible for gear, which Mick, of course, knew to his cost. All of this was prior to the release of 'Hitchin A Ride'. The band had had two hits previously with 'I

Live For The Sun' and 'Early In The Morning', which kept them gigging relentlessly. When "Hitchin" was released, it was an instant hit everywhere, which only made the situation worse as far as gigs were concerned. More clubs, better pay, same musical differences, more arguments.

My living arrangements, however, were troublesome. No problem, of course, when we were on the road, but I had to have a base in London or somewhere close. For a time I stayed in a caravan, which was awful, until I moved in with Trevor's mum and dad in Rochester, Kent, about thirty miles south east of London.

Then the band hit gold in America. The record reached the Top Five and a tour was planned. This would break the mould and the monotony for everyone, band, road crew, management. Dick came to see me and gave me the worst news possible. I wouldn't be going. CMA, the American Agents would put together an American crew and only Mick Minto would go as tour manager. I would be left behind on a retainer. I was gutted, heartbroken, pissed off and everything in-between. They added to the heartbreak by asking me to fill in the time by going home to Shields and to clean all the lipstick messages off my beloved Ford Transit! So back to Warwick Road and to me Mam and Dad's and driving around in an anonymous blue van to boot! Once they were back, the lipstick returned, thank God, and I felt better especially as I had taken the opportunity to fit out the cab with a big set of speakers! Well, a roadie has got standards, you know! However, I did secretly vow that, given the opportunity, I'd leave Vanity Fare and tour America myself, which was my dream. In a funny way, Vanity Fare had done me a very big favour.

Vanity Fare's stage act bore no resemblance to their hits, which were short, ultra pop three-minute jobs. The show was way more interesting. They were bloody good singers and more than adequate musicians, but the combination was terrific. It contained mainly American band covers ranging from Three Dog Night, to The Doobie Brothers, to The Beach Boys to Blood, Sweat and Tears. Some of that was way over the heads of your average cabaret audience, but the band knew how to 'sell' a song. Dick and Barry were forever 'discovering' what was new in The US charts and pushing the rest of the band into putting the songs into the show. There was little resistance, as the other three had no fresh ideas anyway, content to have a great life with little effort off stage.

The band did lots of TV work and must have appeared on 'Top Of

The Pops', the top rated UK chart show a gazillion times. They were special days as, for me, it was a piece of cake. No back line as it was either just singing 'live' to back tracks or a straight mime. Drums, keyboards and guitars were just props, so to speak. It took all day, which meant a 10am call for a show that went out live at 7.30pm that night. Eight hours of tedium would be the most fitting description with a five-minute spell of semi-excitement. The studio was always full of nubiles, just waiting to get laid, but who disappeared immediately the show finished. I guess they were really there for the thirty minutes of fame on screen, rather than us lads, but you only realise that years later!

Strange but true moment. At one of Vanity Fare's recording sessions, the trainee engineer at De Lane Lea Studios was Martin Birch who was working under Roy Thomas Baker. He was later Purple and Rainbow's engineer, co-producer and went on to work with Iron Maiden among others. It's a small village, isn't it?

Strange but true moment No. 2 - One March night in London, when the band had a night off, Dick and Barry went with Status Quo drummer, John Coghlan to see a new band showcasing at the Speakeasy. They'd heard some album tracks of the band at De Lane Lea and wanted to check them out. You guessed it, Deep Purple - Ritchie Blackmore, Jon Lord, Ian Paice, Nick Simper and Rod Evans. Dick said that Paicey was staggeringly good and he had seen Blackmore with Screaming Lord Sutch and Lordy with The Artwoods before and knew their worth. It was a night to see the reality of where Vanity Fare stood long-term and if it had a future, as he had just seen the future of rock music, and it was Deep Purple, not Vanity Fare.

One year on in October 1970, we all trouped back to South Shields, not to do a gig but to attend the wedding of Dick and Diane. Today, thirty-four years later, they are still together and are my best friends. A big change had also come about for my sister Carol and her husband David who by now had two sons, Paul who had been born in 1965 and Stephen three years later. David had decided that he should leave the legal profession for a higher calling and went off to Theological College in Birmingham to study. After his 'graduation' as a Methodist minister, he and Carol would devote their lives to the pastoral and actual care of seafarers by running "The Royal National Mission to Deep Sea Fishermen" in some of the most remote and wildest fishing ports up and down the British Isles. Quite a contrast to my life and pretty humbling when I think about it. Way to go, sis!

By this time, my living arrangements back in London had became somewhat fluid and I had changed to sharing a flat in Ealing, West London with my old school chum Billy Borthwick from Shields with his girlfriend and dog. My favourite living place was years later, (before I moved to America permanently), in Westbourne Grove near Central London where I shared a three bed-roomed flat. More of that later.

With Billy, fate took a hand. He was, by now, also a roadie with Matthews Southern Comfort and was set to tour the States. They'd just had a massive hit with 'Woodstock' on both sides of the Atlantic. Yet Billy, mad as ever, was busted walking down Earls Court Road in London in broad daylight smoking a joint. He walked right past a policeman who had no option than to spoil Billy's day. That meant no visa, no job and MSC short one roadie. Billy, being the thoughtful chap I'd known half my life, asked me to cover for him. Step into the breach Mr Hart, this is your lucky day! Billy, bless him, put me forward, I subsequently got the call, got the positive nod, and out I rushed to get a visa. Now I had to tell Vanity Fare! I went to Dick who did all the band's admin (whether he liked it or not), and, much to my relief didn't make a fuss. He realised how choked I'd been when they'd gone to the States without me the year before and to Australia after that and felt this was an opportunity I should not miss. Little did he know I had my visa already and the job with MSC, so I would have gone anyway! (*Well I do know now! Dick*) This was 1971 and my exciting future beckoned, although just how exciting, I of course, had no idea. You know how you want things in life so bad that you kinda dismiss the uncomfortable bits that just might go with it? Well, touring the States for me was a big; I mean a huge ambition, so taking the job with MSC was, well, without any regard for 'the small print' really. The small print being that I was their roadie, their ONLY roadie on a rather large tour of a country I'd never been to before. Oh, well? What could go wrong?

CHAPTER THREE
FACES I SEE

Heathrow, passport and visa, bag checked. My first flight, ever, Pan Am 101 to JFK New York: A mixture of elation, blind terror and pure undiluted excitement at the great adventure on which I was embarking. I arranged to meet MSC's tour manager at Heathrow and off we went for, what I believed then, was a short two-month trip of a lifetime. The band was not on the same flight as they were to travel the next day. When we got to "Kennedy", we went by cab to a U-Haul Truck hire company in Queens where I was given a wad of dollars, a slap on the back and given an address on the outskirts of Boston. The simple brief was to get the truck, come back to Pan Am freight, load the gear and drive 250 miles due north and that was before my tea!

Never one to flinch or dodge a challenge, I smiled, probably mumbled 'no problem', and then disappeared in the same cab into the fleshpots of Manhattan to await the bands arrival. Now, I know, to some, Queens in New York is home, but to me it was 'the badlands' of mythical proportions. That was and still is the trouble with me, I read too much and I also have a vivid imagination, so on this occasion I felt a little, shall we say, uneasy. I told myself not to be so daft. I'd driven down the notorious Scottswood Road in Newcastle in the dead of night without turning a hair, so just what could Queens dish up that hadn't jumped out at me on a Saturday night after Newcastle United had lost at home! Absolutely nothing! Whistling a happy tune, I swaggered into the truck hire emporium. I don't know quite what I expected - something big and well, American. All chrome and testosterone. Ah Colin, not for the first time and believe me, not for the last, you heard the Laurel and Hardy 'let down' refrain. You know how it goes "Wah, wah, wah whaaaah". Well, it wasn't big, but was certainly American, had terrible rusty chrome (I think) and had an absolute, and distinct lack of balls! It looked as if everything in New York, at sometime or another had backed into it. It was paid for up front by a voucher that was in the pack I'd been given, so brief formalities over (no such thing then as "please check your vehicle over, kind sir, before you leave"), just a nod in the general direction and an unspoken take it or leave it.

I gave a cheery wave, as only us Geordies can, and headed in the general direction of the airport, feeling pretty deflated. Now you have to remember I'd just flown seven hours and, to my little body clock, it was around ten at night plus I'd sunk the odd one or two cold ones on the flight. The prospect of finding the Van Wick Expressway to the airport, finding Pan Am Freight, loading the gear, connecting to the right freeway out again AND driving on my own to Boston was, to say the least, a tad daunting. It was a baptism of fire and the first hard lesson in what was to be expected of road crew by management and bands. I silently vowed that, in the future, if it was up to me, my decision, I'd appreciate the time a task would take the crew and budget the time and expense accordingly. There would be many tough times ahead when good employees were to be our strength. Treated right they came through for you, treated like beasts of burden and they would not.

Feeding on adrenalin, I navigated the back streets of Queens and out to "Kennedy". In fairness, the truck hire guys had given me a map of sorts and good directions. Mastering the knack of driving on the wrong side of the road and on the wrong side of the truck, however, was another matter, although I had previously driven in Europe with Toby Twirl in a van with right hand drive and driving on the right, so it wasn't too bad. I eventually rocked up at the freight dock of the airline. Carnet papers in hand (which, thankfully, I had also encountered before with Toby Twirl on a couple of occasions), I offered them to the customs guy with as much confidence as I could muster. He looked me up and down like they did then and despite an obvious mistrust of long hair, stamped the forms and directed me to the gear.

In comparison to what would develop with Deep Purple, there was not much to sweat over. A standard backline amp rig, standard drum kit and guitars including one nifty pedal steel guitar. No big task, which was a good job, as there was only me to load and it was a very small, aged truck. (We were set to use house PA's on the warm up gigs).

I'm blessed with a wonderful sense of direction, which has got me out of many a problem over the years. I can picture where I am and where I have to get to by imagining I am, say a mile above ground, like looking down on my location and understanding where each landmark is relative to me and especially where north is. A bit like SatNav today! It's hard to explain, but it works. Getting from "Kennedy" to Boston meant sort of drifting right, but not too much, otherwise I'd be heading out to the nether regions of Long Island. Eyes glued to the road signs with trusty map on the passenger seat, I found directions to Interstate 95 and basically never wavered from it. Four hours later, totally knackered, I reached the Boston 'burbs'. I found a small motel and was out for the count instantly.

The next day I found the club, which was a pretty seedy little affair in Framingham. I introduced myself and began to unload and set the gear on to a rather small low stage. Problem number one - I'd never actually seen MSC work so I had no idea where anything went. Were the bass player and lead guitarist left and right of the drums or the other way? Where was the pedal steel player? Oh Shit! So I decided to just set it up how I hoped the band would be happy and prayed they'd turn up to sound check with enough time for me to change it around if need be. Setting the pedal steel for Gordon Huntley, who I was to room with, was a nightmare. I had absolutely no idea, as this was an instrument I had never encountered before (or since). So I just stuck it on its legs and hoped for the best. Why had I not checked this out with Billy before I left England was a small irritating thought that I pushed out of my head. After all, he had been with them for six months. Bit bloody late now!

The band duly arrived and was, thank God, totally without ego. After some small adjustments, everything was set and the smile on my face would have lit up a small village. Hell, if this was the big time it was going to be a breeze. The show went well and MSC were really pretty good. Gordon was a fantastic guy, both as a musician and socially. He was, truth to tell, in his mid forties, (so really old to this young twenty something), happily married and not one for sampling the 'fringe benefits' of the life of a rock star. Quite how he'd found himself in the band to start with was a mystery probably to him more than anyone else. He was a man steeped in country music and a sought after session player. I suppose, like a lot of things in everyone's life, it seemed like a good idea at the time. That, for the rest of the tour, folk assumed he was my father, caused much amusement to him, to me, and the rest of the band. I'm sure I embarrassed him many times when I'd return to our room to 'entertain' a young lady and he'd be there snoring for England. I have to say the young ladies fell into two distinct categories. They were either highly amused and weren't bothered or disappeared into the night wondering just what they'd walked into with this British roadie and his patently exhausted dad!

We did about a week of these warm up shows, finishing up over the border in Canada prior to the first show of the tour proper in Toronto where we would be third on the bill to the headliner Rod Stewart and the Faces and Deep Purple. This was fantastic. I mean I was a fan, I had their records and now I could rub shoulders with them and be part of their inner circle. I pinched myself quite a lot on that first tour, I can tell you. I'd show up with this piddling little truck and park it next to this larger truck belonging to Purple which in turn was parked up beside this massive truck belonging to The Faces. There was just me for MSC and two guys with Purple's gear and then quite a few more in charge of the Faces gear. It all worked very well with no divisions of labour, everybody mucking in to do a type and scale of show that I'd never done before with Vanity Fare. It's not that they had never done arena shows; they'd just done them without me earlier that year in, once again, America.*

The Faces gear went on first and they sound-checked followed by Deep Purple and their check and lastly me to rig in front of everyone else, sound check optional depending on time. I always watched from the side, (probably as I'd been told to stay out of the way and keep quiet) when both the bands sound checked. They were so good to watch. The charismatic Stewart cheerleading a troupe of merry pranksters who could boogie with the best of them, they just never let up with, well, having a good time, even though at times I'm sure they were seriously hung-over. Deep Purple ran through, I guess the word is, efficiently with the enigmatic Blackmore, never more than a heartbeat away from a scowl.

Their crew, at that time, was Ian Hansford, who was their tour manager and soundman, (and travelling with the band) together with Rob Cooksey and Ron Quinton, who both drove their truck and did the gear. We soon worked out an efficient system for the good of all. Rob and Ron would help me get my gear off after MSC's set, pack it away and lock it in my small truck, and then I'd help them set for Purple's show and clear away afterwards. The three of us would then go back and watch Rod Stewart who drove the crowds wild. Purple were doing a great show however, and some nights the kudos went to them, not The Faces. Purple were building a large and loyal audience steadily, having had chart success with 'Black Night' and 'Strange Kind Of Woman' prior to this tour. The "Caravan"

---

* Dick Allix: "*When we did our tour it was with Neil Diamond, Tony Joe White and the Grass Roots - sorry to rub it in, mate*".

wove its way across Canada to the West Coast of America via Minneapolis and then down into California playing 5000-seater ice arenas, basketball stadiums and small theatres.

It wasn't before long that Rob, Ron and I decided that we were missing a trick and that it made more sense (well, I would, wouldn't I!), if we traded in the two trucks and got one bigger one that would take both MSC's gear and Purples and that way we'd save on gas and be able to share the driving. Not daft us roadies! The truck was big enough to take three in the cab and was in way better nick.

Life on the road was hard work, but, at twenty-four, doing something you love, it was dead easy. After about ten shows into the tour, I was introduced to Deep Purple formally; after all, they'd seen me lurking around and knew I had a function of some description. They were smashing guys from the very first hello - none of the " I'm a star, you're only a roadie" - we were all in it together. The after show social life was fantastic too, a gigantic party every night, and the booze flowed back at the hotel as much as back stage all the time. It was a male 'club' in all respects, a drinking club! Purple and especially Rod and The Faces were not exactly shrinking violets. My capacity for booze and my bodies capacity to recover from it, improved daily!

In fact at the Minneapolis after show party Rod and Ritchie started a food fight, and dumped Warner Bros representative Russ Shaw in a laundry basket and Ritchie wrapped a fire hose around the hotel manager! I was there for a while… it was very amusing to say the least. Russ was the unfortunate recipient of many practical jokes back in those days.

Ironically Rod Stewart incidentally had been considered as Purple's original vocalist in 1968, although they had not been impressed with him. Blackmore had apparently been quite condescending when their paths crossed later that same year. There wasn't any noticeable friction between Rod and Ritchie during this tour, but in general, they kept a respectable distance, so to speak.

Following the West Coast jaunt, two long months later we were back on the East Coast and Ian Hansford approached me saying that there may be a job for me with Deep Purple, once we were back in England. I took this with a pinch of salt frankly, as I considered that, once back, Billy would reclaim his spot with MSC and I, after a short break, would rejoin Vanity Fare.

On the plane back to England I reflected on what a great time I'd had and that probably, sadly, I'd never make it back to the States. At Heathrow I rented a car, said my goodbyes to Rob and Ron, and drove home in the early morning September sun to South Shields, to Warwick Avenue, to my Mam and Dad and an uncertain future. Could I really rejoin Vanity Fare and go back, as I was now seeing it, to cabaret clubs? Well, the very next day after I'd returned, my clothes still in the suitcase, the phone rang. It was John Coletta, one of Deep Purple's two managers, the other being Tony Edwards. I'd met them during the tour, although like most managers, they'd only appear at the prestigious shows, never in "Bum Fuck", North Dakota. When it was New York, Los Angeles and the like, they'd be there two days before and three after! Ah, those managers, they're too much, aren't they!

Coletta said that the band had expressed a wish that I should work for them and did I want the job. I thought long and hard for about a nano second and said, "YES". I'm hard to get, me! Ian Gillan has documented that after he saw me dump a mug of beer on Rod Stewart's head one night in a Holiday Inn bar after a show, he just had to have me as part of their crew! I knew that (though I remember it not)! They wanted me to be in London as soon as possible to pick up their truck and drive it to Zurich. I put down the phone, picked up my case full of unwashed laundry and explained to my parents that I had to go right now, I had a job.

Looking back, that was harsh, but Eddie and Bettie, God love 'em, just smiled, congratulated me, even though I knew they were pretty upset, and off I went, with them waving in my rear view mirror. I know I owed them, big time, but their love for me, I know now, was totally unconditional. They knew I was so happy at what I'd managed to achieve in such a short time from leaving the Town Hall and my happiness was theirs. In the years to come they would often be at Purple concerts and my dad and mam were on first name terms with Ritchie (and, trust me, there are not many in that club!)

CHAPTER FOUR
ON THE ROAD TO GOLDEN DUST

I drove back to London punching the air at my good fortune. I dropped the car off and took a train to Gerrards Cross, just outside London, to the home of Rob Cooksey, where I stayed the night. The next morning, he tossed me the keys to a massive 7 ton diesel truck, gave me an address in Zurich, Switzerland, some cash float, ferry tickets and all the necessary documentation for customs. I asked if I was replacing anyone, fearing that perhaps Ron Quinton might have been canned, as plainly Rob hadn't. He said no, the crew was expanding (and boy, would that get out of hand later). I was in my element and drove to Harwich for the ferry to the Hook of Holland. It seems now that I drove without a break, high on adrenalin, across Holland, Germany and into Switzerland, although realistically, I must have stopped to eat and catch sleep breaks in the cab. However, it must have been a fast journey as I got there thirty-six hours before the show was due to start!

My first European tour! Ian Hansford with the band and me with Rob and Ron in the truck with the gear. The album 'Fireball' had just been released which they had recorded before the tour with the Faces, so there was plenty of promotional activity to do. The band would often take off with just guitars with Ian to fly to, perhaps, Bremen, Germany to 'lip sync' on the TV Show 'Beat Club'. The same boys club atmosphere from America prevailed and none of the inner friction, which was to be the future nemesis of the band, was in evidence. We played all the major cities as we journeyed across Europe and I revelled in the family, albeit male, camaraderie of Purple on tour.

By mid-October, we were back in England for a few days of well earned rest and then to the States once more to start yet another tour. After only two shows, Ian Gillan started to look decidedly peaky and by the third show in Chicago, he went from peaky to a nice shade of yellow. He went to hospital and was diagnosed with hepatitis. As it is not something that a couple of Tylenol would cure, it was decided to cancel the tour and head back to England.

Not wanting to waste any creative time, Ritchie called me up telling me to pull out his gear and Paicey's glitter kit and take them to a small studio off Holland Park Road. This was a little strange, as Ritchie and Paicey were not exactly the practising types. Imagine my surprise when Phil Lynott of Thin Lizzy appeared in the studio too. The three of them were there for a couple of nights. I had to load in and out each day, as the studio had not been block booked, only by the session. Apparently, this was all an idea of John Coletta "just to see what would happen" as Ritchie was a long time admirer of the Irish bass player. It is common belief that the resulting tapes were not good and only half finished, lying in a long forgotten vault. Not true, I think John Coletta or Tony Edwards had them and they were finished, all four songs were great. Perhaps they will surface one day? There was an actual name given to this little "band" and it was called "Baby Face".*

I'd met Phil a few times before that, once at one of the Thin Lizzy shows at the Rainbow Theatre in London and again at his mothers - Philomena, or Phyllis, as she was more commonly referred to. She ran a rather unique boarding house for travelling musicians in the greater Manchester area. She was a charming lady, but wouldn't take any crap from anyone, so staying on her good side was a plus and you stayed healthy.

My ever fluid living arrangements had by this time changed again and I'd moved into an apartment in Tooting, South London with Tony Jarrett, Vanity Fare's bass player, his girlfriend Jenny, and Micky Minto, Vanity's roadie. I had the front room for about a fiver a week. Vanity Fare's career by this time was on the skids. Dick had left to work with producers George Martin, Ron Richards (Hollies) and John Burgess at The Air Studios in London as a trainee publisher, and keyboard player Barry Landeman was about to leave to go to university. Tony played house while Jenny went to work and Mick often stayed back in his hometown of Birmingham, so, when I was home, it was just Tony and I.

* In an interview for the Deep Purple Appreciation Society, Derek Lawrence (who produced Deep Purple's first three albums) recalled *"the three of them recorded at The Music Centre at Wembley. I have no idea how many or what happened to the tracks. I seem to recall Ritchie telling me that they cut a track by Johnny Winter called 'Dying To Live'."*
Blackmore gave a different account of events in a more recent Greek magazine interview, confirming they had made some demos, but after a couple of days playing, they didn't like the results and decided not to pursue it. He also commented that he did not feel the demos were of high enough quality to ever release. The recording date was supposedly November 22nd 1971.

By now, plans were afoot to do yet another album for release in spring 1972. 'Fireball' had sold well, going to No. 1 in the UK charts, so naturally we, the road crew, looked forward to a reasonable respite from the physical excesses of touring rather than the social ones, which went on unabated no matter where we were or for what reason - very civilised attitude, I thought. The Stones Mobile had been hired to record and Claude Nobs, promoter and entrepreneur extraordinaire, had fixed up the old casino in Montreux as the venue. Why a drafty old casino you ask, instead of a comfy studio back in England? Well, Ritchie is the answer first and last. You see he hated the standard studio because they were so open to folk dropping in unannounced and that ruined the focus, in his eyes, essential for the recording process. Anyway, everything packed and organised, we drove to Switzerland and the Hotel Eden Du Lac where we were to stay.

On arrival, I parked the truck and we considered loading in to the casino that night, where recording was due to start the next day, but, found out that was not possible as The Mothers of Invention with Frank Zappa were playing the last show before it was to close up for the winter. That was, of course, why we could use it for the album. We all decided, band and crew, to go and catch the show as Claude had arranged a private box. As we went in, I checked that the Stones Mobile has also arrived and was parked up beside the casino in readiness for the next day's start. The casino was a multi story building, a magnificent old place, with the ballroom on the ground floor and the casino and restaurants on the floors above.

Half way through the concert, as is well documented, some idiot decided to set off a flare gun, which sent a flare into the suspended, acoustic ceiling, consisting of overlapping straw matting (in an effort, I assume to give that all essential 'Polynesian straw hut' feel, so chic for the time). Also, to soak up excess echo: Looked great (for a death trap). It would never have got planning permission these days, but then things were pretty lax then. Not unreasonably, it went up like the Fourth of July, flames shot in all directions. Frank Zappa, mid song, very calmly said "fire" in an almost John Cleese / Fawlty Towers fire drill way with no panic in his voice what so ever. Then, his tone went up an octave in controlled panic to shout a tad louder, "err, fire". He directed everybody out to the exits.

There was a big plate glass window overlooking the lakeside of the casino ballroom and Zappa strode up to it, grabbed his guitar by the neck, and smashed it to bits to allow the crowd a better and faster exit. He was a real hero that evening, so calm. All the rest of their gear of course went up in the fire. Before long, flames were shooting through the roof and the sides of the building were getting very hot. Unfortunately the Stones Mobile was parked against one wall and the sides of it were getting very hot too, so the crew jumped aboard in an attempt to drive it out of harms way, but it got bogged down, its tyres spinning on the grass made wet by the fire hoses. We got the fire crews to ply their hoses over the mobile as well as trying to put the fire out, and thankfully it came out of it, slightly scorched, but otherwise unscathed. We all went down to the lake, which is where we stood and watched this building go up in flames with the smoke drifting across the lake. You can see from the photograph on the album, this great tower of smoke. It was a total loss, but no casualties, which was a miracle really. I don't think they even caught the phantom flare firer!

So, once back at the hotel, we sat down and wondered what to do next. John Coletta suggested that Claude should be contacted to see if he could source another venue, despite the fact that poor Claude had rather a full agenda at the time! Fair play to him, despite being up to his eyes in police, fireman and insurers he did manage to come up with a small theatre come casino; Le Pavilion, which had a small stage and was like a small club really. It too, was closed for the season, but would open for us for the six weeks we reckoned it would take to complete the album. Unfortunately it was really echo ridden with a glass wall running its full length on the lakeside. Not unreasonably, the band didn't take to this and suggested we put drapes along this one side, which sort of did the trick.

With equipment set up and the mobile cabled in, the band began to jam and this is where the world first heard the immortal intro to 'Smoke On The Water'. Roger had written a poem overnight and then together with Ian developed it to the lyrics that we all know today. The jam initiated that powerful intro and the rest, as they say, is history. However, the troubles were not over. Half way through that first evening session (the band nearly always recorded late, about 10pm till 4am), the police showed up! Purple at full throttle had got the locals fired up. Well, the casino was opposite The Palace Hotel and we had residential buildings either side. They quite simply, but firmly told us to desist immediately.

Soooo… back to poor old Claude yet again and the plea for another suitable recording site. Hell, the man was a solid gold trooper. After much searching he, eventually, came up with another 'closed for the season' venue. Just how many were there? This was The Grand Hotel, a deserted, massive, cold… grand hotel! The band decided to give it a shot and we, the crew and the mobile's tech guys set on to sound proof the place with mattress's, curtains and old drapes. We built a little T-shaped studio, using parts of three corridors that met, fixed mood lights everywhere to create atmosphere and ran the cabling downstairs, out through the lobby and into the mobile. This was parked unfortunately and unavoidably on a steep hill so that when you stepped into the back you nearly fell through to the front! It wasn't ideal, far from it. It was quite a schlep from the studio to the truck, involving a stroll through a hotel room, out onto the balcony, into another bedroom, out into the corridor and down the stairs to the lobby and out to the truck!

So the band got into the habit of doing multiple takes, then trekking to the mobile to hear all the playbacks. Yet, it was worth it, as history bears witness. Our official photographer, who did just about all the live and posed shots of the band was Didi Zill, a really nice German chap. He did the album photography there too and really did a great job especially with that aluminium sheet onto which he used the reflection of the band members as the shots for the front cover. This was despite someone accidentally treading on it, which bent it and gave it its warped effect. Art knows no boundaries, you know!

By Christmas, it was nearly finished and everyone took off to have a well-earned break. Claude got me a secure spot to park and lock the truck whilst the mobile left for England. The band flew us home to the bosoms of our family. Imagine my horror when, on my return, I discovered the truck had broken locks. Worse still, all of Jon Lord's keyboard set up was missing. My heart sank. "This is just great," I said to myself ashen-faced. I rang Claude, ready to read him the riot act. I was shaking with a mixture of anger and fear. Claude, however, was calm. "Don't worry, Colin. Jon has them. As you know he went to Zermatt for Christmas and got bored, I guess. He missed his keyboards, he wanted to do some jamming with others staying at the hotel, so he sent someone down to get them, who had to break the locks. Sorry, we forgot to tell you". I seethed for about a week, but another little episode broke the spell: I got arrested on suspicion of murder!

We had taken (unsurprisingly for Purple), to frequenting a small bar opposite the Grand Hotel for the odd sampling of the local brew. Not unnaturally, where rock bands congregate, the local female population soon gravitates. It soon became a fun place to be, to unwind. One evening in the middle of recording, in walk four Inspector Clouseau look-alikes who ask for me. I was totally stunned when they requested I accompany them to the station, which was at the bottom of the block from The Grand. They couldn't speak great English and I instantly regretted neglecting my French studies. An interpreter was found, who proceeded to explain that they were conducting a murder enquiry.

Seemingly, the story was that I had been seen leaving the bar with two girls, which was true, one of whom turned right with me towards the hotel, the other taking a left and saying her goodnights to us both. We then walked back to my hotel, the Eden, where she spent the night. Her friend sadly never made it home. She had been raped and murdered. Thankfully, the girl I was with substantiated my story, otherwise my explanation would have been hard to corroborate. I was in shock and John Coletta actually was the comforting presence for me, assuring me that all would be fine. John stayed with me for most of that afternoon. I don't think even Claude could have fixed that one. I heard much later that a local man had been tried and convicted of the girl's murder. And so, 'Machine Head' was wrapped up and we all headed home.

****

John Coletta and Tony Edwards were 'old school' managers, which meant that rest periods for their artists were not on the agenda. Whether this was from a fear that it would all disappear like an early morning mist tomorrow or from sheer greed, I have no idea, but come January we were back to America for a month of shows with Buddy Miles Express, as our support. I know this took a toll on the band, especially Ian G, who wasn't keen on John and Tony to start with, although the others seemed to have a reasonable relationship with them. I, however, found the two of them to be charming guys and I loved touring, so I was very happy with the schedules.

It was still Ian Hansford, Rob, Ron and yours truly, although this was set to change later in the year. On American tours, we had to hire loaders at each venue and, depending on how strong the union was in the hall, let them rig the show with us supervising. We called it a "pull up and point" show. Not too physical for us, but the promoter had to foot the bill for the labour. The unions, at that time, had a virtual stranglehold on any venue with regard to non-union labour, which meant us, despite it being our gear. It's not much better today, thirty years later, but I kinda respect it anyway and once there's a mutual respect, hall labour to crew, the shows get set up really quickly.

It was on this tour that Ritchie got hepatitis and was sent home. For whatever dumb reason, the management thought he could be replaced and we proceeded to set up an audition in a small theatre on Staten Island. Al Kooper had been auditioned and rejected and Randy California had been suggested and he duly turned up. He was fine, not quite Ritchie, but he'd do for the number of shows left on the tour. On the way back with the gear to go to La Guardia Airport, Rob Cooksey and I were driving the truck back over the Varrazano Narrows Bridge when we noticed a car behind us giving the full flashing headlights treatment. Rob told me to slow down so that he could give the driver some choice English 'verbals' and a possible slap or two. When the car drew level, before Rob could utter a word, the driver yelled, "the back of the truck is open, Buddy, you're losing your load".

We swallowed hard, we were in the middle of the bridge, so there was no way we could turn round or stop, so we gingerly drove off the bridge to the first exit and pulled up. Sure enough, the back was open where the bottom slat of the roll up door had sheared, leaving the lock in place, but only attached to the sheared slat leaving the rest to roll up. I could see immediately that a Roland piano case had gone together with Ian Paice's trap case. We secured the back with rope and drove hell for leather back over the bridge. As we got all the way over we could see in the opposite lane Jon's flight case sitting in the middle of the road just at the precise moment an 18-wheeler turned it into matchwood. There was wood, piano keys and odd bits of wire everywhere, what a mess. Rob found a phone, (no cell phones in them dark days) and called the police who, at first, were mildly interested. "You've lost some gear off the back of the truck on the approach to The Verrazano Bridge? What sorta gear?" the dispatcher said in a very bored, heard it all before voice. "A piano" said Rob in a clipped English dialect. "A FUCKING PIANO!" came the reply.

Attention duly grabbed, half of Queens traffic police got very excited and raced to the scene. All was destroyed, however, and we never found Ian's trap case with hi-hat, cymbals, sticks and his favourite snare drum amongst other goodies. Now we had to tell the band who were staying at The Warwick in Manhattan. We reached La Guardia and, taking a deep breath, I rang Jon first. "Jon, its Colin. We've had a slight accident. The Roland came off the back of the truck and is, err, somewhat damaged, in fact it is no more" I winced, holding the phone away, ready for a high volume onslaught which oddly didn't come. "Colin, that's very careless," he said in a very measured relaxed voice as if I'd just interrupted his afternoon nap, maybe I had? "Just phone Roland in the morning and get another" - soft click followed as he hung up.

I couldn't believe it. He was a prince among men. Now for Paicey who loved his kit... well, like Ritchie loves... well, you know. "Ian, its Colin, we've had a slight accident and your trap case has disappeared." I didn't wince as much and Ian, nice as pie told me not to worry, and was I okay? Are these guys for real? "Just phone Ludwig in Chicago and get replacements sent to the next venue." How nice, how civilised! All Rob and I were grateful for was that we packed Ritchie's guitars way up the front of the truck, as Randy California would not be touching those! I somehow believed that, under the same circumstances, Ritchie would not have been as understanding as Jon and Ian.

It was a measure, however, of how money had ceased to be tight and that manufacturer's would bend over backwards to please Deep Purple. The tailpiece to the story was, unfortunately, Randy was a complete disaster from the get go. Sure he could play, but he was no Ritchie and that's who the crowds wanted to see. So, after just one show, we cancelled the tour* and headed home to await the recovery of Mr. Blackmore, who was by now eating boiled chicken under the strict supervision of his then second German wife, Babs.

* They had managed nine shows before Blackmore took ill, then did one show in Michigan as a four-piece before the one and only show with Randy California in Quebec, Canada.

CHAPTER FIVE
HIGHWAY STARS

April 1972 and 'Machine Head' hit the streets running, to instant acclaim. No.1 in the British charts, No.7 in America and a massive hit pretty much everywhere in between. For us roadies, the reflected glory was blinding!

In late July, we headed off for Rome to a chateau on a hill to start to record what would eventually be 'Who Do We Think We Are'. It was the usual format, the Stones Mobile plus our 7-ton truck. There was one small problem that had been overlooked and that was the size of the Stones Mobile and size of the ornate entry arch to the chateau. One was bigger than t'other and the chateau was not the larger. This meant parking up the mobile outside the gates and cabling up for what seemed miles into the chateau. Shades of the Grand Hotel in Montreux, in that it was a day's march from the studio to hear any playbacks.

The band soon got fed up with this, having tried out some test recordings of daft songs just to see if the miles of cabling would take the feed successfully. Ian, Jon and Roger recorded a little Gillan penned opus called 'Smelly Botty' and the classic standard 'It's Only Make Believe' with Jon playing a classic wrong chord deliberately a la famed English comedian Les Dawson and Ian matching him with the vocal. It was hilarious and I know Roger still has tapes of that event. Copious amounts of wine were drunk and many intense card games, Shoot Pontoon being one, between management, band and crew for a couple of weeks, before it was decided that it really was not going to work and recording was abandoned. Only two good tracks ever came out of it, one of which one was 'Painted Horse' which made the album 'Powerhouse', an odd album of tracks released five years later.

In August, we set off to tour Japan and recorded the live album 'Made In Japan'. The album was a huge seller made even more remarkable by the fact that we did not use the best equipment or have the best facilities to record. On one occasion at the Budokan we had to use a back stage dressing room as the control room, which meant no vision between the engineer, Martin Birch and the band on stage. It really was a 'seat of your pants' kind of deal, but sometimes that's what makes things work. Martin had pre-ordered what he needed as there was no chance of getting the beloved Stones Mobile to Japan and he got the gear closest to his request list.

Whilst there, I met the love of my life. It was the last day of the tour, we were in Tokyo and I was at breakfast with the crew. Scoping the room, as you do, I saw this girl with long blond hair down to her ass with her back to me. I kept staring at her, willing for her to turn round and confirm a beautiful face matched the hair. She did and it did. Eye contact, but no more. We left to do the last show, returning late in the evening. As was usual, we all headed for the bar, but I returned to the lobby hoping to see her. It got very late and I was about to give up when she came into the Hotel. Bold as brass, I went up to her and asked if she wanted a drink. The Hart magic at full flow, she accepted. We went for that drink and I introduced her to the band and other guys, and then took her for a walk in the hotel gardens, which, for anyone who has been to Japan, are always a haven of peace and serenity. We just talked, her name was Marlene and she was from Miami where her mother ran a jewellery business. They were here on a buying trip and she was nineteen. I eventually walked her to the elevator and we exchanged addresses and phone numbers. I'm sure she believed that would be the end of it.

Up early the next day for the flight home, I wrote her a note and left it in her box at reception. Back in England, I wrote her a long letter and over the following months, rang her many times. We became close, albeit via transatlantic phone and kept in touch constantly wherever I happened to be. Two years later in 1974, she came to England with friends, to backpack around Europe. I, by this time, had moved out of the Tooting pad into a flat in Westbourne Park Grove, West London. Save it to say, Marlene skipped out on some of the backpacking adventure, moving in with me instead. It was shared with two other roadies, Phil Macdonald, then head roadie of Fleetwood Mac and John 'Magnet' Ward, ex-Led Zeppelin, who was now on the Purple road crew, too, along with a new face, Baz Marshall. The flat was handily above the management offices of Fleetwood Mac, though handy for who is debateable. Phil, I know, felt he was never 'off the clock'.

In October, we packed everything off to Frankfurt, Germany to finish

'Who Do We Think We Are' after the abortive attempt in Rome. We stayed at The Park Hotel. Once again we bowed to Ritchie's penchant for the Stones Mobile and recording in a club where we could effectively 'lock out' any unwanted observers. During the sessions, as usual, we favoured a particular bar with our patronage and enjoyed its hospitality and brew to the maximum. Unfortunately one evening Ian Gillan and I had indulged a bit too much and, once back in the studios, decided to see if we could punch a hole in a sound baffle. After many attempts, this was found to be impossible, but Ian, true to his nature, would not quit and ran full tilt at the baffle and gave it one last mighty punch. Alcohol has a wonderful way of numbing pain, we all know this, but there always comes a point where the brain sends a desperate signal to the body that it is now damaged. Ian turned round, looked at his hand and calmly said, "Colin, I think you'd better take me to hospital, I may well have broken this"

The knuckle of the small finger of his right hand was way further back towards his wrist than nature had intended and so, sobering rapidly as you do, we ventured to the hospital where his damaged hand was put in a cast, alas not that successfully as, even today, that old knuckle looks like a mutant cousin to its brothers. Ian then finished the album looking like he was auditioning for the part of "The Claw" in some B movie. In truth, it wasn't one of their best. Ritchie, I know hated it, but it did sell, reaching No. 4 in the UK charts, but less well in America peaking at No.15. There was a distinct air of frustration developing between Ritchie and Ian during the making of this album. Fuel for the fires that would burn in later days.

It was now November 1972 and strangely, you may think, we started yet another tour of, yes, America! This time the tour support was the Texan rockers ZZ Top, who at that time were beardless, but still had them big arse hats and just loved their beer, booze and women. As you would expect, dates blur into dates, but I remember one ridiculous show in Ithaca, in upstate New York. We'd flown to Syracuse and then had a long limousine ride to Ithica. It was partly in the open air with a tarpaulin as a roof for the stage. ZZ Top went on and did their thing and two of Purple, who were with me to get the feel of the place, saw the rain pouring onto the stage off the 'tarp' and understandably refused to go on, not that we'd have let them anyway. Simon and Mad John, our sound engineers, from Tycobrahe and Pirate Sound in Los Angeles said: "Everything is wet through and we're getting terrible interference, its madness".

The decision to pull the plug stood and when the crowd heard about it they just tore the place to shreds. They jumped on the twelve-foot high stage and wheeled a Steinway grand piano right off it and Lordy's organ Leslie speakers met the same fate. Of course, some of the crowd were less destructive choosing to loot instead. Speakers and amps just walked right out the door in front of the security. "It's okay, man, we brought these in with us…" Many years later, I'm told, some of them resurfaced in a second hand music shop in the area, even marked up "Ex Jon Lord of Deep Purple". Some balls, eh!

We were forced to cancel Atlanta the next day, whilst we sourced replacement gear, but at the gig the day after that, equipment restored, we discovered that Ritchie's No.1 guitar did not leave Ithaca where we stayed after the arena debacle. So, being the understandable gentleman he is, he refused to go on, despite having all his other six guitars. That was unless, of course, somebody went to fetch it? I established quietly with his guitar tech that Ritchie had in fact, left the guitar in his room. Just whose ultimate responsibility it was to get it picked up, was still a bit debateable, but the fact remained, no guitar, no show. I was ultimately responsible for everything, so I took the flack, as usual. $5,000 later, for a small hired jet plane with one roadie, Ron Kilburn on board, who was another addition to the entourage as my assistant for this tour, and the guitar was restored into the hands of our maestro and show commenced. Ron, bless him, accepted the responsibility for the mislaid guitar, but to be honest, it wasn't his fault. You may think that $5000 is a bit much, but consider it saved a fee of $30,000 and it takes on a new perspective.

The tour continued its less than merry way across America as tensions between Ian Gillan and Ritchie became more apparent and deteriorated rapidly. The boys' club atmosphere struggled to stay alive, although to the ticket buying public, nothing outwardly was wrong. If Ritchie chose to be morose and maybe not do the odd encore then it was passed off as rock stars just being rock stars. Things got so bad that Ian announced that he would no longer travel with the band, meaning with Ritchie, and took to travelling separately with is own personal German roadie, one Ozzy Hoppe. They, together with Ian's Girlfriend Zoë, would take separate flights and travel, stay at separate hotels and only show up at each gig about ten minutes before showtime. This made life pretty stressful for yours truly who always had to ensure that the band; ALL the band made each show. I would far rather, obviously, have had them all where I could, figuratively, if not actually, see them. I continuously had to check with

Ozzy where Ian was and what time I would like him to put in an appearance, something that I felt made a hard job just that more difficult.

Sound checks for Ian were now out of the question. I had to inform back stage security what limo to look out for and at what time. It would arrive; Ian would emerge already dressed for stage and walk straight out to do the show. Once over, he would go straight back to his waiting limo and, with Zoë and Ozzy in attendance disappear into the night to reappear at the following show in an identical manner. Just how Ian resolved this behaviour with Roger who was his closest friend, having been in Episode Six together prior to joining Deep Purple, I had no idea. When I tried to discuss it with Roger, he just shrugged sadly and asked me to leave it to work itself out. Rock stars, don't you just love 'em?

By the time we got to Dayton, Ohio, however, the problem of the unending touring and the widening rift with Ritchie determined that Ian would resign, giving six months notice. He set the leaving date for June 1973, which really was pretty fair, acknowledging that a Japan tour for that period was contracted. Most, brought to the brink, would have walked there and then. Prior to the personal road manager and alternative travel arrangements, I had sensed the bad feeling and tension between Ritchie and Ian for some time. It was okay seventy percent of the time, but you instinctively knew when to make yourself scarce. Then, the okay times would gradually decrease over the months. They are two very proud men who, in fairness to both, have got attitude problems of equal proportions. My job was to get the show done and all the guys looked after so that the journey was as problem free and as pleasurable as possible. After all I had the welfare of five guys to consider, not just two, and that was what Ian and Ritchie failed to appreciate a lot of the time.

It has been oft reported that Ian Gillan was also the only member of the band that ever queried accounts and that this too had a bearing on his decision to leave. Well, Ian had, and still has, a big rival in the "where's the money been spent" stakes. Stand up Ian Paice, bless him. Paicey, quite rightly, in my view, inspected the tour receipts, not at the end of each tour, but DAILY! No sooner were we on the bus or in the car after a show and he would summon the tour accountant or, in the earlier years, me, to check the door receipts to see by how much we had broken the guarantee, what deductions had been made, how well merchandising had gone in terms of what lines had sold well and how many had been 'comped'.

In the reunion years he needed to keep up to date on numbers of crew

Above: Dad performing with his banjo.

Above: NALGO Holiday camp, Cayton Bay, Scarborough, North Yorkshire.
Middle row, me fourth from left, with school pal Geoff Tate, fifth from left.

Left: Geoff and I doing our Peter Cook and Dudley Moore routine on stage at Cayton Bay, 1966.

Right: My other best school friend, Billy Borthwick.

Left and above: One of my first roadie jobs was with local band The Jazz Board who regularly played at the New Cellar Club in South Shields. It was also where I met Hendrix, who played there on 1st February 1967.

I showed up in the afternoon, having 'disappeared' from the Town Hall, to get a look at a 'real' band in action. I met the roadie, and offered to give him a hand getting the gear up the stairs. He was delighted when I provided him with much needed fuses to get Jimi's Marshall rig running and nipped out to the van to get some.

Below: My first professional roadie job came with another local band, Toby Twirl.
L-R. Nicky Thorburn (guitar), Barrie Sewell (keyboards) John Reed (drums),
Dave "Holly" Holland (vocals) and Stu Somerville (bass).

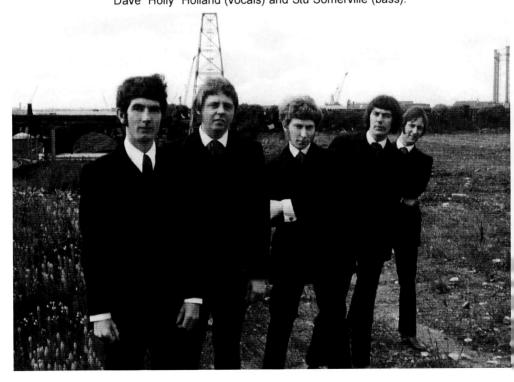

Left:
With my fellow Purple crew mates.
L-R: John "Magnet" Ward, me, and Baz Marshall

Below:
Pigging out on the Starship, and with one of the lovely stewardesses.

(Starship images, Fin Costello)

Backstage in Paris after Ritchie's last Purple show, 7th April 1975.

Left:
L-R. Ian Broad (Ritchie's assistant), Graham Nolder, who worked for Purple Records in London, me and Ritchie.

Below:
With Purple's engineer and producer Martin Birch.

Left: With Coverdale and Paicey.

Bottom left: With RB.

Bottom right: With Glenn Hughes & Jon.

Above: One of the very first shots of Ritchie Blackmore's Rainbow, taken at rehearsals in ollywood. L-R: Ritchie, Ronnie, Craig Gruber, Mickey Lee Soule, Gary Driscoll. *(Fin Costello)*

elow: Ronnie at rehearsals at Pirate Sound Studio in Hollywood, Los Angeles. *(Fin Costello)*

Above: Me, Nicky Bell and Rob Cooksey
taken at Deep Purple's rehearsals at
Pirate Sound Studio, Hollywood, Los
Angeles, June 1975.
Rainbow was rehearsing in the
soundstage next door and Ritchie "sent"
me in to spy on things. (Fin Costello)

Right: Cozy Powell at Rainbow's
rehearsals at Pirate Sound.
(Fin Costello)

Left: Ronnie and Ritchie enjoying a liquid lunch at the Sans Souci hotel in Ocho Rios. Jamaica. We were down there doing some overdubs in Kingston. *(Hart)*

Below: Rainbow during rehearsals at Pirate Sound.
L-R: Ritchie, Ronnie, Tony Carey, Jimmy Bain and Cozy *(Fin Costello)*

Above: Cozy confronts an Albino kangaroo in an animal sanctuary outside of Sydney, Austral
(Hart)

Below: Ronnie and Wendy's wedding in Connecticut, 7th April 1978.
L-R. Me, Raymond D'Addario, Danny Padovana, Ronnie, Wendy, Bob Daisley, Ritchie and
Bruce Payne.

Above and left:
Ritchie and Cozy in
Copenhagen, October 1977.
The captions were added by me, but
written by Cozy. He and I would add
captions to any photos we found lying
around... because we could!

Below:
Ritchie boring Bruce Payne to sleep,
also in Copenhagen.

(Ross Halfin)

Left: Cozy on a moped he found in a shed, riding in the pool, as one would at Le Chateau de Pelly De-Cornfeld in France. The locals were not amused.
(Har

Below: The same chateau, where most of the *Down To Earth* album was recorded. It was horrendously expensive at around $25,000 per week. It was close to Geneva in Switzerland from where I collected prospective vocalists. Eventually we discovered Graham Bonnet. It was to be his one and only Rainbow album.
(Har

Above:
Roger after joining Rainbow with Tony "Sarge" Mazzucchi,
who anchored the lighting crew for most of the Rainbow years.

Below:
Graham and I sorting out the worlds problems after a show.

Right:
On one of our dive trips in St.
Croix, U.S. Virgin Island. In
the foreground is Rainbow's
publicist Jenny Halsall.
Cozy sits on the back of the
boat tanning his legs.
(Hart)

Newcastle City Hall,
February 1980

Left:
Roger backstage
with my nephews,
Stephen and Paul
Mann, and holding
his daughter
Gillian
(Hart)

Right:
Paul, Ritchie,
Stephen, and
David Mann, my
brother in law.
(Hart)

Left:
Graham Bonnet
and Don Airey with
Paul and Stephen.
(Hart)

Above:
Cozy backstage at Newcastle City Hall, February 1980 with my nephews Stephen & Paul Mann.
Little did we know then that Paul would one day conduct the LSO alongside Deep Purple,
performing Jon Lord's *Concerto For Group & Orchestra*.

Inset: With my sister Carol.

Below:
Cozy and I were out for a walk in Tokyo when he was mobbed for autographs.
(Hart)

Above left: Roger, I believe in Killington
Vermont, at a Christmas party.

Above right: Our lovely lady backing vocalists
for Rainbow; Lynn Robinson and Dee Beale.

Right: Lita Ford and my dad, backstage at the
Whitley Bay Ice Rink. He had a big crush on
her, (didn't we all?)

Below: Joe Lynn Turner at the filming of the
Stone Cold video in New York City.
(Hart)

Le Studio, Morin Heights, Canada during the making of the *Straight Between The Eyes* album.

Above: Ritchie adding his ideas to the string arrangements for Eyes Of Fire.

Below: L-R. Nick Blagona, Roger, David Rosenthal and Ritchie adding the strings. *(Hart)*

and how much they were paid too, information that he got from Barbara at Thames Talent, our agents. Then he would feed it into a little account book and, in the future, a laptop in order to predict his eventual 'take home pay' from the tour. It's just how he was, all done with a smile, not on a whim, though it was serious stuff to Ian. You didn't pull the wool over Paicey's eyes, well, not where money's concerned anyway.

1973 kicked off with a similar incident to the one in Ithica a couple of months earlier. As previously documented in 'Black Knight' The Ritchie Blackmore Story, at Amsterdam on 28th January 1973, violence erupted amongst the audience on a scale never before witnessed at a Deep Purple concert. Due to Purple's growing popularity, the venue (De Oude Rai) was the only building in the city big enough to cater for ticket demand but it was an old wooden cattle hall, and furthermore had insufficient power supply for Purple's PA set up. On arrival at the hall, once they were made aware of the problems with the power the band was ready to walk out but in the knick of time somebody came up with the solution of feeding electricity from the Okura Hotel next door. Whilst the power problems had been sorted out, with 12,000 crammed into the hall with an estimated 10,000 capacity, concerns over the lack of security once again threatened the cancellation of the show. After checking everything over several times Hansford gave the thumbs up for Purple to go on stage.

With the band finally ready to leave the comfort of the dressing room, Ritchie instantly spotted the poor organisation and immediately headed back. Eventually an hour later they finally went on stage but after only an hour one of Ritchie's guitar strings broke at the end of a song; he threw the guitar in the air and left the stage. The rest of the band soon followed. Following an announcement that there will be no more, the house lights were switched on but the crowd got even more restless, throwing beer cans towards the stage again. The minimal security was unable to control matters, and I remember the after effects, trying in vain to defend the equipment from the crowd who were determined to wreck it. I had a mic stand in my hand and was persuaded to just give in and not try to be a hero, which could have resulted in some serious injury, or worse.

For some time, the ever-faithful Ian Hansford had been having problems at home with his wife who, quite understandably, was not happy with the time he was spending on the road. In fairness, the band said she could come on the road too, all expenses paid, but she declined and reluctantly Ian left which, of course, created a vacancy as head roadie (or as they are known today tour manager).*

I went to John Coletta and threw my hat in the ring, as they say. To my great surprise and pleasure, it got the 'nod' from the band. I was henceforth No.1 after little more than a year with Deep Purple. Well, I must have been doing something right. It helped that, unlike Ian, I had no ties and could be at their beck and call twenty four/seven. I'm sure they saw this too and exploited it to the full for the foreseeable future, but hey, I was very willing, so no criticism. I worried at the time how Ron would receive the news, as he'd been with Purple when I joined. Rob had already made the unbelievable leap into management, so the tour manager gig didn't interest him, but Ron said he just wanted to stay with the gear and not have to be a "nanny", as he called it.

This meant now, of course, that, as well as being with the band in the limo, and not driving the truck, I was introduced to the responsibility of mixing. Not that I didn't believe I could do it technically, I knew I could. It's just this position is the most political in any band. You see, the perception is you can make or break a performance, but only in the eyes of one or other of the band who believes you have pulled down their fader or pushed up one of a band mate, whilst in truth there is a perfect balance. The first few shows were a horrendous experience. Gillan marked my card from the off, when he announced from the stage, "I want everything louder than everything else, please."

At the time, we had a complete custom Marshall set up through a sixteen-channel desk, which, for its time, was state of the art and seriously loud. Of course, I had to ensure when Ritchie's guitar solo's came along, the fader went up as far as it would go. Real Spinal Tap stuff! I, thankfully, did not keep this 'kiss of death' part of the job very long as sound engineer, as the band graduated to hiring specialist sound companies in each country, who had their own engineers, leaving me to "supervise". It was a joke, really for me to be out there trying to oversee a real sound engineer, but Ritchie always seemed to trust that I would be sure his solos were not missed, and believe me, they never were. (Was I that bad!)? Specialist lighting companies would follow too, so we soon carried a lighting designer and a soundman as permanent crewmembers. The cast of 'thousands' was not far off.

Not long after I became tour manager, it was one of my jobs to check

---

* Ian Hansford's last show with Deep Purple was at the Liverpool Stadium, 28th February 1973.

the box office and pick up the money. Now if we broke the percentage, which was becoming increasingly a regular occurrence back then, I could walk out of a venue with $100,000 or more in CASH. Now that was scary shit! I had to count it first too! It was then a very quick trip back to the hotel and into their safe before depositing it the next morning into whatever bank account was ordained by Coletta and Edwards, and later Bruce Payne. It wasn't every night, granted, and it all changed later on, thankfully, to bank drafts and certified cheques after Led Zeppelin was ripped off in New York a year later at the end of their momentous 1973 U.S tour, when the door receipts deposited by manager Peter Grant and tour manager Richard Cole, some $200,000 from the show at Madison Square Garden, 'disappeared' from the Hotel safe overnight. I guess some hotel staff were becoming wise to the amount of money some rock bands could have on them and temptation was getting too hard to ignore!

Bruce Payne, who became Purple's and Rainbow's manager in later years, hated Ian Paice looking at the books on the road. He far preferred Ian looked at them when the management had prepared them, after all tour expenses had been accounted for. I sympathise with both camps actually. Paicey, at times could be a real pain with it. At least Bruce did properly audited tour accounts, although sometimes a little too late for some. There was never such a thing with Coletta and Edwards. They'd just tell the band that the tour had gone well and their share was about ex-amount. That's what riled Ian Gillan, infuriated him. He'd once or twice posed the question to them, "How come we're still riding the tube (subway) or begging for £20 gas money to go to rehearsals, when you're riding around in a Rolls Royce?" Fair comment, wouldn't you say?

At one stage, I shared Ian Paice's big flat at 11 Harbledown Road in Fulham, London, when he was still single, and on Friday afternoon, if we were home, I'd go to the management offices to pick up my wages. On my return, Ian, without fail, would be waiting for me with, literally, his hand out for the rent. Even on our days off, he would plan the evening out where I would chauffeur him in his XJ6 Jaguar, first to The Greyhound on Fulham Palace Road, then at closing time, to The Speakeasy until the early hours, leaving when he was ready and with a two pints of beer limit for Harty! Whose night off was this?? Did I always do it? Yes! Did I ever complain? No! Well, somebody had to look after him!

So, Gillan had finally resigned with a six-month notice period. Oh boy, wasn't that going to be fun! To cap it all, I was getting the distinct impression that our Mr Blackmore was also eyeing the exit door, but then Ritchie never, ever did anything without planning and much deliberation!

We returned to England just before Christmas for the holiday break. Throughout my time with both Deep Purple and Rainbow, Christmas and New Year have been totally sacrosanct. No band commitments of any kind for any reason and they have been offered sensational money over the last thirty years to do one-off Christmas Eve or New Years Eve concerts. The answer has always been an emphatic, but polite "no". Being with the family (of the moment for some), had always been their only concern at this festive time of the year. It also gave me time to get home to South Shields for a brief hello to Eddie and Bettie. My visits were becoming more infrequent as time went on, only seeing them if the band played Newcastle or I managed to get them to a show further a field. Billy had not returned home either, moving out of London to the coast at Harwich with his missus, Linda and the kids, where he'd become a full time truck driver. It was something he hated, but he could just not get back into the music business. He did a brief stint as a bass player, but had to look after the family first. Poor Billy! If you're out there, Billy, gimme a call!!

The impact of Ian's resignation sent the band into a period of self-doubt and unease. Ritchie and Ian Paice's recording stint, which I'd been at, with Phil Lynott, had increased the feeling that perhaps they would jump ship too. Certainly Coletta and Edwards, along with Roger and Jon Lord, held this view and the two managers made moves to nip it in the bud by sitting down with the drummer to persuade him that it would be absurd to throw all that Purple had achieved down the drain for an uncertain future with Lynott, especially when Thin Lizzy's career was taking off anyway. Paicey was persuaded and with Jon and Roger and the managers, sat down with Ritchie and more or less told him that, with Ian gone, he had the box seat, as it were, and could exercise pretty much total artistic control. Ah, control, Ritchie's favourite word. The search for the singer began.

Wolverhampton band, Trapeze, had been knocking on the door of the big time for quite a while, but the door was just not opening. Jon and Paicey went to see them at London's Marquee Club and were impressed by their singer, one Glenn Hughes. Apparently Ritchie liked him too, but more as a bass player than a singer, although skill in the latter would be great to augment a full-on lead singer, he thought. Poor Roger now saw that the writing was on the wall for him and realised that he, too, would be out the door with Ian, after the tour of Japan. He was mystified, very hurt and very low in that spring of 1973. You may ask why did Jon and Paicey not fight to keep Roger? Well, that's not them, they went with the flow, which was kinda disappointing to Roger, I'm sure. Ian Gillan was the fighter, the righter of wrongs, not Jon or Ian Paice.

Personally, all I cared about, bottom line was that I continued to have the greatest job in the world. If Ian was leaving, sad, as it would be to see him go, I wanted Deep Purple to carry on. I asked Tony Edwards what was to happen with the band, and specifically me. He assured me that it would carry on with a new singer and that there would always be a place for me in the organisation. Roger's departure was harder personally, as he had become a really close pal. What's not to like? He is one of the few guys I know who has no bad side to his character. His Ex-wives may disagree with me, but his small problem is he just loves everybody, which, I suppose, can be, shall we say, 'misconstrued', where the fairer sex are concerned. Doesn't mean he's a soft touch, just he would always see the good side in anybody, even though it might be a real stretch to find one. He was and is a man of infinite patience too. A prime requisite for the future producer of Ritchie Blackmore and Deep Purple.

August soon arrived and that last sad tour of Japan. At the last show in Osaka, Ian Gillan walked out on stage resplendent in a white jacket with his long black hair and recently grown black beard, all very John Lennon, which annoyed Ritchie big time. It just was not his idea of the rock 'n' roll image, precisely the reaction Ian had planned, no doubt. Ian sang the whole show with his hands in his pockets whilst Roger, true to his big heart, played the show of his life. After the concert, back stage in the dressing room, Roger just sat in the corner and unashamedly cried his eyes out. Jon, Paicey, and Ritchie just silently unwound deep in their own thoughts. Ian just walked out and went straight back to his hotel room. A little while later he rang down and asked if I would come up to the restaurant on the top floor of the hotel and have dinner with him and Zoë. He said how much fun it had been, but he just had to go. He asked if I would be going with him to the airport the next day. I, of course, agreed. The sadness in the room was colossal; you could touch it, wrap it up and take it away. The next morning, I arranged for the transport for the entire band and crew to wherever they wished as it was 'vacation' time. I got Ian and Zoë in the limousine and took them personally to the airport to say our goodbyes. I did not see him again for eleven years.

CHAPTER SIX
WHAT'S GOIN' ON HERE

Back home, once the word was out that a new lead singer was being sought, the Newman Street offices were bombarded with tapes of 'hopefuls'. These in turn were sent on to Ian, Jon and Ritchie. As I was living with Ian at the time in Fulham, I got to hear them too. You know, some guys just cannot be hearing the reality of their own voice! Some were good, some bad, some bloody awful, but they did all get a fair hearing. This one tape, however, kept on doing the rounds; the singers voice just had something. It went from Jon, to Ritchie, to Ian and back again. Ian Paice played it to me over and over asking me what I thought. In Ian's mind, this was the guy. The best of the bunch and his name was David Coverdale from Redcar in Cleveland: A northern lad like me, who was gigging around his local area in semi-pro bands doing covers by night, and working in a boutique by day.

He was duly contacted and invited to travel down to London for a real listen in a session with the band. This they did at a rehearsal studio under the Capitol Radio Studios in London. On the day, we all sat in the studios awaiting the arrival of this hopeful. The tape had been great, but you never really knew what the reality would be and, of course, he'd have to fit in socially. We certainly didn't need another Ian, God bless him, who would clash from the 'get go' with our Ritchie. That would not have been progress at all. David arrived. He was, eh well, okay on first sight. Tall, a tad plump and with glasses with an unfortunate squint or wandering eye. The song from 'Paint Your Wagon' briefly entered my head; you know "I was born with a wandering…" Ah, never mind. This was all forgotten when he sang. Wonderful, better than the tape, better than we could have ever imagined. Yet he was painfully shy which under the circumstances was understandable. He was an amateur, never been professional and here he was in the presence of, well, greatness. He was crapping himself, but you knew he'd very quickly, with careful nurturing be capable of equal greatness, with perhaps a little bit of help from outside sources. The band continued to run through a few bluesy numbers, after which they just kinda said "thanks". At that moment, no confirmation that he'd got the gig. David was sent back to Redcar and his job in a boutique probably believing he'd blown it.

Two weeks later they decided he was the one and this time he got the real treatment - his first class train fare (he'd paid his own way down the first time!) He met the band once more in Coletta's office and signed on after agreeing to a few conditions like lose weight, grow his hair, change his wardrobe and get his 'wandering' eye fixed, those outside sources I alluded to. It wasn't a hard choice for David to make. He signed and three months later including a short stay in a Harley Street eye clinic, he emerged the perfect rock star. He had also come with an unforeseen, yet welcome bonus, he could write great songs! Many years later, it was apparent that David's contract with Coletta and Edwards was pretty onerous. It was a long one and they had made David very aware that if he did not sign he would be on his way back to Redcar. In David's defence, what would anyone do faced with the option of joining one of the biggest bands on the planet or returning to oblivion, flogging cheap togs in a boutique on the outskirts of nowhere? Mmmm, now let me see, what would I have done!

By this time, of course, Roger was gone and Glenn Hughes was installed, so the new line up was complete and they all went off to Clearwell Castle to rehearse and write for the new album, eventually to be called 'Burn'. I say 'they' because I only went there for the set up. Ritchie had a huge bug up his arse about me. He was under the impression I didn't like him for some reason, when in actual fact I was scared to death of him most of the time, as were so many others. Anyway, HEC Management had other plans for me, which was to look after two new signings to the Purple label, so I cannot recount to you any of the intimacies at Clearwell, sorry!

These two bands, however, were Elf and Tucky Buzzard. Elf was fronted by the diminutive, but perfectly formed body of one Ronnie James Dio. Ronnie from Cortland, New York had started out his musical training on brass instruments such as trumpets, which probably gave him such an immense set of lungs, his voice could be heard for miles and of course helped give him one of the best rock voices around. The rest of the line up was Craig Gruber on bass, Mickey Lee Soule on keyboards, Gary Driscoll on drums and Steve Edwards on guitar. I mention these gents, as they will re-emerge later on in this tale of mine. Roger Glover, who hadn't drifted far from the fold was to produce their next album, 'Carolina County Ball', so my day-to-day contact with Roger happily remained intact. It was recorded at The Manor Studios, where my love for Ronnie and the band was set in stone. We had a fantastic time at the studio and at the pub down the road, of course. Even got Ronnie to play football a couple of times. I enjoyed playing when I wasn't being "ordered" to play, no matter what!

Into 1974, and 'Burn' was about to be released in the February, but by now there was a cast of thousands on the new crew. I was announced as tour manager for the new boys, Tucky Buzzard on the 'Burn' world tour, supporting Deep Purple, of course. Well, many questions were about to be answered. Would the band be as good without Mr. Gillan and Mr. Glover or, hold your breath, would they be better? There was no doubt that Ritchie was a happier man. After all, he now had a lead singer, unlike Ian, that he could bully (well, for now at least), and he had control. However, in life as in rock, nothing is forever.

The tour should have started in Aarhus, Denmark, but that was cancelled and we started the first show at the K.B. Hallen in Copenhagen. The tour ran until June 27th then resumed a month later on July 24th at the Orange Bowl in Miami running on until December 17th. The usual Christmas break, then from January 25th, through Europe ending April 7th at the Palais de Sport in Paris, (which would, unbeknownst then, be Ritchie's last with that line up.)

Glenn, as you would expect of a seasoned musician, shifted into gear effortlessly, standing his ground when necessary and contributing on an equal level with Paicey, Jon and Ritchie. David was, naturally, more unsure of himself, not in the vocals department, but more in the 'pecking order'. He was very aware that he was the new kid on the block not only as far as the band was concerned, but also as a professional musician. Ritchie took full advantage of this, that control thing you see. Jon would often sit with David and be his counsel and sounding board, offering advice where necessary or simply 'being a mate'. Just Lordy being what he is, a thoroughly nice bloke.

Many, many years later when David was the true rock god in Whitesnake, Jon Lord and I dropped in on him in an upstate New York hotel suite just to say hi. He kept us waiting in the lobby for a considerable time before we were granted an audience. I found this terribly insulting to

Jon who had been his mentor, protector and best chum. But then he was with Miss "Kitten"* at the time, if you get my drift! "How easily and quickly they forget," I thought. I was all for leaving, but Jon, ever the gentleman and super cool guy said to wait. We were eventually ushered into David's presence in his suite where he was serenely being served tea. I just looked for the nearest sick bucket!

Anyway, I digress. The album was a big success, but I just started to get the feeling that this would not be a long-term relationship. Glenn, no two ways about it was a 'white' soul singer, a brilliant one and, given the chance, would try to influence the band in that direction. David would write with Glenn and so the songs that resulted had that soul tinge. Ritchie, like Queen Victoria, was "not amused' and the familiar friction began to appear. True to form, Jon and Paicey just sat on the fence. They never really voiced their true feelings. Perhaps they may have felt too that the Deep Purple of old was gradually being hijacked. Perhaps, they didn't care or were happy at the change in direction? Yet, if they didn't speak up or wouldn't complain, wreck a hotel room or two, who was to know?

After rehearsing at Shepperton Studios in North London, they hit the road supported primarily by my Tucky Buzzard and later ELF and The Electric Light Orchestra (ELO). This is when I met for the first time that rock family without equal - The Ardens headed up by the father (Godfather?), the infamous Don Arden, with his son David and (pre-Ozzy Osborne) daughter, Sharon. Don, by hard earned reputation, was a tough guy and just loved the reverence this afforded him. Son David was thankfully with the band more than his father and was a real nice, easy to work with guy, but when Don was due to appear at a show, the ripple of anticipation akin to fear, that ran through ELO and its crew, was palpable. Fair dues, Don got great deals for his clients, not to say great for himself too. I mean how could you say no? Don came from the same school of management as Led Zep's Peter Grant.** No fear, no prisoners and absolutely no misunderstandings. Sharon was a great laugh and a really nice lass.

A bit heavier pound-wise back then than she is now in her high profile nip and tuck TV persona, but what's a girl to do? I really admire what she has achieved with Ozzy. When she married him, Don, I know was not best pleased with what his little girl was getting into and they didn't speak

---

* American actress Julie "Tawny" Kitaen who Coverdale married in 1989. They divorced in 1991.
** Grant had in fact worked for Arden in the sixties as tour manger for Gene Vincent.

for the next twenty years, but today, well, it's all turned out more or less okay, well for Sharon and Ozzy certainly. Don as it turned out did, shall we say, take more than he was entitled to from ELO. Sharon subsequently settled with Jeff Lynne for this discrepancy, which amounted to a considerable sum.*

ELO's act was wonderfully orchestral, surprisingly so when you consider they had only one cello and two violins, yet the full orchestra sound at times defied that slim line-up that seemingly produced it. Their soundman certainly earned his wages! Jeff Lynne, their leader was very quiet, a musical scholar heavily into his art who would go on to even greater things than the highly successful ELO, as a producer for Tom Petty and the Travelling Wilburys to name but two. No TV sets out of windows for Jeff after the show, probably just a cup of cocoa and a good book and trust me, that is not a criticism, far from it. Some come into this business to savour the life, others come for purely the music. Jeff definitely falls into the last category. Dick, my writing buddy here can remember Jeff when he fronted 'The Idle Race' back in Birmingham and they supported Vanity Fare at a gig at Birmingham University. All he wanted to do was discuss harmonies and such like. I suppose I was there too, but I guess Dick's memory is better than mine.

Anyhow, still in charge of Tucky B the summer found us travelling America on the famous 'Starship',** like all true rock stars did at the time. Well, it was expected! Coletta and Edwards informed the band in an almost nonchalant way that they could afford it. It did, in its defence, have the overriding advantage that you're travelling times were not dictated by airline schedules or that you had a heavy check in routine in a crowded terminal, which were two big problems with Deep Purple's rising star status. The daily routine of hotel, airport, show, hotel, airport, never varied that much throughout the tour.

It was apparent that the job was not that different from a parent trying to placate five teenage rich kids, all with different likes, dislikes, personalities and paranoia. From Ritchie with his 'control' thing and

---

* In 1979, one of Arden's artists, Black Sabbath, sacked vocalist Ozzy Osbourne who began to date Sharon, who then took over his management from her father. Arden was livid. Sharon married Osbourne and had no contact with her father for twenty years. In 2001 under Osbourne's insistence, Sharon and Arden finally reconciled. In August 2004 she announced that her father had Alzheimer's disease. He died in Los Angeles on 21 July 2007. She paid for her father's care in the last years of his life.

** The Starship was a former United Airlines Boeing 720B passenger jet, bought by Bobby Sherman and his manager, Ward Sylvester, and leased to touring musical artists in the mid-1970s.

perfectionism to Glenn with his ever increasing attraction to recreational pharmaceuticals. Jon was the tours librarian, so to speak, always accompanied by two cases, one for clothes, and the other for books. In later years, a third case would be added, the music case, in which was a small stereo system and enough CDs to satisfy his tour needs. Rather heavy, it was! He was an avid reader from the latest novel to philosophy and history - whatever he fancied at the time. The rest of the crew waited for him to finish the latest novel for it to be handed on. The 'book' case would get lighter through the tour only to get demonstrably heavier once Jon had hit a particularly good book store.

Many years later, even when Waterstone's and Barnes & Noble stores sprung up everywhere, Jon's addiction was never quite sated. Paicey was the gadget man, always after the latest piece of technology that would keep him in touch with home and specifically English football. It was standard practice, in later years, in any hotel, to book him into a south facing room (for northern hemisphere or north if in the southern hemisphere), the highest possible and preferably with no high rises opposite the room. He carried with him his own personal receiver dish, which he could direct towards whatever was the appropriate satellite to get his fix of soccer. Armed with a video recorder he'd never miss a match. It was a common sight, on booking into a hotel for him to be beside me with a compass. He'd ascertain where 'south' was, point and then look at me in expectation as I directed the receptionist to where Mr. Paice's room had to be. What has this to do with rock music? Absolutely nothing. With rock stars? Absolutely everything. David Coverdale kept very much to himself in the beginning, as he brought his then girlfriend from up north with him on the first section of the tour. She was very rapidly replaced by a hoard of available women, poor lass.

The American tour eventually took us to California where Purple headlined one of the biggest festivals ever, The CalJam in Ontario, California playing to over 400,000 people, supported by Black Sabbath, Emerson, Lake and Palmer and five other lesser names.* It lasted all day and we were shipped into the tournament site by what appeared to be an ex-Vietnam type helicopter. Quite a trip! I was primarily in charge of Tucky Buzzard for Purple Records, but I aided anywhere and everywhere,

---

* The full list of performers was Rare Earth, Earth, Wind & Fire, The Eagles, Seals and Crofts, Black Oak Arkansas, Black Sabbath, Deep Purple, Emerson, Lake & Palmer. Although it was Purple's gig, ELP was allowed to close the show, primarily as it gave Purple's crew more time to get to the next gig the following day in Phoenix.

as needed.

The whole show was a nightmare of disorganisation. The stage was a mess, backstage a bigger mess. Managers were arguing with other managers and collectively with the promoters, which didn't make for a great atmosphere. It was, in comparison to the present day festivals, a complete amateur cock-up. There was no dressing room coordinator like today. Then, it was whatever room is free you take. Get it, grab it, and keep it! It didn't make for a friendly band to band camaraderie either. True to form, Ritchie, ever the scene-stealer, on arrival at the festival site, locked himself in a free trailer and refused to come out until dusk. The whole show was running, unusually for a festival, ahead of schedule. Ritchie wanted the impact of sunset and full impact of lighting for Purple's grand entrance.

In fairness, Sabbath and ELP did not kick up too much fuss because they knew, either it would be futile where Ritchie was concerned or simply because they, at that time, deferred to the headlining act. The promoters started to get really antagonistic towards Ritchie for his delaying tactics and then towards the road crew as we were visible and his lordship wasn't. Whilst everyone was trying to cajole Ritchie to make an entrance, Ossie Hoppe went on stage and whipped up the crowd to expect Deep Purple at any minute. This cunningly diffused any notion the promoters might have had to axe Purple from the show altogether as the crowd went ape shit in expectation. Ritchie decided it was time at that point and made the grand entrance. The band stormed through a magnificent set.

Ritchie had planned the grand finale too. By now he'd become known for trashing Fenders at the climax of any show. This time he wanted something a little more spectacular. He'd blow up the Marshall stack at the point of impact of the 'Fender'. This had been done quite a few times before at previous shows and Ron Quinton was used to using a little flash powder and a dash of gasoline to just blow the front of a 'dummy' Marshall speaker cabinet. Ritchie wanted this to be special so he told Ron to double up on everything. The appointed time arrived and the detonation was truly spectacular, too spectacular, too much petrol and too much damn flash powder. Result - one very deaf and singed roadie in Ron Quinton, when the back of the speaker cabinet blew off. Poor old Paicey's glasses were blown clean across the stage, which by now was ablaze quite nicely and the force of the explosion nearly blew our guitar maestro off the front of the stage, setting him alight into the process.

Ritchie looked very shaken, but quietly considered how cool it was and how very effective it had been! Could never happen today with fire marshals, health and safety inspectors and very litigious promoters. Amateur times they may have been but they did allow a certain freedom of expression! If you watch the video of the show you can see all this quite graphically as you can also when Ritchie's destroys a television camera that got too close. He just hates cameras in his face and this one, on a track, kept getting right in front of him, so he decided to eliminate it by repeatedly ramming the lens with the guitar head. The film director must have told the cameraman to stay put, as he made no attempt to back off. A nice filmic moment and a nice hole in Ritchie's personal purse to the tune of around $20,000: In 1974, not chump change, not today either come to think of it! Tour over and we all came home weary, spaced out and happy.

****

In August, the band started on the new album at Clearwell Castle. Many months of touring had created a song writing bond between David and Glenn with the result that they come up with a selection of songs for what would be 'Stormbringer'. Problem was the songs were even more soul and funk slanted and this drove Ritchie insane. He hated, what he dubbed 'shoeshine music' and I could tell that his heart was not where it should be. He was losing that all-important control. He'd jammed with Ronnie James Dio and Elf on tour many times and had even secretively cut some tracks in Minneapolis, when we'd had some days off on that tour. I sensed that he would have preferred to maybe be with them where he could regain control over musicians and musical direction rather than stay and fight for control on a daily basis with Glenn and David.

In truth Elf had given Ritchie his escape route. Sadly Jon and Paicey could not be counted on to sway the balance in his favour. Worse still, Glenn was trying to get the gross national product of Peru up his nose! An unwelcome by-product of coming from no money to lotsa money. Glenn just loved cocaine, no doubt about it. I can remember sitting up with him at The Holiday Inn, Swiss Cottage in London one night while he played me songs on an acoustic guitar. He was so high, racing so fast he could just not stop talking and playing. Many times I got up to go to bed only for him to stop me and play me one more tune which he was obviously making up on the spot and it was pure drivel. I kept on giving him more booze in an attempt to induce sleep, but it had no effect on him, but I got quite drunk. It was dawn before he eventually nodded off and by that time I had to start to get on with the business of the day, knackered. Tour managers, we never sleep!

In America, Glenn had a regular supplier in a guy called Roger the Hat who would show up just everywhere, hotel, airport, and show, so great was Glenn's need, so important a customer for 'The Hat'. It wasn't as if the whole band were coke fiends, far from it, Glenn was not the lone user, but by far the heaviest. Me, I'm a Geordie - strictly beer! But then, as I found myself with more money, I could afford to hoist the occasional Scotch and coke, too. (Coca-Cola that is.) Ian Gillan and Roger liked the odd toot of herbal tobacco, but they were pretty much straight alcohol guys which probably isn't very rock 'n' roll, but then the music always came first with Purple, the lifestyle second whereas some of their contemporaries lived the life style first, the music second.

Ritchie took a lot of pride in always being in control of himself, let alone others. That slipped occasionally, but not very often. He would hardly ever go on stage worse for drink, in fact over the thirty years I have looked after him, I can count the times on one hand he's been "shitfaced" during a show, usually caused by a late running start due to technical problems. You see, he had a strict ritual before going on stage. Being fairly nervous about performing (shocked eh!), I always had to have for him a bottle of Johnnie Walker Black Label whisky unopened and sealed in his dressing room. He would mark the outside of the bottle where he knew he could safely drink down to in order to kill the nerves, but still be in total control.

It never ever varied. I had to give him the 'ten minute to showtime' nod, so he could reach the preordained level in the bottle. During the show he'd stay off the whisky and just have a bottle or two of Becks or Heineken handy, more to replace fluid loss than to get pissed. Scary, but sorta cool eh! The other guys were a tad more relaxed about alcohol intake and perhaps were a bit unnerved by the guitarists 'preparation'. Perhaps guitar 'gods' are more aware than most of what is expected of them by the fans - it's a very high bar to jump over EVERY night and Ritchie would never willingly settle for second best from himself.

He often thought the audience didn't deserve him though, which is why he often ducked an encore saying, "They don't deserve one, they (the audience) weren't good enough". I used to ask myself what he'd heard that I had not, as the crowd had gone berserk, erupted. By what or who had he been upset? Was this the ultimate cruelty that he could deal to his fans, maybe the ultimate control? Whatever, he'd show no remorse at all that he'd pissed off 5,000 to 10,000 fans. Ho Hum. After the show was finished he'd return to the hotel and maybe have two or three more bottles of beer, rarely more. That was usually when he became human. If it had been a good show and Ritchie was high on the adrenalin buzz, he could be a very funny sociable mate, no other words to describe it: Great company, nice and gracious to all. He'd egg me on to tell his favourite jokes or reminiscences, which I did, not needing that much encouragement, maybe I told 'em better. Come the next morning though, the mask would be back on.

Alas, through the escalating musical differences between Ritchie on one side and Glenn and David on the other, one way or another the band was doomed. One of the basic problems, looking back, was that they never sat down together to talk about what was going wrong like adults would, but there's the rub I guess: Too many egos, too much pride, and no courage to open up and express their personal feelings to each other. For Ritchie, in particular, that would have been and still is impossible. He is unreadable and to quote Glenn in later years, "He's got his mystique and loves to live in that, he's comfortable with it". Give me an amen!

At this time the management of Deep Purple had come to a head. I had heard the suspicions of Ian Gillan, twelve months before, that the finances of the band had, shall we say, been 'neglected' by Coletta and Edwards and had grown into full blown confrontation, and the band was refusing to renew its contract until there had been full disclosure. Their agent in America had been, right from the first tour I undertook with Matthews Southern Comfort, a guy named Bruce Payne. Then he had been with ATI Agency as their vice president even though he was pretty much my age, but soon left to set up his own company called Thames Talent, taking Purple's North American representation with him.

When I first met him in those days he had hair down to his arse as we all did, very much the hippy image, and so unlike the dapper debonair businessman persona he would acquire in later years. He compiled a roster of acts including Elf whom he had managed in earlier days. Bruce impressed the band with his hard work, undoubted savvy and depth of knowledge of the business. Thames Talent and Bruce acted as pure agents for the band, dealing direct with Jon and Tony, but on long treks across the States and Canada John and Tony were often absent, only showing up at prestigious gigs whereas Bruce was constantly around. Bands are like spoiled precious wives or girlfriends - they want constant attention and are high maintenance. Start neglecting them and they'll soon stray to the first available 'silver tongued devil' that fusses over them and is a shoulder to cry on.

Bruce had a 'golden tongue' and broad shoulders! They soon asked Bruce if he would look into their financial situation just to see if their suspicions were well founded. With their contract with Coletta and Edwards due to expire, Bruce popped the question and Purple walked up the aisle. It would prove to be a long lasting relationship for Bruce, maintaining and constructing Purple in all its component parts and, in turn, that turned out happily for me too. At the start Bruce and I were very close, almost equals and in the early years of the relationship, I protected Bruce on many occasions when the band, faced with some fuck up, would, as a knee jerk reaction, blame Bruce when in reality it was not his fault and I said so. I kept him well informed and well protected at all times.

As the years progressed from Purple to Rainbow and back again, Bruce transformed from the savvy hippy to the cold businessman and our closeness fell away to become very much, employer / employee. Bruce changed and I had not. Maybe it was me who was caught in a time warp and I couldn't or wouldn't change? Nothing ever stays the same. Maybe I expected too much, but my loyalty to Bruce over the coming decades would never be repaid. I guess I expected to be taken into Thames Talent as some point as a full time employee on the management side, but Bruce would always keep a tight ship and never expand the agency and management company. Empire building was not on the Bruce Payne agenda. Absolute control would be his and his alone with no delegation of decision making whatsoever. 'Tour manager' was as high as anyone could ever get on the Thames Talent ladder to the top simply because there was no higher rung. Bruce was next up and he was not for changing, ever!

****

With "Stormbringer" finished the inevitable world tour followed starting in America in November '74. Ritchie was becoming more and more distant, insisting on a separate dressing room and Glenn's drug intake was reaching alarming proportions. Behind the scenes, the whole structure of Deep Purple on tour had become a huge ridiculous monster.

Even the roadies had roadies! There were guys hired just to do luggage, guys just to do driving, guys just left behind to pick up forgotten luggage that played catch up throughout the tour, and guys just to work for roadies answerable to them and not the band. It was bizarre. There were an awful lot of people, posing around, not doing much. Worse still the band and its management sanctioned this ridiculous overhead. I was now devoted full time to Elf for Purple Records and we were on this tour. We were loving it, but I just knew Ritchie would leave very soon. He was looking for his exit. I also felt that when he baled out, Deep Purple would be finished.

As the tour continued through Europe, it was apparent to me that it was over and in Paris in April, Ritchie told the band, prior to the show, that this would be his last and that he was teaming up with Elf to do his own thing. A certain panic began to form deep within me. What would happen to me? God forbid, would I have to return to Shields and the borough engineer's office, the dream over? Rob Cooksey, who was now managing Purple with Bruce, came into the production office backstage and said that Ritchie wanted to see me in his dressing room. Once there, they explained in front of Ritchie that there was a proposition for me, which involved Ritchie's plans to form a new band with Elf called Rainbow and was I interested in being its tour manager? The inner panic disappeared instantly as the words 'Yes, of course' sped past my lips. I went from despair to euphoria in two seconds flat.

Ritchie played a blinder that night, I guess because it was all out in the open, unlike the preceding dates on this tour where it was patently obvious to band and fans alike that he didn't give a flying fuck anymore, often playing behind the amps or off-stage altogether and refusing encores. Jon and Paicey were mortified by Ritchie's declaration, yet they could hardly be surprised. The atmosphere in the Deep Purple dressing room after the show was seriously 'down' whereas next-door in Ritchie's room it was euphoric as he posed for photographs with Elf.

CHAPTER SEVEN
THE RISING RAINBOW

I had packed up in London and moved to Cortland in upstate New York quite some time before, to be close to Elf and we continued to work our Elf dates. I thoroughly enjoyed my time in Cortland with Ronnie and the guys. We all got along so well and it seemed like the whole town were our extended family. We had a little time off now to prepare for the big change in our lives, especially mine. I rang Eddie and Betty, explaining the situation and they, as ever, were totally supportive. Ritchie's plan was to have us all move to be close to him and work his new dream. We were summoned to move cross-country to California. Everyone... myself, roadies Raymond, David Needle, Gerry "Ox" Oxford and Mickey Lee's wife Ramona.

No sooner had we settled in than we decamped back to Europe to record the bands first album in Munich at the famed, although now defunct Musicland Studios, with Martin Birch producing. This was just prior to Ritchie's final tour with Purple. 'Ritchie Blackmore's Rainbow' got mixed reviews, disappointing Purple fans and perplexing those of Elf to whom the sound was not unnaturally closer (but not for long).

We all moved into our new accommodations at the north end of Malibu, near the Ventura County line: Very nice, too. We all shared two beachfront condos, apart from Ritchie, who rented a house in Oxnard for himself and his then "between wives" girlfriend, Shoshana. Ronnie had his own condo in the Malibu Bay Club, the next complex to ours. We rented Pirate Sound in Los Angeles, which was a sound stage and offices on part of the old Columbia Pictures Hollywood lot, and rehearsals began.

Even at rehearsals before we had done one show, I knew the signs of discontent in Ritchie were surfacing. He has this thing he does which, although he says nothing, his actions shout, reverberating around the room. He simply stops playing, slowly turns round, slips his guitar over his head and lays it on top of the stack, switches off and walks slowly and silently away. He did quite a bit of that at rehearsals. He admired Ronnie, of that there was no doubt as a singer and a lyricist, but he was used to virtuosos in Purple and I think he missed that, more than he would ever admit. He was funding Rainbow personally, so I guess he took the view that he had made his bed and he would have to lie on it for the time being. To start changing musicians at this early stage would scream 'panic' and give Purple, who were back in England trying to fill the gap, way too much satisfaction.

One day, noticing that a large amount of equipment was being shipped to the stage next to ours, I, inquisitively as ever, asked who it was. "Deep Purple for four to five days" came the amused reply. "They start rehearsals next week". I told Ritchie who also saw the irony and ordered a week off to avoid any embarrassment to anybody, despite him still having to pay a daily rental to the studios. Nevertheless, Ritchie asked me to 'drop in' to spy on their rehearsals and report back, which I dutifully did. Bolin was good, very good and fitted into the jazz funk direction that Glenn and David were determined to follow. Ritchie's curiosity could not be contained and I drove him down to the studios one afternoon. We quietly entered our sound stage and like two sneak thieves stealthily cracked open the double doors leading to Purple's stage. They were in full flow. Ritchie's face showed no emotion and he listened there for nearly half an hour. He finally looked at me, just shrugged as if to say, "No competition there" and said, "Okay, lets go"

By August, the first casualty was bass player Craig Gruber. Ritchie just could not suffer him any longer. This was made worse by Craig's obvious belief that the guitarist had hijacked Elf and his antipathy showed. Ronnie seemed unfazed on the surface that his band was being ripped apart; no doubt the obvious financial implications had a bearing. Next to go were keyboard player Mickey Lee Soule and drummer Gary Driscoll. The Rainbow 'revolving door' was firmly installed. Ritchie decided to hold auditions for drummers and bass players rather than go on recommendations and told me to go to the Musicians Exchange in LA with, if you like, an identikit profile of the archetypal rock drummer, bass and keyboard player, even down to how he, (forget she, as Ritchie would have never considered a woman to fill this role) should look. Every day I would scour the registers, which listed a photo and playing record; take addresses for guys that seemed to fit the profile; fix an audition date and see what happened.

Ritchie had Pirate Sound booked solidly for these auditions, already set up with amps, keyboards and drum kit although most discerning drummers brought their own. He had a pool table installed to the side slightly in the shadows and we waited for the players to arrive, playing pool to while away the time. Some never made it past the front door. I'd sit with Ritchie in the half-light by the pool table. If the very first visual impression did not please, he'd just say, "Tell him to go now". One poor guy turned up with his own roadie who then set this mammoth kit up while he changed into a full leather jump suit complete with black leather gloves. Ritchie just watched in the shadows, a faint smile of amusement playing on his face. I looked at him, he looked at me. "Get rid of him", he said and got up to play pool once more.

It was tough to be me at times like this, I can tell you. Down I walked, armed with the famous Geordie Bonhomie to tell this poor sap that he should go. It's a wonder I escaped unmarked and the look of rejection on his face haunted me for, well, at least a day. A scant few actually got to play and Ritchie would plug in, tell the drummer to keep up and then launch into a fast, very fast, boogie type shuffle. Not many kept up and the old guitar over the shoulder, place on top of the amp, switch off and walk away in silence routine was my signal to say, "thanks, we'll get back to you". Of course I knew full well we wouldn't. Cruel? Absolutely. Necessary? Of course. Could have been kinder? Not Ritchie's style. Funny? Fucking hilarious!

By this time, Scotsman Jimmy Bain from the band Harlot had been recommended as a likely contender for bass and Ritchie liked what he'd heard and invited him back to Los Angeles. Jimmy got the job and attended most of the auditions keeping pace with his new employer and saying pretty much nothing, so we were moving forward, at last. By this time, mid summer, most of Purple too, had moved to California with the remainder of their crew. It was an odd situation, to say the least, to see Jon, Paicey, Glenn and David plus the old crew around socially in the clubs on the strip in the evenings, but kinda cool too. There was absolutely no animosity. It also brought sadness. Ron Quinton, he of the exploding speaker cabinet at Cal Jam, who had moved to L.A. too, met an untimely end. One night, Jon Lord threw a big party for "everyone" at his condo, which was a beautiful three-storey end unit in the same complex as Ronnie and everyone rocked up. Purple, Rainbow, crew, just everybody (except Ritchie there!) Ron, considerably worse for drink, decided against all advice to drive himself home to Hollywood. He drove down Pacific Coast

Highway, a drive he'd done many, many times before albeit not drunk. He took a bend on the wrong side of the road and hit another car head on. He was dead, as they say, at the scene. Poor Ronnie, a great guy. He'd cheated death however the year before, falling asleep at the wheel on the A4, just outside London, but had survived that wreck. I guess he just run out of luck.

It was now September and we still had to find a drummer and keyboard player and time was running out with Bruce talking about tour dates from November. The Musicians Exchange route to recruitment was proving fruitless; so Ritchie, a tad reluctantly, told me we should, first of all, perhaps find an established name drummer, who would be a known quantity. I think he felt uneasy with this, as it would mean possibly inviting another competing ego into the fold that could perhaps kick at his domination over Rainbow. He wanted pliable non-confrontational players, that's for sure. We threw names around and one of our guys suggested Cozy Powell. Ritchie visibly brightened at he thought of the drummer who had growing respect in the business for his past work with Jeff Beck, Bedlam and as a session drummer. He'd also had a solo single out called 'Dance With The Devil' which had been a considerable hit and caused the drummer considerable embarrassment to his 'street cred'.* He certainly did not want to be remembered as a latter day Sandy Nelson. Cozy was contacted and duly arrived accompanied by his own roadie, Bob Adcock who'd been with him since his days with Jeff Beck in 1971. Usual audition routine, even for someone of Cozy's stature. Ritchie and Jimmy set off at an awesome paced 'shuffle' and Cozy kept right there with them for about twenty minutes. Suitably impressive to all, he was hired on the spot! Part of the deal was that a place had to be found for Bob in the scheme of things, so, with Bruce's agreement; he became my assistant, which pissed Bob off no end.

A few weeks after Cozy had joined, Jimmy Bain recommended Californian keyboard player Tony Carey who he knew. (Just why he had not mentioned him before, was a mystery, but he's Scottish and forgetful, go figure). Tony was a classically trained, Juilliard School of Music type guy and all that. He came, he auditioned, he kept up, he was hired. We were a complete band again. All through this summer of recruitment, preparation had being moving forward back in New York for the

---

* 'Dance With The Devil' reached number 3 in the UK charts in early 1974.

construction of the giant 'Rainbow' that was to be the centrepiece backdrop to the live show. Built by the lighting company 'See Factor', it consisted of four sections of aluminium and steel, accompanied by two risers for either end for the bigger stages. The drawback was that it severely restricted the working stage area, but as it was a 'great idea' dreamed up by Ritchie and Ronnie, it had to be used, but like all 'great ideas', the practicality sometimes escapes the joy of the originators. It was like the Brooklyn Bridge and as heavy. In truth, it never, ever worked properly. It consisted internally of thousands of light bulbs all worked from a computer, the idea being that the 'light' would shoot from one side of the arc to the other. When the light 'whooshed' across, the amps joined in with massive interference and static.

The only time the interference ceased was when all the lights were on (or off!) It looked great and the effects were stunning when it worked properly, but the gremlins could never be permanently ironed out. John, the technician in charge of it on the road, spent his whole life inside it, trying to sort it out, replacing bulbs and tinkering with the computer. It drove him, me, Raymond (D'Addario) and certainly Ritchie to distraction. Its inclusion meant the rig time for any show extended to around seven hours to get this bloody thing erected and it took up half the capacity of a 40' trailer tractor rig to transport it. Can you tell I wasn't a fan? Rainbow persevered with it for many years until it was eventually dropped from the show. It subsequently languished in storage in New York for years and was rumour has it, eventually sold to a disco in Mexico. Any Rainbow fans on holiday down Mexico way may well bump into it or have it cause annoying interference on your hotel TV screens!

Rehearsals started in earnest and in tandem with working up material for the new album. As we shared the same agency, I was aware that Deep Purple, Tommy Bolin safely installed, were away on tour in the Far East. Tragedy struck them in Jakarta when Patsy Collins, one of Purple's long time security men, suspiciously fell six floors down the hotel lift shaft to, not surprisingly, his death. Rob Cooksey, who by now was tour managing the band also got severely beaten up immediately after, when he tried to shed some light on the incident. Various tales drifted back of rioting fans and out of control police. Save it to say that Jon Lord has consistently refused to go back to this day. There is a brotherhood between road crews and we were all pretty down about it.

My private life around this time was getting difficult. Marlene had been with me in London all through my time working for Purple Records and looking after Elf and Tucky Buzzard. She had moved with me to Cortland, New York when Rainbow was formed and then onto Malibu. We were great together, but she knew I would soon be away pretty much constantly from now on and she wanted stability, not a relationship conducted by phone. She knew I loved my job and rather than give me the ultimatum "the road or me", she quietly ended it and moved out. What's the phrase? "If you love them, set them free". She had a job and got another apartment for a while. Later she moved back to Miami to her mom's place. The memory of her walking away haunted me for many years to come.

As the band had developed and most of the imported "Cortlanders" were now history, the accommodation arrangements had changed. The beach condos were let go. Cozy moved into a house in the hills behind the Capitol Records building with Bob Adcock, and rented the attached apartment to Jimmy Bain. Ronnie rented a house in Encino and Ritchie rented a house in the Hollywood Hills, up behind the Hyatt on Sunset. I moved into the Sunset Marquee Hotel, which became my home for quite some time, while we prepared to tour.

By late October, we were pretty much ready and Bruce gave me the first series of dates for which to prepare. We headed to Canada, to the Montreal Forum Concert Bowl where we were supported by Argent on 10th November. The show was not a sell out, but Ritchie was fairly philosophical. After all, this was a new beginning. Even he did not expect to attract crowds of Purplesque proportions, well not quite yet. The rainbow arch did not perform well either, surprise, surprise. Two days later we were at The Beacon Theatre in New York, once again with Argent. Russ Ballard was their guitarist and writer and would figure later in the direct success of Rainbow. The tour set off crisscrossing America, the shows often blighted by that bloody rainbow arch and also demonstrating that booking agents don't know their geography. The East coast, the West coast and back again with seemingly no logic to it. Ritchie was paranoid about his personal sound and just would not go on unless he could see me at the sound desk beside the engineer, Davie Kirkwood, with my hand poised over Ritchie's fader.

Once I had got them all on the side of the stage ready to go on, I then had to rush into the auditorium to the desk. Some nights this could take some time. Once I signalled I was in place, the show would start, bless him, but he'd always look to my direction from time to time to check I hadn't slipped away. I was often tempted to get a cardboard cut-out of myself and stand it next to Davie, but balked at the idea in case Ritchie wanted me to wave. It was daft really because Davie was very competent, more so than me in the sound department, but Ritchie just had to have me there in plain sight. By the end of December, we wound it up in Tampa, Florida. Christmas beckoned back in California and there was an album to record come the New Year.

A month off for tour managers is in reality, being at home at the beck and call of the band, which meant Ritchie. However, I did go briefly home to Shields for the Christmas break for some good old home cooking and to see Mam and Dad who just did not seem to change. At a pub in Shields I bumped into John Miles, also home for Christmas. He lived on and off in London where he was trying to get a record deal off the ground. I wished him well, which may or may not have done the trick as he was No.2 in the UK singles chart by April with his one (and only) hit "Music". January and I was back at The Sunset Marquee for some quality time even if it was, at times, interrupted by the business of the band. I had to set up the recording, scheduled for February at Munich's Musicland again, in the basement of The Arabella House, which was a hotel and apartment house. I had to organise the flights for the band and get the crew and equipment in place as well as ensure producer Martin Birch was in the loop.

Why Germany when there are gazillions of places way better to record? Well, simply put, Ritchie just loved all things German and had it in his head, convinced even, that in a former life he was a German nobleman or some such. It was a Ritchie thing and you just went with the flow on this with him, you just didn't goosestep in his presence and attach little moustaches under your nose, he'd take it the wrong way! He speaks German fluently though, has been married to two German women and has lived there off and on since his teenage years learning his chops on Hamburg's Reeperbahn in the sixties, so I guess it's not a passing fancy. In later years, he would change his recording venues to somewhere hot and near a soccer field. Well, you can take a thing too far, you know!

Anyway, back to the plot, Martin Birch was becoming an increasing presence and had in later years become the sound engineer on the road for Purple as well as the recording engineer/producer, before he was sweet-talked away by Iron Maiden. The recording, of what would become 'Rainbow Rising', only took ten days, no time at all really with the tracks each taking no more than two to three takes, such was the immediacy and cohesion of this, my favourite Rainbow line-up. Ritchie and Cozy became very close, the former allowing the drummer a totally free hand to interpret Ritchie's ideas, a pretty unique arrangement for the guitarist, which was a measure of his musical trust and respect for Cozy. It was a happy time 'cos, as was oft said; "If Ritchie's happy, we all happy!" 'Rainbow Rising' surprised everyone, including the band as to its quality and raw power. Now we had to translate that to the live show.

Returning to California I began, through Bruce and Thames Talent, to set up the 'Rainbow Rising' tour and it was to be a mammoth trek of Marco Polo proportions. The band members returned to their respective homes to get to know their families again and recharge the batteries for many, many months on the road. One day Ritchie announced he would throw a party at his house in the Hollywood Hills. Not any old party, but a slick suave soiree with good food, good wine, classical music and a select close group of like-minded friends. Eh, not very rock n' roll Ritchie? I was invited to be barman and chief usher / door opener. As it is said, it's all in the timing.

Alas Led Zeppelin were in town staying at the Hyatt (Riot) House on Sunset. Led Zep meant John Bonham, who could sniff out a party from three states away and the word was out that Ritchie was to have a party with a strict guest list and Bonzo was not on it (as he had the unusual habit of getting a bit out of hand when drinking!) The party was in full swing, the heavily candle scented air accented by the lilting music of Bach. I dispensed cocktails and wine, the ever-dutiful barman. The doorbell rang and I glided to the door. There stood Bonham and his ever-present shadow Richard Cole. "Good evening" says he in his heavily accented Birmingham brogue. "I hear there's a bit of a piss up going on here". "Do come in," I said, not wanting to piss him off or indeed be the one to shut the door on one of my all time heroes. It was also the slightly lesser of two evils - pissing off Ritchie came ever so slightly second. Ritchie spied him from across the room. "What's he doing here? Can't you get rid of him?" (Like that was an option now he was in) Poor Ritchie!

He had tried so hard to make this a tasteful affair and he could see his plans going down the gurgler. I served Bonzo large neat vodka as he enquired, "What's with the morbid music? Isn't this supposed to be a party?" he said exhaling heavily. It was evident that this was not the first watering hole our drummer boy had visited this fine evening. He wandered over to the stereo system and, with that wonderfully, destructive scratching noise that can only be made with a stylus dragged over vinyl, yelled, "What the fuck is this shit? I want to hear that 'Silver Mountain Man'," referring of course to 'Man On The Silver Mountain' the current Rainbow single. Well it was close. He rummaged through RB's record collection until he found the album and put on the track after a few more stylus scrapes. He then cranked it up to eleven and started to enjoy himself, a broad smile across his face, as did most of the other guests.

Ritchie, visibly infuriated, went to his stereo and replaced his own album with Bach once more. Bonham, stopped short in mid boogie, stormed back to the stereo with a very irritated look on his face, frisbeed Bach across the room and returned the sounds of Rainbow to the assembled and bemused guests. You'd have thought Ritchie would see the compliment that this icon of rock was paying him, that a man such as Bonham would demand that he hear the latest work by Ritchie and of course Ronnie James. Well, alas no. Ritchie returned once more to regain his control of the music. Bonzo came back to me for a refill and I could see the devil in his eye as he began to liven up the proceedings in his own inimitable way. Into the pool went most of the females who were within pushing or pulling distance along with whoever tried to impede him. He then followed clasping the nearest three people close to him.

The party now took on a whole new dimension with semi-naked women and some extremely wet braless tops on view. Ritchie glowered silently, spun around, gave it up and disappeared to another quieter part of his home, his evening in tatters. Bonzo, after a few more large ones emerged quite naked from the pool, tucked his clothes under his arm; beckoned to the smirking Cole and got into his car. The equally inebriated Richard Cole then got into the drivers seat and they were gone into the night. I heard the next day from Zep's crew that they had got right back to the Hyatt without mishap and pulled up outside. Bonzo then got out totally naked, walked through the lobby saying a polite "good night" to all the stunned staff and guests and entered the elevator, about turned, waved and retired to his room. Back in the Hollywood Hills at the Blackmore's, the party went on for several hours with a much more loose feel about it. It was a great success, the talk of the town for weeks, but Ritchie never mentioned it again. The evening went with a bang and ended with one for me too, literally!

****

On June 6th, the tour kicked off in Stateline, Idaho which might seem strange, but it was thought best to start the 'warm ups' out of the glare of the music biz to avoid any rustiness being misconstrued as the real deal. Thin Lizzy, who were a hot band at that time with 'The Boys Are Back In Town' in the charts, was to be our main support, and along the trail Southside Johnnie and The Asbury Dukes, Heart, Mahogany Rush, and England's Gentle Giant joined us at various points. However at the last minute Lizzy withdrew due to an illness to Phil Lynott and the band flew back to England.

On some dates we did the supporting role to arena bands such as Jethro Tull, as Bruce began his task of elevating Rainbow to larger audiences to regain the status held by Deep Purple. Tull had a great set up and road crew led from the front by tour manager Andy Truman who was one of the best in the business. I learnt so much from him about the job. He was a businessman from Yorkshire, England who was a personal friend of Ian Anderson, first and foremost, and had been persuaded by the flautist to run Tull's tours. He taught me backstage diplomacy in that you'd achieve far more far quicker if your dealings with people, particularly venue staff and owners, were done with a willing smile and warmth rather than with the usual rock star 'attitude'. It was pure manipulation, but very effective. Once again though, the bookers had lost the map of America! I hate to think of the unnecessary expense of continuously retracing our steps. The US dates eventually finished on August 3rd at The Starlight Bowl Amphitheatre in Burbank, California - home at last albeit briefly!

Three weeks later and the caravan reached England with the first show at Bristol's Colston Hall followed by dates in Leicester, Liverpool, Edinburgh, Manchester and finally three nights at The Hammersmith Odeon in London. It is expected at British dates, more than anywhere else, that friends, acquaintances, hangers-on, free-loaders, record company rep's and just folk you've never heard of will contact the band and thus me for tickets and passes back stage, under any pretext imaginable; yet another intrusion into your tour manager day. I've always tried to accommodate everyone as I see it as an important part of the band PR. So many people work behind the scenes to make stuff happen that to deny them the kudos of getting backstage is being pretty shitty. However, there is "backstage" and really "backstage". I'd arrange a separate room away from the band dressing rooms and recreation area where "backstagers' could congregate with a few beers and sodas. The band would then 'drop in' to this room after the show.

What I've always tried to square with security is the 'roamer'; these folk are a problem and believe the pass is 'open sesame' to every area. Nooooooo! That's a pass that says 'Access all Areas' and is strictly monitored. Ritchie, true to that part of his mystical character, rarely met 'back stagers' leaving that socialising to the rest of the band. He gave me on this occasion strict instructions that if Deep Purple came a-callin' he was not at home. He didn't mind them backstage, but they were not to call on him and especially not David Coverdale, who had been derogatory about Ritchie in the press and the maestro was not pleased. Jon Lord, Paicey and dear old Roger did show up, but thankfully not David. I was really glad to see them and it was mutual. We spent a good time reminiscing. It was obvious however that all was not well and Purple had fallen apart.* They had done some dates in England earlier in March and Bolin had 'frozen' on stage in Liverpool. By this time, Glenn's and now Bolin's drug intake was out of control. According to Paicey, Tommy Bolin just crumbled on stage and fled back to the States straight afterwards unofficially breaking up the band. Little did we know then that three months after this show Bolin would be found dead in a Florida hotel room from a heroin overdose, which sort of made it official.

Our tour then continued through England, eventually stopping at Newcastle City Hall on September 14th. It was always good to come home especially with Purple and now Rainbow. It was, if you will, confirmation that I had made something of myself. Playing to a sell out 'home' crowd, so to speak, gave me an immense buzz. Eddie and Betty were my very special guests and would always sit up front right through every show. I bet their ears rang for a week, but they never said a word of complaint, happy I guess that my big gamble had seemingly paid off. Ritchie was extraordinarily kind to them. His dressing room door was never shut to them. He'd even seek them out if he knew they were back stage, chatting away to them like they were his own. Back at the hotel he'd sit with them and talk to Eddie about anything under the sun. Eddie took me aside once and said how nice Ritchie was, but a bit of a lonely lad who was into funny stuff like the occult. Not daft my old man, very perceptive! Yet, today, with Eddie and Betty long gone, I'm grateful to Ritchie for being, well, so gracious to my parents. He didn't have to be which is why

---

* Deep Purple's split was announced to the press in July.

I appreciate it all the more. He sure is an enigma.

The tour continued on through Germany, Austria, Switzerland and up into Scandinavia supported mainly by emerging Aussie rockers and renowned drinkers AC/DC. Whenever we encountered a new band as a support who were beginning to get a reputation, Ritchie would observe quietly from the wings, the longer he stayed to watch their set was the level of how much he considered them worthy of their spot. AC/DC got about thirty minutes, which is a long time for Ritchie even though he did find Angus Young's stage wear a little amusing. Bon Scott, their singer was, he thought, tremendous. When we were in Frankfurt after a show, I was driving Cozy back to the hotel through a very seedy part of town when we spied their drummer Phil Rudd staggering along the street absolutely arseholed and having an altercation with some of the local populace. We stopped and told him to get out of the area and stop being a dickhead, but he just wanted to stay there, stand his ground and not go back to his hotel. How wonderfully Australian! We quickly bundled him into the car, as this was just not the part of town to pick a fight especially as he was not the biggest guy in the world. He very reluctantly allowed us to take him back, but the next night and the others after that he would repeat the exercise. Get shitfaced, find the local badlands and try to rearrange the locals. It's called a death wish, which happily was not granted then or since.

Guitar demolition was now the expected finale and ritual to a Rainbow show. This sounds like sacrilege, I know, to a wonderful instrument, but as you would expect they were either Fender Stratocaster seconds or cheap Japanese imitations from which a roadie had erased the name prior to each show. We even tried to recover the bits of the Fender seconds, if they were not too damaged, to glue them back together, but I guess about 80% were beyond repair. The guitar tech roadie would loosen the screws to the neck on these to ease the breaking point so that destruction would take place at a critical point for reconstruction. Sorry to shatter any illusions, but Ritchie just would not destroy a pukka Fender Strat, well not on purpose! One tragic night, Ian Broad,* who was not his guitar tech, but happened to be closest to the guitarist, tragically handed Ritchie his number one guitar and not the dummy. Ritchie played it for a few bars then went into full demolition mode. He realised after a very short while

---

* Blackmore and Broad, a former drummer, had played together in 1964 in The Wild Ones (also know as The Wild Boys), and in 1966 they toured Italy in a band called The Trips.

that this was not a dummy, but the real thing. He didn't miss a beat and completed the task, with a tear in his eye no doubt, considering that way better than stopping half way through for the audience to suss the error.

Full destruction of Ian Broad occurred shortly after the show finished, maybe a touch unfairly, but who said this was a fair business. Yet, deep down Ritchie really loved "Broady" and would forgive him almost anything. Safe to say the error was never repeated! You have to realise what this destruction meant. Ritchie's Fenders were not 'shop bought' in that they were standard manufacture specifications. They had been highly adapted and upgraded by Ritchie, once acquired. The frets, extra fat, would be routed and grooved and the neck deepened between them so that he could bend one string under another. Anyone picking one up to play, (as if) would have to play 'finger light' otherwise it would be out of tune instantly. The pick ups were 'souped up' and his amps modified, (courtesy of a tech guy named John Stillwell of Dawk Sound from Ithaca, New York), so much so, that we often picked up passing cab drivers 'chatter' and any one else on a similar frequency within a radius of twenty miles.

Only John was ever allowed to work on Ritchie's guitars and amps and was flown anywhere in the world to Ritchie if there was a problem that a mere mortal guitar tech could not solve. In later years John Stillwell would be let loose on Jon Lord's keyboard set up. All this modification had an adverse and opposite reaction as it caused colossal buzz through the PA systems so much so we employed a buzz tech whose sole job was, once all the gear had been rigged, to wander all over the stage with it all on, full bore, guitar in hand to eliminate the inevitable buzz. Sometimes he just did not succeed and Ritchie would sing a familiar song "I ain't going on (until you lose that buzz)". We always did, to a certain acceptable Ritchie level, but it would be touch and go.

Anyhow, back to the plot. The seconds and copies were not cheap and initially their purchase was at Ritchie's expense, but as the tour continued he changed the cost to a 'band expense' as he considered it was part of the show and should be registered as an official tour overhead. Nobody, of course, dared object. Touring was fun again. Ritchie and the band were playing so well, and it reflected in the 'off duty' times. Yet the boredom threshold of our guitar hero was notoriously low and I felt sooner rather than later he would start tinkering with the line-up, eternally seeking that perfect blend, but, you know, this line-up was the closest he would ever get.

Ritchie admitted one day to Roger Glover in later years that he simply could not bear other people being happy. If he saw it, he had to upset it and cause chaos, then he in turn was happy. Spooky eh! Bruce and I eventually used this to our advantage. We'd often find ourselves together before a show with everything pretty much handled and under control, having a quiet cup of tea or a beer (which Ritchie hated as it looked as if we had nothing to do and were, God forbid... enjoying ourselves!) If Ritchie appeared Bruce and I would start arguing and gesticulating, blaming each other for some imagined crisis. He'd saunter over and ask if everything was under control. Bruce would rant that everything was fucked up, but he and I would move heaven and earth to fix it. "Excellent" Ritchie would simper, smile at these perceived problems and, happy, get on with his day. We too, were then happy and all would be well with the world of rock.

The European leg of the tour was coming to an end in Paris in mid October. Erik Thomsen, our European agent was the butt of many of Ritchie's practical jokes, which I have to say he always took in good heart (that Ritchie? so funny!) Well, in the top three of 'Erik stunts' was having him 'flown' over the audience buck naked in a harness in that city of romance and elegance, quite stunning! Now obviously this was not an impromptu performance, as we had practised the routine with a couple of fully dressed roadies at the sound check just to ensure that the harness was safe and that Erik could not fall or wriggle out. This was, of course, mandatory for the roadies not a choice, they were only junior roadies after all, quite expendable.

Now Erik was always game for a laugh, either out of sheer bravado or because he wanted to keep the business. Is that too cynical of me? A little worse for wear, which was understandable given the task at hand, Erik allowed himself, after one almighty struggle which he knew he would not win, to be strapped in to the harness during the encore and, much to Ritchie's delight, was flown above the band from our Rainbow arch, swinging helplessly, quite naked, his Danish 'credentials' for all to see. Every camera in the place scanned to vertical and Eric was immortalised. The trouble was his five minutes of fame were rubberstamped on the front page of the Danish papers the very next morning. The result was his bank manager called to say that they could no longer do business together, which proved beyond doubt that the Danish have no sense of humour. (Not all of them, anyway!) Erik was mortified and I think even he thought we had gone too far.

It wasn't only Rainbow that 'got' Mr T. Eric Clapton, on a later tour, actually travelled through Europe to each show by train (as you do) and Mr. Thomsen was once again the European agent. Clapton had his own carriage, which was hooked up to the regular service from city to city. Unhappily our jovial Dane was once more persuaded to divest himself of all clothing (It's a Scandinavian tradition, obviously) and as the train stopped just outside of some far flung European snowbound town, he was dumped naked from the train as it moved once more, never to return, or certainly not for the guy in the birthday suit. The things you do for love and commission! He was one of the world's greatest promoters and a great friend.*

Cozy, however, gets first prize for the worst (or best) prank on dear Erik in Gelsenkirchen, goaded on naturally by Ritchie. First of all, I was given the task of stealing his room key. Not difficult, if you know Erik. He checked in and we invited him down to the bar. On arrival he threw his key onto the bar, in expectation of the first bevy of the day. I slipped the key into my pocket and the crew, with Cozy, proceeded to totally empty Erik's room of every piece of furniture, leaving only the carpet and the phone. He went back to his room much later in the evening and quite naturally complained to reception, bitching like hell. They apologised and he was given another room. He then came back to the bar and without much trouble I picked his key from his pocket and the new room was reduced to total emptiness like the first. On retiring for the night, Erik's consternation at yet another empty room was overcome by his fatigue, so having scrounged a couple of pillows he bunked down on the floor for the night.

Was that the end of it? 'Fraid not. Cozy, who was an athletic lad, found a fire extinguisher and scaled the outside wall of the hotel intent on letting it off through the open skylight balcony window of our long suffering promoter just to emphasise, well, I really have no idea what, except how boorish British rock stars can be? Now it goes wrong, gets out of hand like all good schoolboy pranks. Cozy, bless his heart, never the sharpest blade in the draw, counted the rooms wrongly. You know how it goes, "Its eight floors up and five along Cozy my son". He scales the wall

_____
* Erik Thomsen died in 2006.

chanting the mantra "five floors up and eight along. Five floors up, eight along".

Problem number two, the fire extinguisher like all good German products was the state of the art, top of the range oxygen depleter type deal, NOT your regular foamy type that would just get Erik, well, foamy (if it had been his room which it wasn't). The German business man occupying five up and eight along never knew what hit him other than he knew he was running out of air fast which was not quite what one was accustomed to in a five star hotel in wonderful Gelsenkirchen, in the middle of the night. The poor chap, slowly asphyxiating, managed to crawl flat to the floor to the door where he duly collapsed and was rushed to emergency. Oops! The next morning I was summoned by the manager of the hotel to accompany him to this poor guys room which was covered in a film of grey powder with his outline quite discernable on the bed and his desperate drag marks to the door. Cozy was mortified and immediately went to see the recipient of the prank to apologise profusely and beseech the chap to not involve the police. Unbelievably, Cozy's begging worked, his grovelling was accepted and it went no further. Who said the Germans can't appreciate British humour?

On reflection, God knows what would have happened if he'd got the right room and Eric, in his drunken slumber, had not woken up. It doesn't bear thinking about and the 'pranks' subsided for quite a while after that. Well, apart from a car race one night in Germany between Erik and Cozy; the drummer challenging the Danish promoter to who could get back to the hotel the fastest in their individual cars. Erik, like the loveable fool he was, accepted. Surely he suspected a prank; after all he'd been the object of most of them from most of the bands he'd toured. They set off in a Le Mans style start racing for their 'chariots'. Unbeknownst to Erik, during the show, the road crew had tied several rows of stacked chairs to his back axle with enough slack to give him a good start. Cozy was out the back lot of the arena and away into the night, Erik was hot on his trail until the avalanche of chairs that zoomed after him took up the slack. He slowed considerably and created a tremendous noise as they whacked off the walls, trash bins and odd vehicles that were unfortunate enough to be in the locale.

Over an hour later Erik entered the hotel bar, shame faced to a smiling Cozy with his feet up. The local promoter was not amused and Erik had to pay up for all the damage. All I can say was that Erik must have been making a good profit on all these tours to be able to pay the damage that was caused. I think he judged that if it kept his clients amused, it was worth it. By mid October we had completed Europe with a final date at the Congresgebouw in Den Haag, Holland. We waved our Australian mates, of whom we had become quite fond by now, goodbye and set our compass for Australia. How coincidental!

The two-week gap before we arrived in Perth, Western Australia was a time to recharge batteries for the band, but for yours truly there was no such luxury. An immediate flight back to California, which by now was losing its appeal, a furious two weeks of planning equipment hire, arrangement of visas for band and crew and just maybe an odd moment to myself to reflect on my non-existent personal life was the scheme of things. Ray D'Addario, a survivor of the Elf road crew, was in charge of the backline and together with Bob Adcock, my trusty right hand and Cozy's batman; we got everything and everyone to Australia for the first show at the Entertainment Centre on 4th November.

Australia's a damn big place where nobody lives if you consider that in a country the size of the U.S.A the total population is about that of New York City alone! Still, we managed eleven pretty much sold out shows, interspersed with much sunbathing for the band and, for me, visiting embassies to fix the visas for the next part of the tour - Japan, a country Ritchie seemed to hate, but in which he never refused to perform. His reasons were, I'm sure, nothing to do with Japanese fans, more to do with Japan's overbearing authorities who never allowed the fans to express their exuberance at the performance. Because of this, Ritchie found it a sterile land with no vibe at all.

Tony Carey, however, was not holding it together on the road. It was a given that he was an excellent musician, but he did not tour too well. He became too often the butt of Ritchie's 'humour' and never retaliated which, of course, encouraged the guitarist even more to even greater pranks of humiliation. Tony retreated into drugs of any kind he could obtain, not hard stuff, more of the pill and amphetamine persuasion. If a bum offered him some on the street, he'd buy 'em and swallow 'em, then ask what they were! Crazy!

I'd warned him prior to departure to Tokyo that Japanese Immigration was very strict and he must not be carrying anything that he shouldn't. He then had the good taste to swallow everything he had on the plane. Literally, everything he had! Of course, normal folk flush 'em down the toilet on the plane prior to landing; Carey flushed 'em down his throat. Hey waste not, want not. I said to him as we got off the plane, "hey, Tony, you've got to pull yourself together to get through this immigration. These guys are tough. Be cool, I'll be with you, stand next to me in the same line and we'll walk you through". The rest of the band and crew went to other lines keeping Tony and I at a discreet distance. Thanks!

I was called to the line and the next thing I heard was Cozy's voice saying from the adjacent line, "he's behind you on the floor". I winced, turned and looked down. Not only was Tony on the floor, but he was also curled up fast asleep or unconscious, it was hard to tell. I rushed back and pleaded for him to get up, slapping him. "Next", the immigration official shouted (or a Japanese approximation of it). "Tony, get up. I'm gonna fucking kill you," I whispered loudly in his ear. "Whaaa, whereeee, ummmmmmmm, whoooaaaaaaar youuuu". This from a Juilliard graduate, phish! I turn to the Japanese official explaining that my friend is very sick and he shrugs and incredibly, impossibly, accepts this. He stamps his passport and I manhandle Tony through. Must have been the end of the officials shift and he was on a promise from mamma san. Fair play though, Tony had taken me at my word. He had nothing on him... in him? Oh yes.

The Japanese dates went off flawlessly with dear old Martin Birch yet again recording the live show for posterity at Bruce's behest, more I think as insurance in case it all went tits up for some reason. Bruce is nothing if not cautious, but maybe he knew something I didn't? The 'Rainbow Rising' tour came to a final halt at the renowned Budokan in Tokyo on December 16th after an arduous six months non-stop touring. We all went our separate ways. I went home to Shields for Christmas, fine ale and the company of my family and friends. What next I thought?

CHAPTER EIGHT
BALANCED ON THE BRIM

The last six or so years had been fun and I tried over that time to keep in touch with folk back home, especially Dick and Di who had moved to Kent following their marriage. Dick had left Vanity Fare in the autumn of 1971 to come off the road to a job at Air Recording Studios in London. After a short while he went on to train as a booking agent first with General Artistes and later with Impresario Arthur Howes. He'd run European tours with Marvin Gaye, Stylistics, Kool and The Gang and most other Motown acts right up to October 1976 when he and Diane moved to Yorkshire to be close to the disco band Heatwave who he was to manage. He also tour managed the very first UK Tour by AC/DC in the spring of '76 - prior to them touring with us - small world, eh!

January 1977 dawned and, refreshed, I returned to The Sunset Marquis in L.A. and called the office. Just to spread Christmas cheer and reward for a good tour, I learned that Bruce had phoned Jimmy and Tony over the festive break, no doubt at Ritchie's request, to 'thank 'em and sack 'em'. Well, beats the old Christmas box and bonus, eh? I guess it's like a soccer or football coach at the end of the season. Time to tinker with the line-up, bring in new talent, and freshen things up a tad. Gotta win some medals this time around. I might seem a bit flippant here, but really, I understood what drove our Man In Black - the perfection he demanded of himself, he demanded in those band members that surrounded him. If any of them fell short in his eyes they were history, as simple as that.

Bruce was not to blame either and who knew what conversations went on privately between him and Ritchie. Ultimately Ritchie employed Bruce, not the other way around. Bruce gave good counsel, he was a great manager, but if the client, Ritchie, was dead set on a course of action, it had to be carried out despite what private reservations Bruce may or may not have had. I was sad to see Jim go, he was a really nice guy and was perhaps stifled in his creative contribution to the band by the inner sanctum of Ritchie, Ronnie and Cozy. Those three drove the band creatively and spiritually, specifically because they were on a par in terms of skill in their respective departments and also because Ronnie and Cozy didn't take any shit! Tony, a great musician, just needed to get off the road, fast! Who knows, his sacking just may have saved his life.

Bruce decided to bring a little light relief into my life at this time. He was involved, professionally I'm quick to add, with Playboy model turned singer Barbi Benton. For whatever reason, she was short a driver for a couple of weeks, so Bruce, considering either I was at a loose end, which I wasn't or that I needed some female company which I did, asked me to take her around to her various engagements and meetings in the Hollyweird neighbourhood. So I took a cab from the Sunset Marquee to her place, knocked on the door to be met by her boyfriend, singer/songwriter, sometime actor John Prine. Now Prine is a BIG guy, very tall. Don't forget I'm six feet three and he towered over me. Barbi had lived with Hugh Hefner at the 'Mansion' for the several previous years, so I guess he was a little suspicious of anybody rocking up to the front door, especially looking like me. "What in hell is this coming up from her past?" he must have thought. Anyway, he looked me up and down and just grunted. Either very Shakespearean or very Bob Dylan, it was hard to tell. He left me there on the step without another sound. I felt very uncomfortable. I mean, was he going to fetch Barbie or a gun? Then, deep joy, out bounced and I do mean bounced, our Barbi. "Hi Colin… lets go!" she chirruped.

Be still my beating heart, she was just ooooooooooweeeeeeeeeee. Ever seen the film 'The Mask' with Jim Carey when he first sets eyes on Cameron Diaz? That was me! She gave me the keys to her BMW and away we went into the Hollywood hoopla that was her life. To be fair, she had more brains than most and had done a few movies, mostly B's truth to tell, and guest appearances on TV shows like Marcus Welby M.D and McLoud. She started off, I think, on the kids show Hee Haw. Sure didn't have the likes of her on TV back home when I was a kid! Of course, she also did three cover spreads (I know, unfortunate word) in Playboy, which is still a record, or so I'm told. After our brief encounter, she went on to a long career in TV shows like Love Boat, Charlie's Angels and Chips. Hardly stretching for an actress, but hey, it worked well for her. They were two glorious weeks and she was so nice, so natural. Best present Bruce ever gave me! I saw her recently on VH1's Where Are They Now? She's well, rich and living very nicely thanks in Aspen. Oh, Barbi.

By February, it was official that Rainbow was short of two players. Jimmy was replaced pretty quickly with ex Uriah Heep and Jon Hiseman's Colosseum bassist Mark Clarke who we'd known from the year before when he'd been in L.A, also rehearsing at Pirate Sound. That place was getting like Piccadilly Circus - stay there for a few months and pretty much everyone who mattered would pass through.

It was now time to record the follow-up to the highly successful 'Rainbow Rising'. The original plan was to return to Germany, but I was asked to find a suitable venue, preferably a chateau or castle in Europe somewhere. Quite a broad brief. Ritchie had a book on such matters; you guessed it - "Chateaus and castles of old Europe" (kidding!) I browsed through it, set up a short list and set off by plane and hire car. I saw some great places, some gothic, some medieval, some distinct copies of the first two, but great nevertheless. We eventually found Chateau d'Herouville near Paris, which suited the brief in that it could accommodate all the band and crew and had been fully converted into, a then, state of the art studio. By May it was all set to start. Unfortunately the search for a replacement for Tony Carey had been unsuccessful, so he was rehired. Some folk just never learn! I cannot to this day understand what possessed him to return. If it had been me, I would have told Bruce to tell Ritchie to stick it where the sun don't shine, but I guess his love for the band or the money it brought, probably a bit of both, overrode any misgivings and he thought he could stay the pace. Was he ever wrong!

May in the countryside around Paris is a real cool place to be, but not too conducive to the creative endeavours of the recording kind. Progress was slow and became quite boring. It did not help Ritchie's humour to hear Fleetwood Mac over all the airwaves with tracks from their soon to be gazillion seller 'Rumours'. This once dyed in the wool blues band had reinvented itself with a vengeance and I'm sure our Ritchie got slightly yellow at their success. To alleviate this Ritchie began to get up to his old tricks. The occult and all things from the, shall we say, the dark side had always had a certain attraction for the man in black. Séances were now his new big thing. The chateau, reputedly haunted (aren't they all), just suited Ritchie and his girlfriend, down to the ground in this respect. We were asked each evening to set out a large table and chairs in the recording room itself because it had the best vibes (?). We laid it out with upside down glasses at each place setting and with the regulation ouija board in the centre. I didn't like this at all and consistently refused to get involved.

Why? Dunno, It just felt wrong and I had to go on my instincts where this type of deal was concerned. I guess I was right because some inexplicable stuff happened.

We generally tried to record during the day, avoiding the evening and the night. Can't explain it, it just felt wrong once dusk set in and the whole band, crew and Martin Birch felt it too. Tracks that had been laid down transferred to different tracks by the next morning. Faders went up and down of their own accord and spookily the 24-track machine once started up all on its own and ran out until the tape was flapping with the onlookers gob smacked. One night when I was walking up a large spiral staircase to the studio, a large chandelier just dimmed almost to nothing and returned to full brightness once I reached the top. It had no dimmer switch, just plain old on and off, odd eh? The whole place would also get incredibly cold to the point of freezing for no reason then slowly get back to normal. This is in early summer, people. That can't happen! The weirder it got, the more Ritchie loved it.

The band however was becoming unravelled in the shape of bassist Mark Clarke. As I've said before, Ritchie cannot and will not tolerate bad musicianship. For whatever reason Mark seemed unable to keep his bass in tune. The confrontations in the studio went from bad to worse. Mark said he was in tune, Ritchie said he wasn't and was furious that Mark couldn't hear it. In the end Ritchie lost patience and came to me one evening and told me to go to Mark's room and get his bass guitar. I knocked on the bass player's door and said "Ritchie wants your bass guitar now". "Oh Fuck," he said knowing full well, I guess, what was about to happen. He handed it over and I took it to Ritchie who then went back into the studios with just him and Martin and recorded all the bass parts himself on three completed tracks.

You see, Mark had this crazy habit of bending the neck of his bass once he'd tuned it and thus throwing it out of tune once more. He also tuned his guitar to tuning forks striking them in the traditional manner and holding the fork to the neck of the guitar. Ritchie thought this absurd and often said the he didn't care if the guitar was in tune with itself it wasn't in tune with him or the keyboards. Cruelly whenever Mark was around the band and Martin Birch would say, "here comes…" and then hit the table or desk top with their finger and hold it to their head going ding". The neck bending must have been an unconscious nervous habit, but he did it nonetheless, despite being told and was quickly history. Recording carried on with Ritchie now playing both lead and bass parts.

Tony Carey kept himself to himself and became, as a result, more and more isolated. He stayed in his room when we weren't recording and this to Ritchie and his court jester Cozy was an invitation to visit mayhem upon the luckless Californian. Woe betide him if he left his window open during the night as he would be visited by the nerveless drummer who was completely unfazed by heights and would think nothing of going over the roof into Tony's room and either leaving something unmentionable or removing certain items. It all got too much and Tony called his father one night expressing the fear that they (the band) were trying to kill him. Knowing Tony's predilection for pharmaceuticals, I'm sure these increased his paranoia.

You have to remember that Ritchie hated drugs and resented anyone, especially band members whose intake had got out of control and they could expect no mercy from him as a result. The persecution of Tony increased in direct relation to the drug intake. Tony couldn't take it any more and fled during one night. The first I heard of it was at breakfast the following morning when the chef, who we employed, sidled up to me Clouseau style and said, "Monsieur Tony, ee leave". "What?" "Monsieur Tony, ee leave at three 'clock this morning, ma gurlfren tak heem to the Areoporte. Ee fly awayeee". I rang through to Ritchie and explained. He was totally unconcerned. Some hours later Bruce rang saying he'd had Tony's father on the phone anxiously explaining that Tony believed he was going to be murdered in his bed. Stifling a laugh, I explained to the perplexed Bruce, who was well used to the pranks, what had gone on and asked him to be gentle and diplomatic with Tony and his father, but he was out of the band. Bruce, as always, went off to smooth things over.

What appear to be 'practical jokes' to Ritchie are, to others, the height of cruelty, bordering on sadism - Ritchie just loved 'em, especially when we were recording as they often relieved the boredom. Martin Birch was one of the initial targets, but made it very clear from the start that he wasn't having any of it and would not tolerate any of that kind of shit. Being a karate expert of the ultimate Dan, Ritchie of course acquiesced to Martin's wishes and moved on to other less potentially aggressive prey, be it engineers, roadies and his fellow band chums. He rarely 'got' me because I simply knew him too well and suspected everything. It made for a twitchy kind of life, but at least I did not get caught unlike Tony Carey who he tortured mercilessly. On the road, it didn't let up and I was always the one to placate the hotel management and make good for any damage the next morning.

One outrageous prank in Detroit was to place a fresh human turd, possibly from the Maestro himself on top of Carey's bedside light shade prior to him stumbling "shitfaced" to bed once more. Tony, totally fucked up as usual, fell asleep with the light on. The next morning I was summoned by the stern faced hotel management to inspect Mr. Carey's room. Knowing what I was about to encounter, I put on my best 'shocked yet concerned' face. The smell was horrific and poor Tony was embracing the porcelain television in the bathroom very noisily. Whether that was from the stench or from the previous day's intake of drugs was immaterial. I explained that someone had a grudge against our Mr. Carey and we would make every effort to find the culprits and, what would the damage be to get the room back to normal. $500? No problem.

In San Antonio, Ritchie did finally get me. Whilst at breakfast before leaving for the next city he super glued a band member's door shut. With the bus ready to go, the poor sod kicked open the door, grabbed his bag and fled to the bus. Whilst I was explaining this to the hotel management and yet again reaching for the trusty cash float, Ritchie ordered the bus to leave, stranding me. Revenge however is sweet. I still had my briefcase, although no luggage. I sat down, had another slow coffee, read the paper and took a limo to the Airport. I bought a first class ticket over the phone by credit card and flew to rendezvous with them at the next gig. I arrived refreshed, if not a little merry from the on board champagne. Took another limo to the hotel, checked in, took a nap and used the pool. By late afternoon, the tour bus arrived with the band hot and tired to be met by yours truly, a large cold one in the hand. "Ritchie, old son. Did you misplace your credit card?" Revenge is sooo sweet!

******

So, down to the famous three and the album was obviously going to be delayed and tour dates would have to be put back. We returned to America and began auditions in L.A. Same old routine and there were, as usual, a fair number of keen young men who, although aware of Ritchie's fearsome reputation, still wanted to play alongside him, such was the kudos. Eventually Ritchie flew out an unknown keyboard player from Toronto, David Stone. He was pretty good, but most importantly would follow Ritchie wherever he went musically. You know, in most respects Ritchie was looking for Jon Lord and, more than once over a beer, the question was mulled over about him being approached, but then dismissed almost in the same breath. Next up, bass players and we looked at what seemed like hundreds though in truth it was probably around thirty. Australian Bob Daisley had been around the block quite a few times, playing in Chicken Shack, Mungo Jerry and lately Widowmaker. Ritchie met with him in L.A. through a mutual friend, Dick Middleton and Ritchie and Bob hit it off from the start. Ritchie seemed to like his style and attitude and so we were complete once again.

We began those rehearsals for about a month in L.A., once again at Pirate Sound, the old Columbia Studios, with Bob staying at the Sunset Marquis with me. We had to fly in Bob's wife, Vicky, to get him to stay for the required time. Before we began to rehearse Ritchie dropped a bombshell. He'd had enough of West Coast life and announced that anybody who wanted to stay with the band better get his arse to the East Coast. It wasn't a problem for me or for anyone else. In retrospect, it's the best way to run a band as in my experience, making decisions by consensus rarely works. Benevolent dictatorships are way more suitable and successful. Not surprisingly, nobody declined. I flew to Connecticut first, staying with Bruce whilst I looked for suitable properties for some of the band. I quickly found a house for Ritchie in Darien, Connecticut and also one for Cozy and I in nearby Weston. That was the routine, which went, "Go and find me a house, apartment, with a pool, stable, close to a bar, strip club…" Their wish was my command. Ronnie rented a place in New Canaan. However, no sooner unpacked, we repacked and flew back to England to Shepperton Studios, the rehearsal venue prior to kicking off the start of the 'On Stage' world tour in Europe. Would the new band gel? Well, David was very quiet, softly spoken and polite, being whatever Ritchie wanted him to be whilst Bob was a typical Australian, full of fun and into himself, but in a great way. I wondered what fun, frolic and furore was in store for us all and who would stay the course, for I always considered that the band were temporary, it was always just a matter of time.

It was about this time that a certain gentleman named Jack from California began to show up at Ritchie's home and occasionally on tour. One memorable morning Ritchie appeared with a shockingly vibrant head of luxuriant black hair. We looked on in silent awe. Ritchie's hair had, for some time been thinning alarmingly and now it was, well, big and full and not his! Knowing his moods, we all thought it best to not mention it in his presence, but truthfully it looked great, so, well, whatever flicks your switch, eh! Life continued as normal, but you really had to steel yourself to maintain eye contact when you spoke to him. I had to say to myself whenever we spoke, "look at the eyes, don't look at the hair, just do NOT look at the hair, concentrate on the eyes". Hey, human after all, that rascal!

The tour began on September 23rd with a stutter in Finland where we had to cancel due to the gear being impounded at Customs. Great start! Long way to go to kick heels and then we moved on to Sweden, Norway, Denmark and Holland. Rainbow was by now, as big, if not bigger in some markets than Deep Purple, especially in Europe where Ritchie was adored. Germany was almost like a homecoming, the guitarist and the countries fans were like a mutual admiration society. On October 18th we arrived in Vienna, Austria for a one off show at The Stadthalle. All was going well with a capacity crowd. About three quarters of the way through the set, Ritchie noticed what appeared to be a security guard getting far too enthusiastic in his work, holding back the front rows of the auditorium that were on their feet. The guy swung a punch at, what seemed to the guitarist, and was indeed, a young teenage girl. Ritchie ran across the stage and kicked the 'guard' full on the side of the jaw, breaking it. Trouble was it was the hall manager, not that was an excuse for his abuse of the young girl, but it did cause every single door of the hall entrances to be immediately sealed.

The show ended hurriedly as Ritchie had had quite enough. I realised we had big trouble as the whole of the back stage area was suddenly full of police, police dogs and their handlers and security, who were all after Ritchie and it wasn't for his autograph! It was apparent that the broken jawed one had immense power in Vienna; such was his ability to summon at a short notice such impressive 'backup'. I quickly told every member of the band to get ready to leave. Someone had the bright idea of smuggling Ritchie out of the hall in a large flight case. Dramatic? Yes. Doomed to failure? Eh, that would be a yes again. The flight case was rolled onto the back of one of the trailers and one police dog went berserk, barking at the case. Ox, our man mountain roadie sat on the case as the police asked him what was in it. "None of your fucking business" came the reply. Not being quite the answer the police were quite looking for, Ox's head then hit a police baton, not once but repeatedly, which was a might careless of the big man. He got a severe beating as the case was opened to reveal a cowering Mr. Blackmore, who was dragged roughly by his hair ("Not the hair, not the hair") and clothes to a waiting police van where he was thrown together with the now bloody, but defiant Ox. The things us roadies do in the line of duty.

There was nothing I could do to rescue our heroes despite looking for someone sensible from the police with whom I could negotiate. I told the crew to pack up as quickly as possible and drive direct to Munich, our next date, over the border without stopping. Ritchie and Ox stayed in the cells overnight whilst I stayed behind with Bruce Payne and Bob Adcock until the next day to hopefully get them released. The local police were not friendly then either, but did reluctantly agree to release Ox. Ritchie, however, was another matter. He was, as we learned later, stripped of his entire jewellery and trouser belt and thrown into a stone walled, cold, windowless cell, still in his stage clothes. Bruce unleashed all the lawyers, American, British and those nice German ones from Polydor Records. Embassies were alerted and consulted, but no early release was muted. I left for Munich leaving Bruce to his pleadings and Bob with a car to drive Ritchie and Bruce, we hoped, onto Munich.

On arrival at the Olympiahalle in Munich it was obvious that the show would have to be postponed to the next day. It was also to be filmed for Rockpalast, a German T.V. show, so we had a lot of re-shuffles to take care of, while Ritchie enjoyed his gruel in the confines of the Viennese gaol. Not quite the Hilton, that's for sure! I kept in constant touch with Bruce and by the third day, the 20th. Bob phoned to say he had Ritchie in the car and they were on their way. The show was set, but by 10pm, they had not arrived. At 11.30pm. the car roared to the back stage entrance and Ritchie emerged, still in his stage clothes of forty-eight hours ago. He picked up his guitar, sat in his dressing room quietly but with immense relief on his face. He took his customary bottle of Johnnie Walker Black, took just enough and hit the stage to a massive ovation, back to his own arena and played the show of his life.

He was never quite the same again though, never the same prankster, a little more withdrawn, contemplative, realising that at 2:00am in a cold, damp Austrian cell with half of Vienna's finest after your balls, it doesn't matter a row of beans how famous you are. He also started to treat other folk with just a little more respect, not much, but a little. He would refuse to return to Vienna for over four years despite many invitations of the nice kind. Oh yes, all charges went away courtesy of the power of Bruce and a little funding in the right departments. I did not ask, as he would never have said.

From Munich we did further shows in France and then back to England for four sold out dates at the Rainbow in London's Finsbury Park. These were followed by dates in Oxford, Leicester, Stafford and two nights at Manchester Apollo where my sister Carol, her husband David and their two sons, Paul and Stephen paid me a visit. I never was a great letter writer, so a chance to catch up was brilliant. The boys, at eleven and eight respectively were intrigued. Stephen, I'm told the next day had a hard job convincing his young mates that he hadn't been to see Zippy and Bungle.* Rainbow was rocking and Ritchie's love of the stage was probably made more intense by his brush with solitary incarceration.

After the customary, but most welcome Christmas break and full of me mam's Christmas turkey and dad's beer, we arrived in Japan on January 10th. Being at home was becoming increasingly rare and really I found myself more and more apart from that Northern way of life. Nobody had changed, but I had. Dick and Di, with whom I kept in contact by rare phone calls, now had two sons and were settled, yet I was still this nomad, but it was my choice, so no use looking longingly at a 'normal' life. Dick was having success managing Heatwave, who had just been high in The American singles and album charts with 'Boogie Nights'. A different kinda music altogether!

In the land of the rising sun, Rainbow was truly massive in a country of gentle fans and overbearing police. The seventeen-date tour big by Japan standards, started the next day in Nagoya and wound its way across country playing to capacity crowds wherever we went. Half way through the tour at the Nakajima Sports Centre in Sapporo, the crowd were very enthusiastic, too enthusiastic for the security who had still not got the plot about rock audiences. The seating was, unbelievably today, fold-up, unattached seats. In other words they were loose! Health and safety laws today in almost all countries would have shut the show down, but this was 1978 and things were to say the least very lax in that area. The crowd surged to the front and a security-cum-police officer, hard to tell really, walked onto the stage in an absurd gesture to tell them to go back to their seats.

Bob Adcock, who was, at every show time, acting as band security, saw the guard standing in front of Ritchie, who was in full flow. He walked up

---

* Zippy and Bungle were TV Characters on the UK children's show 'Rainbow', who talked funny, were big, colourful and stupid looking, and immensely popular. So no difference there then!

behind the unsuspecting guard and pushed him into the crowd. Thus was born the craze of stage diving (and you thought it came from the punk era, you know nothing). The police guy now had a serious 'loss of face', something that is not taken lightly 'out East'. They redoubled their efforts to quieten down the crowd. Much later, after the show we learnt that a young student girl had been crushed to death under a mess of folding chairs. We were devastated. That's not what rock music is about. It's about having a good time, revelling in exciting sensational music, not to die, for God's sake. Who did I blame? The local promoters, the hall security, certainly not Rainbow, but we were escorted out of town the next day like criminals. Mr. Udo, our Japanese Promoter for the whole tour was inconsolable, seriously contemplating that he would quit this crazy business and he and the ever-present Bruce Payne spent some uncomfortable hours that night with the police explaining Rainbows involvement. Like, what was there to explain? When we arrived at Tokyo airport from Sapporo the next morning we were met by a melee of press, TV cameras and photographers who, as per usual, zeroed in on Ritchie. We had all been told to make no comment, which under the circumstances was not a tough call. Four days later we flew back to America to plan for the assault on America with the "Long Live Rock 'n' Roll" tour.

With three months off the road, but not 'off the clock', I settled down to some sort of routine back in the house I shared with Cozy in Connecticut, although in fairness he was never there, preferring to stay back in England. When he was around, he was not a bit of bother. No arguments, no tantrums, could have been sharing a house with a plumber. A lovely man, God rest his sweet soul. His death many years later was a sad, sad moment to me. Cozy was an extremely fast driver, but always drove within his limits. It will always remain a mystery to me why he died at that time in the early hours on an empty stretch of motorway; he was just never that careless.

I had been with him many times in fast cars especially in Germany where there are no speed limits on their autobahns. I remember one time I was his passenger when he was going an incredible 135 m.p.h. with ease on a two lane road when two trucks pulled level leaving us seemingly with no where to go. Without dropping any speed, Cozy swept onto the hard shoulder with the guardrail inches from my door and blitzed passed the trucks on the inside. As we swung back in front he opened the sunroof and 'flipped the bird" to those truckers, closed the roof and sped on. I didn't know whether to crap, scream or both. He just turned and winked. Sleep well, mate.*

I'd call the office everyday to check what plans were afoot and inevitably Ritchie or Ronnie would call for me to do some 'fetch and carry' stuff. One such crazy request was from Ritchie, bless him. Bruce rang me to say would I go to the nearest Mercedes dealership and buy a top range motor of that esteemed brand with the specific request it be bright fire engine red and a 380 SEC model. I repeated the order, why I don't know as really it should not have been a surprise and off I toddled to the nearest dealer in Greenwich.

On arrival, all long hair and regulation rock star attitude, the sales staff probably thought I had come to ask for a job cleaning the damn things and eyed me up suspiciously. Putting on my best English cut glass Geordie accent (there is such a thing, trust me), I asked to drive the top range motor. Now they thought I wanted to nick one, not wash one and the suspicion quotient racked up a few points. Then I saw, unbelievably, the exact car Bruce had described. "I'll take that one," I said imperiously (well, you have to when you can, don't you). "Eh, certainly sir" he stuttered. "Would you come into the office" thinking now I wasn't a thief, but seriously wacko. "Perhaps we can take a few particulars" thinking this is where the game would be up. "Sure, just phone this number and they will send you a certified cheque right now" handing them the Thames Talent number. Reality dawned that this 'hippy' was the real deal and was a customer! The royal treatment followed including a test drive, which I took, naturally.

Three days later, when it had been prepped, registered etcetera, I returned to pick it up and drove out to Ritchie who, by this time, had moved to Long Island. No bother, it would settle the car in. As I drove down I-95 I kept trying to figure why Ritchie had still never learned to drive, but was buying a car like this. I shrugged and smelt the heady smell that only new cars uniquely have. I arrived and rang his bell, whistling a merry tune. Ritchie was slow to answer the door, but then he always was or whoever he had in the house who was on 'answering door' duties. Ritchie was never a "bounce to the door, come on in" type of guy. The

* Cozy Powell died on 5th April 1998 while driving his Saab 9000 at 104 mph on the M4 motorway near Bristol. At the time of the crash, Powell's blood-alcohol reading was over the legal limit, he was not wearing a seatbelt, and he was talking to his girlfriend on his mobile phone. The official investigation also found evidence of a slow puncture in a rear tyre. It was suggested that this could well have caused a sudden collapse of the tyre with a consequent loss of control of the car.

door eventually opened and Ritchie scowled out, resplendent in his pyjamas, buttoned to the very top, as always.

Now he must have known it was me at the door, spied me from some secret location. He would never just swing the door open in his pyjamas. I could've been anyone. "What?" he growled. (Not "Hi Colin, old chap, what a lovely day.") "I've brought your new car, the bright, fire engine red 380 SEC Mercedes?" He peered over my shoulder, he thought for a bit, said, "Yeah, that's the colour" and he grabbed the keys, slamming the front door shut without another word. "I'll not be stopping for coffee then," I said to the front door, which did not answer. I about turned and walked down his drive out onto the highway, slowly shaking my head at the idiosyncrasies of my famous employer. I had arranged for a friend to follow me so that I could get back, good job really in retrospect. Ritchie did later venture out from time to time in his symbol of German technology chauffeured by his girlfriend of the moment. Ah yes, these rock stars, ain't they something else!

With the album released in April and the single of the same name a month prior, to give it a promotional jump-start, I planned the logistics of the tour based on the itinerary given to me by the good folk of Thames Talent who I fervently, but vainly hoped by now had got a better grip on exactly where some cities were in relation to others. It was Bruce and Ritchie's intention that this tour would once and for all break the band as a major arena box office blitzer. As a promotional curtain raiser we taped the TV show Don Kirshner's 'Rock Concert in a theatre in Long Island. This was a big deal, a big nationwide show. True to form, Ritchie was, to say the least, 'awkward'. He refused to stand on his 'marks' for camera run-throughs and settings, standing moodily behind the amps like the spoiled brat he was pretending and succeeding in emulating.

What's infuriating is that he's not an unintelligent man and knew and encouraged any move by Bruce to raise the profile of the band, yet when it was time for him to do his bit for the cause, outside of the studios and concert forum, he sought to cause chaos, to defeat and delay the very thing he wanted. It was total bollocks, wasn't it? Yet, Bruce, poor Bruce and me, next down the line, just spent our time coaxing and cajoling him - he needed a smack upside the head really! The other members of the band said little, but deep down, I knew they thought that his actions were inexcusable. Not a nice mix - Ritchie and television.

The tour kicked off in Memphis, Tennessee on May 9th 1978, 'Grease' was the big movie and Wings were top of the US charts with 'With A Little Luck' and my old pals Sweet had made it at last into the US Top Twenty with 'Love Is Like Oxygen'. We headlined the first show and then set out on a series of dates that month, either second on the bill to REO Speedwagon or headlining over bands like Black Oak Arkansas (nice guys!), No Dice or Uriah Heep. Ritchie loved to tour, but not as support to other bands, especially those that were a bigger draw, yet in Ritchie's eyes weren't very good musically (which was pretty much everyone). REO Speedwagon fell into this category.

As the dates with them continued, they put a large clock beside the stage so that they could show our boy categorically that he had only sixty minutes to do his stuff and then get off. You see, the later they went on; the more they would run into overtime costs in the arena, which they would have to pay. As they said quite logically, "You wanna pay the overtime, then you can stay on as long as you like" Ritchie did not want to pay, but still arrived later and later to start the set and ran over his allotted sixty minutes. He sure knew how to push their buttons! Their tour manager got so pissed off with it all that, at a show in Atlanta, he put up the house lights when our time was up and cut the power. Not an overly intelligent move! Ritchie did the guitar over head, place on amp stack, switch off routine (not that that mattered as the power was off) that must be familiar to y'all by now, walked to the side of the stage and hit the tour manager with the Blackmore haymaker, which promptly bounced him backwards down the stairs, in a 'reverse pike with twist'. Everybody, as per usual, then piled in to separate the two protagonists to avoid further harm to either. I'm sure Ritchie relied on this happening as I'm not sure he'd ever survive a prolonged toe-to-toe encounter. His first punch was always a cracker though, as I'd seen it on several occasions! I was often minded to let it continue, but I was paid to protect his welfare, shame, sometimes!

Even when we were away from shows, these types of encounters cropped up. Twelve months earlier, I was with him at The Rainbow Grill in LA, just me and Ritchie with his girlfriend of the time, Sue Davis who was, as all his girlfriends, magnificently endowed in the breast department. A roadie for one of the other Brit bands in town was at a table by the exit door and made a comment about Sue's attributes. Ritchie turned to me and asked me who the guy was and I told him. We had finished our meal and beers, when he told Sue to go get the car. Ritchie waited until it was out front, left his table and as he went to go out through the door, hit this roadie with an almighty blindsided whack, which sent him reeling onto the floor behind. Ritchie could not wait for his usual backup, which of course was not around. He flew out the door, into the car, and they sped into the distance, up into the valley and safety leaving me, as always, to clear up the chaotic aftermath. I placated them as best I could but they were staying, like me, in the Sunset Marquis, so for me, there was no escape.

Thankfully, roadies are a brotherhood of sorts and we know full well the shortcomings of our employers. "Its okay, Colin, we know its not your fault, but this is war. If he'd stayed to fight it out, it would have ended one way or another with no ongoing grudge, but to 'punch and run' is not the way to do it". I stayed up until four in the morning back at the hotel with many, many beers placating them and debating the downside to an all out war as it would inevitably involve the respective road crews which would then, no doubt involve the police etc, etc, etc. They grudgingly saw the sense in my view, but Ritchie and I spent quite a few months after that looking over our shoulder.

Anyway, back to spring '78 and REO Speedwagon. After the spat with their road manager the atmosphere between the two camps was frosty and a tad tense especially between the road crews, though why we were dragged in was unfair as the very nature of arena shows meant that crews had to work together. May found us on the West Coast, having finished in Kansas on May 15th. We had three days off before opening at The Shrine Auditorium in Los Angeles and were glad to be back in familiar surroundings. I was hanging out at The Rainbow Grill chatting to Linda the hostess and happened to casually mention that I fancied a new look hair-wise. Robert Plant was a god with golden tumbling locks and I fancied my long, but lank hair, in a similar fashion. Linda, ever the helpful hostess booked me in with her stylist on Sunset. I duly arrived to be met by this chap who was, shall we say, a little light in his loafers, but charming nevertheless. I surveyed a sea of very old blue rinse women and began to seriously doubt Linda's choice of 'barber'.

Anyway, I endured the embarrassment of sitting 'in the line' with these old chicks for several hours until my new look was revealed. I was mortified. I looked like a young white version of Michael Jackson - '70's version when he was black and seriously Afro'd. I pulled my stylist to one side and told him in no uncertain Geordie terms of my discomfort. He told me to keep calm and the hairdo would soon 'relax and drop' provided I kept putting this lotion, that he now hurriedly gave me, onto my hair at every wash. I crept back in the shadows to my room at the Marquis.

The next morning, on looking in the bathroom mirror, my discomfort took a new downward turn. From the front, I had this 'puff ball' look which was scary enough, but 'side on' where I had slept on my back the hair had flattened to back of my head. Now I looked a complete 'tart'. Having had the foresight to buy an Afro pick, I spent the next hour teasing the back to get it looking anything close to a uniform 'roundness'. Now I had to face the band and the crew. Best way was to act as if nothing was wrong.

The whole of the next day and some after, I was met with guys looking away, their shoulders shaking, then talking to me with the eyes on my hair. Some just smirked, others just plain burst out laughing. In the end I laughed along with them. I washed and washed my hair putting this lotion on until I thought the best thing was to get it all cut off. That was a step too far. Eventually after four or five months it grew out, but looked seriously stupid. Moral of the story - never ask the hostess of any hostelry to recommend her hair stylist - it could seriously fuck up your day!

On the 4th July we were on the bill of a massive show at the Edgewater Speedway in Cleves, Ohio. Also appearing were The Outlaws, Rick Derringer, Rare Earth and, wait for it, The Dixie Dregs featuring a young, very young Steve Morse. We never spoke and Ritchie never hung around at shows like these anyway. The Dixies would have been on very early so we would not have been in a position to see them, but weird how paths cross. Little did anyone know that twenty years later Steve Morse would replace Ritchie in a reformed Deep Purple.

The tour journeyed on through July. Springfield, Illinois; Sam Houston Coliseum, Texas; Municipal Auditorium, San Antonio; Louisiana Assembly Centre, Baton Rouge and many more. In Chicago, we had a visit from an old chum in the shape of Roger Glover. With Purple now totally disbanded, David Coverdale and his band Whitesnake had Jon Lord in its ranks, making quite an impact and Ian Gillan doing his own thing in the band of the same name. Roger was producing amongst others Nazareth and having a lot of success, but this was a social call and he and Ritchie seemed to get along great now that there was no 'business' between them, only 'old times' and nurturing a dormant friendship. There was plenty of hugging and backslapping as we parted and I wondered then whether there had been an unsaid agenda between them. Was the hand of Bruce behind this, gently pulling a few marionette strings? Were changes afoot?

These times really were fun times. You know one of the great things about that era of rock 'n' roll was its camaraderie. We had a blast, not only from drinking, but also from the sheer simple joy of being part of a great music show where the fans got a value for money show. This is of course way before the days of $100 or more for a concert ticket. That would have been unthinkable then. We got immense warmth and love back from the fans and it felt... well, wonderful. Today, that feeling is gone, maybe it's my age as I was only thirty-one then, but its now all about the almighty dollar, first and last. Yeah, you're right, it's my age!

August saw us on the East Coast and back with our old Aussie mates, AC/DC supporting us on shows in Long Island, Boston, Philadelphia and New York. This last one at the Palladium turned out a disaster when the dear old Rainbow arch, (yes, still with us), totally screwed the PA and amps with its interference, this time without remedy. The show was cancelled and we refunded all the ticket money, which seriously pissed off Bruce. The days of the arch were numbered! The tour effectively then wound up even though we were due to play one last show at The Asbury Park Convention Hall in New Jersey two days later, but as the arch was one sad puppy and looking like it was beyond repair, we cancelled. We had been on the road for one hundred and seven days and it showed. Rainbow would not play again for over a year and, for some it was their last appearance!

CHAPTER NINE
DOWN TO TWO!

Come September with hardly time to get home and unpack really, Bob Daisley and David Stone got the dreaded phone call from Bruce and we were back to a three piece. Ritchie, I knew, felt he had just schlepped all over America with little effect and at a huge cost. Sure the East Coast was conquered territory, sell out business, but out in the boonies, the Mid West, we were still not headliners and that hurt the guy. He wanted chart success, singles success that meant radio plays and we weren't hitting that market. Time to tinker with the line-up. Ronnie and Cozy at that time said little, biding their time I guess to see who Ritchie wanted in and where he was planning to steer the ship. Ritchie was still bankrolling the band, the guarantor if you want, even though these tours were high grossers, they were expensive to run, so the net profit to Ritchie was not immense. He still relied on his past royalties from Deep Purple to underwrite his lifestyle and they were about to take a jolt.

Purple's and still Ritchie's accountant, Bill Reid, sadly died and he allegedly knew where 'all the financial bodies were buried'. Ritchie took Bill's death badly as Bill was one of the very few guys he trusted, always being on hand to advise on house purchases, what to sell and when. The problem had always been 'Deep Purple Overseas' or 'DPO' where Coletta and Edwards had steered all Deep Purple's overseas earnings. It was a muddy pond and perhaps the main reason for Ian Gillan's mistrust of the ex-managers. Bruce, ably assisted by Bill Reid had been trying, ever since the split, to unravel the financial web. With Bill dead, the trail would become fainter to follow. Bill was a lovely 'Santa Claus' look-alike, always hanging off the end of a fat cigar. I'm sure he woke up every morning in constant wonderment at the world in which he had found himself, contrasting with the stuffy, very correct world of accountancy. That said he enjoyed his new surroundings to the full!

Back in Connecticut, I returned to the old 'fetch and carry routine' mainly for Ritchie and Bruce, but then I was salaried staff, so had to earn my corn as directed, no problem. I was soon informed that Ritchie had approached Roger Glover to help produce and write the next album. Surprised? Yes, in some ways I was, as I thought Ritchie was a 'move on, don't look back' type of guy, but then he was always capable of those surprises too. Nothing against Roger, he's superb, a close mate and I guess it was perhaps more the bassists patience and diplomacy that Ritchie needed, especially when he made it plain to Ronnie and Cozy that he wanted the next album to be more mainstream. He coveted the FM radio singles market and he was going to have it.

I was dispatched once more to Europe "chateau hunting" this time accompanied by Cozy. We got as far as Lake Como in Italy when the drummer baled out and returned to England to his fast cars and fast women, obviously we'd gone a turret too far. On reflection that was a nice time for me, driving through Europe in late autumn looking at stately homes, castles and salubrious chateau's with little pressure, no one on my back and a nice expense account. Eddie and Betty were dead jealous and I bet the lads back in the surveyor's office would have cast an envious eye too! Life was grand. I finally settled on a chateau just outside Geneva over on the French side of the border, Le Chateau de Pelly De-Cornfeld owned by financier Bernie Cornfeld. It was horrendously expensive by today's standards, let alone then, at around $25,000 per week, yet nobody blinked at this cost and it was booked on my recommendation as a location to record for the start of the New Year!

During the break and the introduction of Roger back into the fold, Ronnie had obviously thought long and hard about where the music was heading and he was not keen. Ritchie had been very unhappy with Ronnie's contributions in the writing department. Ronnie sat down with Bruce and Ritchie and he believed it was mutually agreed that the little big guy and Rainbow would part company. However, Bruce phoned Ronnie once again over Christmas (Tip: never take a phone call from Bruce Payne at Christmas time, trust me, it'll be bad news) and told him that Ritchie was breaking up the band and only keeping Cozy, which to Ronnie was like "being pushed before he had time to jump". He was not too pleased, said it put him in a bad light, like he'd been sacked.

So now it was just Ritchie and Cozy plus Roger as producer and writer. This was remedied pretty quickly by the introduction of Don Airey on keyboards, who had been in Cozy's band Hammer and played with Gary Moore and John Hiseman. He came from Sunderland, just a couple of miles from my hometown so he was family, so to speak especially as he had, like me, a passion for Sunderland Football Club and we would spend many an hour remembering great line-ups from the past. It's a soccer guy thing. He came over to Connecticut in December after an invitation from Cozy, his old band mate. I picked him up at JFK Airport and took him to meet Ritchie, Roger and Cozy. It was pretty obvious Don was classically trained which appealed to Ritchie and after a few days of jamming around, he was hired. We all knew Ronnie was out, but it was not public knowledge. Bruce soon took care of that!

We all assembled at the chateau in mid April 1979 to record what was to become 'Down To Earth' this time with Jethro Tull's Mobile. Well, at least lay down tracks as we were still without a singer and bass player although Roger would fill that vacancy in the studios, on top of his producer and songwriter roles. I guess Ritchie thought Roger would write more AOR friendly material, as in 'love lost and found' in comparison to Ronnie's more 'witches, warlocks and hobgoblin' lyrics more in tune to the narrower heavy metal market. It's a moot point really as to which would make more money long term. Ritchie wanted charting singles, which would sell albums, but maybe not as in as large quantities long term as heavier albums, which as a rule did not produce hit singles.

After a short time Ronnie moved on to front Black Sabbath, so I guess everybody got what they wanted, bruised ego's aside. Back in the land of castles and recording, Ritchie and his cohort Cozy reverted to type in their quest to scare the shit out of everybody, especially the newcomers. To me, the old hand, it was becoming a tad tedious. You know, confronted by a ghostly monk in hooded cowl in a dim corridor with lights dimming. "Hi Cozy, how's it hanging?" I'd say as I barely missed a step. "Aw, howdja know it was me" the apparition cursed. "Just a wild guess, mate. You really had me going that time".

Don was not so in step with the tradition and, installed in the old chapel (which he hated) as his living quarters, he had 'visitations' quite regularly which he warmed to quite quickly, unlike some of our ex band members. Maybe it's a British thing? Don was more of a five star Intercontinental Hotel type of guy. Didn't do draughty French chateaus out of choice. The chateau had high turrets and to Ritchie they would be the ideal place to place his 4 x 12 speakers, mic'd from the courtyard below, to achieve an awesome echo effect. He would then think nothing of playing a full four hundred watts of heavy guitar rock across the valley and surrounding countryside at four in the morning. It scared the horses in the adjacent field shitless, but Ritchie was unconcerned and loved the way it echoed off the hills maybe five miles away. Consideration, why? And for who?

The rehearsing went well, with Roger at first reluctantly playing bass, but we still did not have a singer. Many were considered including Brian Johnson, soon to be of AC/DC, but only Marc Storace of Krokus was invited over to meet the band and jam, but it didn't work out. The feel wasn't right. Ritchie, Roger, Cozy, Fergy, (Ian Ferguson, Ritchie's personal), and myself, would sit around after the day of rehearsing was done, trying to figure out possible recruits. Cozy asked if anyone remembered the single 'Only One Woman' by the Marbles and how great the singer sounded followed by the proverbial 'wonder where he is now''. Roger replied that he knew and Graham Bonnet's manager was contacted.

I'm sure Ritchie had this vision of Graham as he was in The Marbles and why not, it was the only vision we all had - all long dark hair, attitude and a killer voice. His agreement to come and try out was confirmed to Roger on the phone and I was dispatched a few days later to Geneva airport to pick him up. Expecting the stereotype rock singer, I nearly missed the besuited, shorthaired geezer in Aviator glasses and a very bright Hawaiian shirt who obviously did see me as the stereotype rock roadie and said, "Allo, looking for me, I'm Graham". My heart sank as I took in this antithesis of the Ritchie rock singer. "Oh boy, he's gonna love you" I thought, as I smiled and extended my hand in welcome. "I'm Colin, head cook, bottle washer and tour manager to the stars, welcome to Geneva". "This is Coverdale all over again," I murmured to myself. "Hope you can sing like a bastard or you're back on the next flight, bonny lad" I thought!

Ritchie's face was a picture as I introduced Graham to the guitarist and the band. Disappointment was written all over it, but fair play to him, he said nothing and was as pleasant as he can ever be. Roger put him at ease and they got on jamming a few songs. Graham Bonnet has one pair of serious lungs and tonsils on him producing a rock voice to die for. The look of relief and pleasure on everyone's face said it all. He was hired. I think the thought was that he had the ingredient that could not be manufactured - the voice. The rest, the image, could be worked on and Bonnet would be styled into that rock star image. Oh, yeah? Not this boy! Graham was not for changing, not for anybody and certainly not for Ritchie. In truth he was a bugger from the start, but canny with it, but read on. I loved him and hoped he would change for Mr. B.

With the album completed, (and it was a great album), the Russ Ballard number 'Since You Been Gone' was picked as the single. By the end of recording Roger had agreed to be the permanent bass player, which was probably the dark plot that had been hatched by Bruce and Blackmore right from the start. Personally, I was dead pleased to have him back. He's one of the very few people I have met in my life who is consistently nice to be around. There are no sides to Roger, no hidden agenda, one of life's good guys. However the overt commerciality of the album did not go down too well with Cozy who grumbled that the guitarist was turning Rainbow into a pop band, an association he hated having tirelessly reconstructed himself from that tag which he'd acquired when he'd recorded for Mickie Most. His discontent was not to go away.

Ritchie loved the album, but then he had a wholly different view to recording and how his band should be. Ritchie was not a 'widdly, widdly, widdly' guitarist in the mould of say Jan Ackerman or Yngwie Malmsteen. His solos are carefully constructed in the same manner as song lyrics are crafted so they 'fit' with the whole feel of the number. If that's 'pop' which I would argue against, then it is the very best of that genre. Fans and phantom air guitarists know his solos backwards and 'sing' them at every concert, so familiar are they and woe betide any of those guitarists who followed Ritchie into Purple in latter years who didn't faithfully reproduce those famous guitar breaks note by perfect note. Cozy respectfully disagreed.

Back home, disaster had struck Dick's band Heatwave, who after their success with the 'Boogie Nights' album and singles from it, had gone to Detroit to record their next. During a break from recording, Johnnie Wilder, the lead singer and leader had been in massive car wreck and wasn't expected to make it. The band was off the road long term, if not permanently; such was the leadership of Wilder. Over the next ten years the band would eventually stumble and fall, but its keyboard player and writer, Rod Temperton, would go on to huge success writing tracks on Michael Jackson's 'Off the Wall' album and the classic 'Thriller'. No more queuing up at the chippy for Rod after that one! The slap in the face for Dick was that the band had not re-signed their management contract when all this happened, so any success that Rod went on to have had no impact on the Allix household whatsoever. Bummer!

****

We now returned to Connecticut for essentially rest and the recharging of batteries for the band before the usual massive tour supporting the release of the album in the July. My week was filled as was usual with running in and out of Thames Talent and playing soccer at weekends. This was Ritchie's second love, and true to his nature they were not just kickabouts for a bit of relaxation and exercise, but full blooded and sometimes, bloody, serious affairs at which he had to win at any cost, usually scoring the winning goal. They were command performances with no choice given to decline. You had to have a very good reason for not turning out. As a confirmed bachelor, I had no other calls on my free time, not that that would have counted, so I played soccer that spring and summer and got fit into the bargain. More of Ritchie's soccer mania later on!

I always kept up to speed on the career moves of my old Purple chums and at this time David Coverdale had persuaded Paicey to go back on the road for one album and a tour with him and Jon in Whitesnake, yet he stayed for three albums and three tours before joining Gary Moore in 1982. Gary had a revolving door for sidemen that included, from time to time, Don Airey and Bob Daisley. Jon had teamed up with David the year before and stayed six years with an album a year. No one really strayed far from the nest, did they?

By August, the route for the new tour was being put into place so my time was spent ensuring all the usual suspects for the crew were notified and equipment, trucking, travel and hotels were finalised. I began liasing with each venue and local promoter to make sure all would be well on arrival. Well, you can never be entirely sure as folk have a nasty habit of fibbing their arse off or simply being economic with the truth. You'd be surprised how many venue owners and managers have a totally false idea of the size of their stages, back stage areas, dressing rooms and loading docks etc etc. Boring crap to you the reader, but pretty essential to our production manager and myself, who were ultimately responsible for everything that ever went wrong. Behind the scenes of rock 'n' roll is just another business in reality. The non-US residents of the band had been flown in to rehearse at the end of August and the tour kicked off on the 20th September at The War Memorial Auditorium in Rochester, upstate New York supporting Blue Oyster Cult.

There was an air of nervousness surrounding the band coming from and about our new lead singer, but this was compensated a little by the immense solidity of the drums of Cozy and the bass of Roger. They really kicked it along and had a terrific understanding. For the next month we trailed all over the east and the mid west. At Cleveland the show finished rather abruptly when Ritchie wandered over to Don during the drum solo and kicked him in the arse… rather a hard kick, too!*

We then split from Blue Oyster Cult on 26th October at The Met Centre, Minneapolis, had a brief ten day rest, then carried on this time headlining with a veritable smorgasbord of talent supporting us including but not at the same time, Gamma, John Cougar (soon to be Mellencamp), and the fast emerging Scorpions. I felt for John Cougar, as it was a classic case of a mismatched bill. He was pretty much booed every night, sometimes only managing fifteen minutes, coming off stage in tears of frustration, his set shouted down by chants of 'Blackmore, Blackmore'. He had a really great band and his talent was obvious, but he was too lightweight for this type of audience, being more suited to the country rock market where of course eventually he would find great fame and fortune. I think at that time he was managed by Billy Gaff, Rod Stewart's mentor who I assume thought Cougar's rugged good looks would get him through - no chance! I spent a few uncomfortable moments trying to calm and encourage John to fight through and not cave in to the audience. Ritchie didn't seem to care.

The Scorpions were another matter. It really was a battle of the bands every night 'cos they were red hot. Ritchie liked them at the start because, of course, they were German and could rock, but Michael Schenker used to bore Ritchie to death with his endless discussions about guitars and music theory when all old Ritchie wanted to talk about (when he actually wanted to talk in the first place) was German beer, women and castles. I remember Eddie Van Halen, who idolised Ritchie, would often track him down on tour and phone him, usually drunk, to talk guitars. Ritchie would just hang up. Nice eh!

This part of the tour was excellent with 'Since You Been Gone' getting massive airplay, boosting the crowds. We eventually finished the US leg on December 9th in Albany, New York and waved a cheery 'Auf Wiedersehen' to our new German chums. We all dispersed for Christmas and New Year with the prospect of joining up in Gothenburg, Sweden on 17th January. Yup, Scandinavia in winter, just the place to tour at that time

* The lead-up to it was a disagreement before the show between Airey and Blackmore, which the keyboard player held himself responsible for, but to this day is still too ashamed to discuss.

of the year. I often vowed to take those bookers with us on dates like these just so they could see the reality of life on the road in sub zero temperatures. Why did we not tour countries this far north in latitude in the spring and summer, too logical I guess? The single 'All Night Long' from the album was about to be released to coincide and hopes were high of a hit single.

On a sad note, news filtered through to us that Bon Scott, lead singer of AC/DC had died back in London from a drinking binge from which he had not recovered and had been found dead sitting in a car. We had toured with him only two years before and our paths would often cross in hotel lobbies or airports. They were on the road constantly and would surely break through soon. Bon was a rocker in every sense of the word from performance to lifestyle and loved and lived every minute of his life. I later learnt that Brian Johnson from Geordie, my hometown band, had joined and I looked forward to renewing our friendship at some point in the future. We all raised a glass to Bon that night which may seem ironic and maybe a bit tasteless, but that's what he would have wanted.

On we went, headlining, naturally, into Germany, Holland, Belgium and back into Germany where at The Olympiahalle in Munich we met our old friend David Coverdale who, by now, was transformed into 'The God of Cock Rock' we now know and love. Now David had been less than polite about Ritchie in many press articles and the guitarist was not amused although he never retaliated in a similar way. Our old friend, promoter Erik Thomsen was great friends with David too and invited him and his German wife to the show. Ritchie, who knew David lived in Munich and would most likely show his face just to get in Ritchie's, gave strict orders to me that the 'Golden One' was barred from all back stage areas. Roger and Cozy said that was unfair as David was their mate too, and they would like to see him. Ritchie was relentless and insisted he be kept away from the backstage area. I advised security accordingly.

Now I don't know what part of 'off limits' they did not understand. David and his wife swept passed them led by Erik Thomsen, who could as the promoter, go wherever he wanted, and right up to Ritchie's dressing room, where David asked out loud in the posh voice he had acquired, along with the blond tresses and contact lenses: "Can I see Ritchie"? Ritchie heard "the voice", his door exploded open and a Blackmore 'haymaker' tried to connect with the handsome, sculptured face of the singer. They went down into a clinch of the unromantic kind and fell to the floor with Erik in the middle, in a mass of hair, heels and tight leather. Security and everyone else pulled them apart and, thankfully, only pride was damaged… and Erik, who took almost all the blows. Who got the instant blame? "Colin, get in here" came the voice from Ritchie's dressing room. "How the fuck did that happen?" "I don't know, what can I tell you, everybody in the world knew David was not allowed past here. I can't be everywhere at once" I burbled, quietly vowing to castrate all security and especially Erik Thomsen.

Ritchie fell silent and I quickly left only to be met by David's wife, screaming at me more or less what Ritchie had just said a moment before, only in a German accent. I tried to shush her, whilst Erik and Roger Glover were consoling David. David thankfully decided to leave, but I was on Ritchie's 'shit list' for weeks. Momma said there would be days like that, momma said!

I've often reflected on why Ritchie had reacted so vehemently and I have never believed it was purely because of those press articles. Many journalists and past musicians had had their say about him since the first days of Purple and frankly he'd almost courted that controversy, adding to his all important mystique. I believe that it was fuelled by jealous rage. He could see that David was about to achieve what he, Blackmore, was finding elusive and that was singles chart success and it ate him up, even though 'Since You Been Gone' had gone top ten in England five months before and 'All Night Long' was looking to break as big, but they didn't break in the all important American charts which killed Ritchie. So here was this boss eyed, knock kneed, jumped up fashion disaster from Redcar to whom Ritchie had given his first chance and this kid was, apparently, pissing all over him in the rock star stakes. A smack in the mouth was the very least he deserved, wouldn't you say?

Whitesnake had been up and running for over two years and at this point and had two albums out; 'Trouble' (1978) and 'Lovehunter' a year later. Now in the spring of 1980, with Jon Lord and Ian Paice in its already impressive line-up, it looked like they were going to be massive (and were they ever!) There again I could be wrong (about how Ritchie felt). It was rumoured some weeks later that David had approached Cozy to join Whitesnake, (revenge?) If the rumour was true it never reached the inner sanctum of the band. What was evident was Cozy's unhappiness at the musical direction of Rainbow, which certainly would not have been assuaged, had he left to join the similar musical direction of Coverdale.

Why would David want to replace Ian Paice with Cozy anyway, he already had the best? Who knows what phone calls occurred in the still of the night (cue for a song?) and what is the secret of life anyway?

Three days later we were back in England for the UK dates and started with two nights at Newcastle City Hall. Mam and dad as usual were there and had their customary audience with Ritchie. Maybe it was because he had such a distant, cold relationship with his own parents that he was so nice to mine. I didn't care as they thought he was wonderful and it appeared to be mutual. Graham Bonnet's hair was by now touching his colourful Hawaiian collar and things were looking brighter if you know what I mean, no pun intended. Just before the show he went into Newcastle and returned resplendent with a buzz cut. I was speechless when I saw him, as I knew what was to come. Ritchie went crazy and called me in for a "how could you let that happen" whilst Cozy could hardly contain himself with laughter. I just sat backstage with my head in my hands wondering just how long this lad would last before he was sacked or got a Fender Strat wrapped round his head.

Samson was our support on this tour fronted by vocalist Bruce Dickinson. I have often reflected over the years the number of young singers and bands that supported Rainbow in that time who later went on to huge fame and fortune, dwarfing that of Rainbow itself. It was and indeed is a funny old life. The tour went on to the usual haunts of Edinburgh, Stafford, Bristol and Manchester where my sister Carol, David and their two sons Paul and Stephen came to the show. Paul, by then at the age of fifteen, was an accomplished and gifted pianist, attending Chetham's School of Music in Manchester, and Don took great delight in allowing him to 'have a go' at the keyboard set-up at the sound check. He impressed everyone including his very proud uncle at how proficient he was, his classical training very evident. It was obvious then that a musical career was in the future. I didn't get to see them that often and to my shame wrote rarely, so hook ups like these were fantastic and to say the least, reminded me of my real family leading a proper life rather than my acquired one.

Next came Wembley Arena where Ritchie specifically requested the sixties pop act 'The Troggs' open the show. It seemed an odd choice, but Reg Presley and the boys went down surprisingly well considering their comparative lack of volume. Rainbow did a storming show and the crowd were baying and stomping for more as the set ended. Ritchie walked off stage into his dressing room and locked the door behind him. "Oh Fuck," I thought. The rest of the band, high on adrenalin were eager to go back on. I knocked on the door. "Ritchie, encore?" "Fuck off, I'm done" came the reply. Cozy and Roger pleaded with him through the locked door, but he was indeed done. I had no idea what had spooked him, but sometimes he did not need a reason. Paul Loasby, the promoter, fearful of a riot tried his luck too - no chance. Outside in the arena the crowd were getting more and more agitated. I reluctantly told the lighting engineer to put up the house lights and it sparked a full-scale riot. The seats were ripped up and thrown onto the stage and mayhem ensued. Security eventually got everyone out onto the outside concourse, but Ritchie had, once more, managed to seriously piss off the very people closest to him, his fans.

This was the first night of two at Wembley, so come the next day, prior to the show Cozy took the guitarist to one side and threatened him physical harm should the same stunt be pulled. Not unnaturally, a full encore was performed to the relief of all. Nevertheless it was Ritchie who had to recompense Wembley for the first night's considerable damage bill. Two days later we played Brighton on England's South Coast and Jeff Beck phoned me for a pass to see his old band mate Cozy. Jeff lived very close to the venue in an Elizabethan mansion where he concentrated on his second love of building American hot rods and driving them very fast through very narrow country lanes more suitable for a horse and cart. I walked Jeff to the sound and light podium, where he sat very quietly, no bother to anyone, throughout the concert.

Afterward he came back stage to shoot the breeze with our drummer, but when Ritchie saw him he just grunted a muted hello and disappeared into his dressing room. Go figure? You would expect at the very least a respectful conversation between two guitar greats. I'm sure Jeff perhaps expected a little more, but sure wasn't going to chase after Ritchie pleading for an audience. Ritchie can be unbelievably insensitive. A few years later in Minneapolis, Eric Clapton got out of a sick bed, seriously ill, specifically to see us and was accompanied by his manager Roger Forrester. I arranged for his car to drive right into the back stage area and I made a comfortable seat for Eric on Ritchie's side of the stage. The concert started and I'd told Ritchie where Eric was and he, unbelievably and to my complete embarrassment, ignored him. Eric, who looked a hundred and three and walked with a stick that day, stayed for about forty-five minutes then signalled he wanted to leave and I led him with Roger Forrester back to his car, which returned him to hospital. Some days weren't nice days in this business. Why did Ritchie do it? I haven't got a clue other than he had little respect for any guitarists and wasn't afraid to show it.

Six days later we wound the tour up in Manchester and Ritchie, Roger and I returned to America, Cozy and Don staying back in England with their families. Japan was next with visas, itineraries and travel plans to arrange: That's for me, not them; they got to rest. The tour this time was short, only eight days playing the cities of Tokyo and Osaka, five shows in the former and three in the latter but I guess you worked that out! Nothing extraordinary happened other than the Japanese organised Graham Bonnet look-alike competitions, which, if you're Japanese ain't a stretch. Take one Hawaiian shirt, aviator shades to hide oriental looks, slick the already black short hair back and voila, you are Graham Bonnet, come on down!

CHAPTER TEN
Cozy's Overture

Back home in Connecticut, plans were being made between Bruce and promoter Harvey Goldsmith for Rainbow to headline a massive "Monsters Of Rock" open-air event at Castle Donington in August, just two months away. Timing being Cozy's forte, he announced to the band that he would quit after that show, a fitting finale to a great partnership with Ritchie and Roger. It had been brewing for months, Cozy just did not want to be in a singles chart band and all that that brought with it. He wanted to be part of a band that had massive album success as he thought that gave him more credibility as a musician. Singles success, he thought, made him look, well, cheap and of no substance - a peddler of three and a half minute 'ditties'.

The supporting line-up at Donington was to be Judas Priest, our German chums the Scorpions, Saxon, Canadian rockers April Wine, Riot and one of Bruce's protégés Touch. After three warm up dates in Scandinavia with Touch, we arrived in London where we would be based. With Ray D'Addario as our production manager ensuring all the equipment was available, I set about making plans for the band to get on site, which was never easy as, like Purple before them and I guess any major band, they all had their own agendas and preferences on a show like this. Roger wanted to experience the whole thing and see all the bands whilst Ritchie wanted to get there his usual thirty five minutes before show time, do the old Johnnie Walker Black Label whisky routine, hit the stage, do the show and fuck off. Cozy, as it was his last show, wanted to make it spectacular and had devised a massive firework and pyrotechnic show during his drum solo of the 1812 overture, so he wanted to be there during the set up and sound check.

This meant me almost running a limo taxi service from our base at the Holiday Inn, Swiss Cottage, London and the festival site, some hundred miles up the M1 motorway. Cozy, as ever the self sufficient, level headed guy said he'd get himself there, leaving me to concentrate on the others.

However I did arrange to be present when Cozy 'rehearsed' his explosions! He wanted the biggest explosion the pyro guys could muster for the finale, so he asked them to demonstrate how loud they could get it from a buried steel pipe. Well, for a radius of five miles, mothers gave birth, hens lay early and to some, World War Three had started, so loud was the explosion. So loud in fact it blew out about twenty speakers of the brand new Quadraphonic PA, literally tearing the cones. They were not best pleased. Cozy, however, smiling broadly said it would do just fine. The road crews then spent a hectic four hours replacing the speakers. It had just not occurred to anybody to set the explosion behind the stage, as it would be on the night and where it would not harm the PA, instead preferring the easier option front of stage.

The show was taped by mainstream TV and radio, so at last Rainbow were getting the exposure they deserved although the critics were less than complementary, but as Led Zeppelin were no strangers to this type of criticism either, most thought we kept good company. The festival sold out, the crowds were ecstatic and they were the ultimate barometer of whether we were 'cutting the mustard' as Eddie would say. It was sad afterwards, saying goodbye to Cozy. He had driven the band, stood up to Ritchie and, with Roger, in my opinion, had provided an unequalled powerhouse and platform for Ritchie. I know he thought the world of Cozy, but, as always, did not know how to say so. Perhaps he had more pressing, personal problems on his mind?

This really was the age of heavy metal. Some weeks after Donington, The Reading Festival was dominated by UFO, Def Leppard, Iron Maiden, David and Whitesnake and Wishbone Ash. Sales of hairspray and calls for hair dryers tripled in London hotels overnight! I wondered at the time if we had maybe done the wrong festival, as I'm sure Ritchie would have fancied his chances at Reading. The challenge to blow that bill off the stage would have been mouth-watering. Ritchie lived for challenges such as that would have presented, as it brought the very best (and worst) out of him. I have no doubt there would have been a conversation on the subject between him and Bruce. The ghosts of the past shimmered in our consciousness in that August of 1980 when the compilation album 'Deepest Purple' went to No.1 in the UK charts, a welcome reminder to Ritchie in the current climate of change that a reunion could always be an option.

Bobby Rondinelli had already been lined up, after yet more exhaustive auditions back in Long Island, to replace Cozy and was at Donington to see what he'd taken on. He had been flown over, met the crew, spent time with the ever-accommodating Cozy and then flew back with me, Ritchie and Roger to America where he lived close to us all, a native of Long Island. Bobby was a skilful basher in the Cozy, 'Bonzo' Bonham mould and would fit in really well, I hoped, for his sake as well as mine. I was getting fed up with this constant 'getting to know you' routine. Too late, in September we went to Copenhagen to begin the next album and it all started to go pear shaped with our Mr. Bonnet.

Ritchie and Bruce decided it was time to prepare for the next album in order to capitalise on the success of the previous one and the two hit singles that had come from it. It was decided that we should go to Denmark, to the Sweet Silence Studios in Copenhagen initially to knock some ideas around and write material. Ritchie, Roger and I went ahead in early September followed a few weeks later by Bobby and Don. Lastly Graham flew in from California where he lived with his Australian wife. He had gone back there straight from Donington to continue recording a solo album. Disappointingly, the Copenhagen sessions were unproductive to say the least.

The atmosphere was heavy as if everyone had no energy or spark of originality. With all respect to Bobby Rondinelli, in my opinion it was because Cozy was gone and it felt like the band was incomplete. Cozy provided a certain spark, a presence that lifted the band and certainly Ritchie, who would now wander into the studios and after an hour look for any excuse to do something, anything else other than record. Graham didn't help matters, as he plainly did not want to be there, feigning illness at every opportunity to curtail the day's rehearsal. Half-hearted tracks were laid down with the only worthwhile song being the Russ Ballard penned, 'I Surrender'. One morning Graham just upped and left, flying back to California, as he felt nothing serious was happening and he was wasting precious time on his own stuff. Ritchie took it as a 'notice to quit' and rang Bruce to tell him it was time to find another vocalist and that he should ring David Oddie, Graham's personal manager and make the break with the singer permanent. No one doubted Graham's ability as a great singer, but that was never enough. Image too, was becoming increasingly important especially as we were entering the video age and MTV. Not that Graham wasn't image conscious, he was. It just wasn't a heavy metal / hard rock image, more a latter day James Dean. With the embryonic

'Difficult To Cure' temporarily on ice, we flew back to Connecticut to find a new vocalist.

Lists were compiled as September drew to a close. Bruce Dickinson, then still with Samson was mentioned and he had often come to Rainbow shows when we were in England as an enthusiastic fan, so it wouldn't be as if high persuasion would be called for. Yet we went through the auditions routine and went to see local bands that had been recommended to us. One such band was local New Jersey cover band Fandango fronted by a young man by the name of Joe Lynn Turner. Ritchie loved him for his versatility, but I thought his voice, good as it was, was not unique enough, sounded like too many great front men, which really isn't a knock, but as my opinion counted for nowt and why would it, Joe was on board. He could mimic anybodies style and did a great Steve Perry of Journey, but where was the real 'Jolene' Turner?

To his credit, he was the consummate professional who constantly strove to improve his art, practicing his scales, exercises and breathing techniques on a daily basis, often in the company of a voice coach. No other singer in Purple or Rainbow had the dedication of 'Little Joe', that's for sure and he could contribute lyrically too, a bonus after Graham Bonnet. Joe spent some time at Ritchie's house in Long Island and emerged as our new singer. Welcome aboard! So, back to Copenhagen to finish the album in the traditionally 'closed' studio, save for engineer Fleming Rasmussen. Even the owner of the studios was barred from the sessions. The kitchen, dining area and lounge were okay, but I had to put a sign up at the entrance to the corridor that led to the studio and edit suite that read:

"NO ADMITTANCE TO ANYBODY OTHER THAN INVITED GUESTS OR PERSONNEL DIRECTLY INVOLVED WITH THIS RECORDING - COLIN HART for RAINBOW"

Hard to take if you own the damn place, but then we did spend a king's ransom there. Joe sang 'I Surrender', erasing Graham's vocals and we all heard a hit single. The album was completed reasonably quickly, spurred on by Joe who had reintroduced the enthusiasm that Cozy had taken with him. He also co wrote 'Can't Happen Here' which would also emerge later as a single. I had instructions to report back to Bruce Payne on an almost daily basis to relay progress and indicate how the new recruits of Turner and Rondinelli were working out. Bruce wanted no hiccups this time as the success of the next album, he knew, would catapult Rainbow to the giddy heights once held by Deep Purple.

We all stayed at the SAS Scandinavia where Joe was introduced to the extracurricular activities of being a Rainbow band member. Trashed rooms, super glued doors were to me extremely passé by now, but Joe took it all in good spirit and the hotel accepted my almost daily 'donations' as a normal part of their routine. One day, however, they pulled Ritchie to complain about the noise the band were making in the wee small hours, instead of telling me quietly. I then would have sorted the problem. Insulted, Ritchie told me to bring a 200-watt Amp and speaker back to the hotel that night. On his instructions, I laid it face down in his room and he treated the hotel to 'real noise' for the next thirty minutes. Their switchboard lit up like a Christmas tree. 'Job done' Ritchie thought, chaos was resumed. I made the customary donation the following morning.

Noise, oddly enough was one of Ritchie's major bugbears. He insisted that hotels, when he wanted to sleep, be monastical in their absence of noise. We had 'noise clauses' in all our hotel contracts whereby the hotel had to declare any construction work that they would have on when we stayed and woe betide them if they broke the deal. Occasionally, of course, the inevitable occurred and I would get a call in my room from Ritchie threatening me with death if I didn't stop the jackhammer or drill that had awoken the guitarist despite it being nine in the morning and a regular working day. That old cash float often did the trick. On the odd occasion this didn't work, Ritchie would immediately tell me to move hotels, not just for him, but also for all the band and crew. The furore and bad tempers I then caused rousting everyone from their beds to move there and then to a new location was stressful to say the least and at times like that, I asked myself if there wasn't another life for me. Captain Chaos had nothing on Ritchie Blackmore.

Of course the noise that he belted out across the French countryside at the Chateau de Pelly de Cornfield in the middle of the night the year before, was an entirely different matter to him. He even complained about wind noises in rooms - like I could get that to stop! Whenever I got him to his room, he would ask me to listen after he had turned off all mechanical noise like a TV. "Listen to the silence" he'd say. Count to ten, Colin. His demands certainly shortened my list of hotels around the world where we could stay and who would agree to my requests for silence before noon.

On December 8th, John Lennon was shot and killed in New York, sixty short miles away from my home and we all became aware of our own mortality. Life was precious, death forever. We were still at Sweet Silence when we heard the news and. like the rest of the music world, I was just thinking about my life and why I was here and it was due in no small measure to him.

Now the entire band except Don lived in America. Thames Talent began to make plans for the next tour to coincide with the release of 'Difficult To Cure'. It would start in February 1981 with a jolly twelve-week jaunt across the States. The start of the tour was buoyed by the news that 'I Surrender' had gone top 3 in England, but Ritchie still coveted American success and was determined that this part of the tour would break the single. He had always been 'difficult' where interviews with press and radio had been concerned but this time he would steel himself to do the rounds of 'daft, inane questions unendingly asked' if it meant a higher profile for 'I Surrender'.

We rehearsed all through January, assembled the crew and the suppliers, which by now was Britannia Row for sound and See Factor for lights. We hit the road at the Peppermint Beach Club, Virginia Beach, which was way bigger than it sounds, on a cold windswept night of 21st of the month. We co-headlined most dates with Pat Travers who really had had only one big hit 'Boom, Boom Out Go The Lights' but he brought in a fair crowd. Many years later Pat would become a neighbour of mine in Orlando, Florida, meeting him quite by chance at the check out counter at my local Publix Supermarket Mart (where all the stars hang out), but in 1981, that was way in the future.

By early March we were in Canada and worked our way west to Vancouver, re-emerging into America on the 18th March at the Seattle Arena. The band was gelling well and Joe never missed a beat or a note, I was warming to him, frankly. We travelled down the west coast through San Francisco, Los Angeles, San Diego, Fresno, and then headed east again into Texas, Utah and Arizona. (The bookers seemingly had got a road map at last!) It was now April and back in England our ex-vocalist Graham 'Hawaii' Bonnet was having chart success with a single from his solo album 'Night Games'.* Meanwhile, in St Louis, Missouri we renewed the acquaintance with Marc Storace of Krokus when they supported us at Granite City and they stayed with Pat and us for the next two weeks - small

---

* 'Night Games' stayed in the UK charts for eleven weeks and reached number 6.

world eh! The tour eventually ground to an exhausted halt on 13th May at Springfield Civic Arena, Mass where we said farewell to Pat Travers and Krokus. Next stop, Europe and Def Leppard.

Support bands to Ritchie were to be tolerated like small children. You knew we had to have them around, but the nanny (me) had to keep them under control and out of his hair (oops, maybe shouldn't have mentioned that word). Unless, of course, they could play soccer! If they could then suddenly they were good to have around, providing they turned out at every opportunity, kitted out ready to rumble. I'm sure any enterprising manager of an emerging rock band could have got them on our tours by dropping a hint to Bruce to tell Ritchie that at least two of the young band had had try outs for England youth soccer teams. They'd have toured the world with us!

Mind you, Ritchie never routed for England at World or European Cups, always Germany and he always watched Bundesliga Soccer, never English league soccer. Strange fellow, but all of this stemmed from his belief that in an earlier incarnation he had been a German Baron or whatever. That's where all the love affairs with German castles came from, his command of the language and his marriages to two German lasses. Even his many houses over the years had Bavarian type bars built in as a standard fitting with only German beer available. Maybe he was right, whose to say different? Anyway, I always say that every guy should have a hobby!

It was June and the 'Difficult To Cure' tour set off once more at The Scandinavium in Gothenburg with Joe (Elliot) and Co (Def Leppard), providing the support and hugely welcomed soccer games! Whether Joe and the boys wanted to play probably never entered Ritchie's head, but maybe the Sheffield lads thought they'd be 'on their bikes' if they refused, so they enthusiastically turned up. As it turned out, Joe Elliot was a fanatic and a brilliant player who still plays to this day. He even turned his tennis courts at his Dublin home into a fully lit five a side pitch!

The European leg took four weeks and included a great show in Madrid where UFO was added to the bill. The next day in San Sebastián, Ian Broad, Ritchie's faithful Liverpudlian personal roadie decided to liven up back stage proceedings: I'm sure at the urging of his employer, by tossing a plate of salad with dressing, over the dressing room partition onto the heads of the spandex attired UFO. Phil Mogg was not best pleased and confronted Ian who, at the goading of the amused Ritchie, swung a punch. Bad idea as Moggie was reputed to be an ex-boxer. Whatever, he could certainly handle himself and all Ian's punches found thin air whilst Mogg's found their target. It was annihilation and Ian was becoming very bloodied and bruised.

I stepped between them saying enough was enough and that it was stupid for Ian to continue. Ritchie grabbed me by the throat, pulling me away and urged Ian, "Get him, you can take him" like a knarled old fifties boxing promoter. This was senseless, but Ian, lion hearted but daft, waded into Mogg once more. Blood was now coming from his ear, from a broken nose and many facial cuts. They went into a furious no holds barred clinch, smashing against the partitions, which eventually fell down. This was now getting like a scene from a very bad western 'B' movie where a saloon bar brawl destroys everything in its path. Broadie eventually raised his arm in surrender whilst Phil Mogg, hardly out of breath, honour satisfied, calmly and victoriously went on stage to play his set. Ian was in a terrible state like a defeated bare-knuckle fighter, but he would do anything for Ritchie and it would not be the last time he'd take a beating at Ritchie's request.

Indeed, some months later Ritchie and Ian were dining in The Rainbow Bar on Sunset in Los Angeles where, as luck would have it the infamous Don Arden (who I've mentioned before), took a seat at the next table. Don, of course, recognised Ritchie from the many dates we had shared with his band ELO.* He leaned over to say hello where upon Ian, god love his quaint Liverpool humour, told the famed manager to "fuck off". Don, not unnaturally, was not amused and, stoney faced, went back to his table. For many, many months later the word was out that Ian's arse was the Dons' and he would be taken care off in a severe way.

We always looked both ways when Ian was around just in case someone from the Don came a-callin'. If Ian knew whom he had addressed in such a manner then he was plain stupid, if he had not, then he was just ignorant and plain stupid. Amazingly it all went away. I suspected Bruce had had words with Don's son David, more for Ritchie's sake than Ian, who after all, to Bruce was a complete nonentity. The deal was for Ian to publicly apologise to Don at the scene of the crime, The Rainbow Grill, and it was my task to set it up. At first Ian was reluctant, as was Ritchie, but I insisted and the date was set. Don was at his table as Ian and I entered. No Ritchie

---

* Arden had also crossed paths with Blackmore in the early sixties. As a top impresario of the day, he had promoted tours that included Blackmore's then band The Outlaws.

you'll note. I pushed Ian forward and in front of everyone (it was a packed evening), Ian said out loud that he was really, really sorry for offending Don and would he forgive him. Don, playing to the gallery, fixed Ian with a steely stare waited a heavy couple of minutes while Ian broke into a sweat and then just nodded and turned back to eat his meal leaving Ian standing there. Way better than a beating, well for Don anyway. For Ian it was humiliation big-time and very public. Yet you had to love him. With a brain he'd have been very dangerous!

We returned to England on the 9th July and, such was Rainbow's pulling power, we sold out two nights at most venues including London's aptly named Rainbow Theatre and Edinburgh Ingleston Hall, where my sister Carol and her husband David came to visit. Carol and David were by now living in the far north of Scotland in Fraserburgh, way North of Aberdeen where David was Chaplain of the Fraserburgh Royal National Mission to Deep Sea Fishermen. There were more sell-outs at Leeds Queens Hall, Stafford Bingley Hall and Hammersmith Odeon.

Rainbow was at the height of its fame despite many voices in the audiences shouting for Ronnie. Joe Lynn Turner was still a bit lightweight for the more avid metal fan, but he soldiered on although at times I could tell Ritchie was a bit disenchanted with him. Why else would he tell him to stop being Judy Garland? On the 20th, we played St. Austell Coliseum way down on the West Cornwall Coast and Roger had a new bass tech in one Charlie Lewis from Cortland, New York. Yes, that place again. It seems if you want to break out of that town you either become a musician or a roadie. After the show, when the band and myself had left for the hotel, the crew began to load out and found a Robin Reliant three-wheel car blocking the load out doors. Despite many attempts to find the owner from the quickly emptying arena, none could be found. Charlie decided, as time was a-wastin', he would move it and jumped into a fork lift truck, gently ran the forks under the offending motor, lifted it and drove it away from the doors to the adjacent swimming pool of the complex, tipping it in. It turned turtle and sank to the bottom.

The blockage removed, the crew carried on. Naturally Harty had to clear this up. My phone rang the next morning with an irate Bruce Payne playing merry hell at the phone call he's just had from the venue about a drowned Reliant Robin and would I quickly find the culprit and fix it. I called Raymond D'Addario who reluctantly admitted that it had been Charlie's rock 'n' roll moment. Charlie who was new to us, but dead keen, 'fessed up' and offered to pay for the damage not only to the car, but also to the pool which by now had all the seeped engine oil gumming up its filters, nice! We took it out of his wages for quite some considerable time into the future, but Charlie was a stayer and eventually became Deep Purple's production manager, but that was still in the far distant future.

Bruce, for some time had been suggesting to Ritchie and Roger that the line-up needed freshening up. An additional guitarist? Keyboard player? A brass section, maybe? Nah none of them, how about two girl backing vocalists! I was a little shocked as it was hardly my idea of Ritchie's rock 'n' roll nirvana. Never underestimate the persuasive power of Mr. Payne had always been my motto and, sure enough, Mesdames Lynn Robinson and Dee Beale, two English singers who had been signed to Purple Records as a band called Reflections, joined our merry throng at Newcastle City Hall. Lynn's other claim to fame was she had once been one of the saucy 'Hills Angels' on comedian Benny Hill's TV Show. Reflections had also been guests on the show. Mmmm, very rock 'n' roll!

They did fill out the vocals no end and to be fair it sort of worked, but Cozy would not have approved had he still been with us and it would have confirmed his worst fears that we were 'going cabaret'. The girls stayed with us for over two years and entered fully into the fun and frolic of life on the road with Rainbow, their gender certainly never saving them from the pranks. Before too long, however, it became obvious to me that Bruce's reasons were maybe not entirely musical for them being with us. He and Lynn were often 'making sweet music' of a more nocturnal and private kind before too many months passed. It amused me that they thought I did not know. After all, one evening at the Brussels Hilton I went to his room for some reason or another, which was pretty usual, only to be told upon him hearing me at the door to "hang on a minute" which was unusual. When he at last let me in, the bathroom door was shut, but the dead giveaway was Lynn's boots on the floor. I looked at them, Bruce looked at me looking at them, and I smiled and left. The next night he took me aside to 'explain' and I said, "Bruce, I know what's been going on. I'd have to be an idiot not to notice, but I don't care. It's nothing to do with me". Still, they were both single, and past the legal age, so why not? They kept their liaison very discreet and I'm not too sure to this day that it was common knowledge to the rest of the entourage, apart from now, of course. Errrrr, sorry Bruce!

After the last two nights at a sell-out Hammersmith Odeon, we took a short two-week breather in London whilst I prepared the visas for all and sundry for the obligatory dates in Japan for the inscrutable Mr. Udo. Nine shows culminating in three at the famous Budokan in Tokyo. Whenever I returned to that city, it brought back pangs of loss at the break up with Marlene who I knew had to be married to someone and, as I was to find out much later, was also the proud mother of twins. More on that later: It hurt, but in life there are many crossroads and I had learned never to regret which fork in the road one chose, as that was a pretty pointless exercise. You should always play the hand you are dealt and never covet someone else's. I had chosen this life a decade ago and for better or worse I had to live it. It was pretty good, all said and done!

From Japan, instead of flying home as was usual, the band agreed to do one last show in Honolulu, Hawaii. At the end of the concert, Don Airey dropped the unexpected bombshell that this was his last show and he would be quitting. The fact that we had all left him on stage mid solo and gone back to the hotel, never to return, could not surely have had any bearing on his decision (least I hope not). Nah! He said that he was bored with the whole thing, that playing old Rainbow and Purple material did not excite him anymore, it was not challenging to him as a musician. So what did he do next? Went and joined Black Sabbath and played their tired back catalogue for a further three years! I think our Don was being a bit economic with the truth.

Rainbow's pay structure was based on the principle of 'unequal shares'. Ritchie and Roger got equal 'lion' shares, but the rest got paid, at best, wages with a small percentage of each night's gross. In most cases, however, it was just straight wages. I'm sure Don negotiated a far better deal for himself with Black Sabbath than he was getting with Rainbow which probably more than compensated for the lack of musical inspiration in their repertoire. I was sad to see him go if, for nothing else, I would miss our chats about all things Geordie, not less the soccer.

We all headed home to Connecticut for the fall of '81 including Lynn and Dee who, after much persuasion from Bruce, I agreed for them to share my house that I had now rented in New Canaan. Rent free, I may add, which I was okay about really, as they were great to have around and often took to sunbathing topless on my back garden deck, which was a very welcome bonus, not only for me but also for my landlord who lived next door. He could just about see if he stood on a chair in his kitchen! Lynn, especially was a sight to make brave men weep, bless her.

CHAPTER ELEVEN
STRAIGHT BETWEEN THE GOALPOSTS

L ife returned to normal for all of September and October as Ritchie and a now somewhat restless Roger began to search for a replacement for Don. Touring for Roger was a love / hate deal in that the long treks took their toll on his health. He had always suffered from bad migraine headaches and stomach cramps and the longer the tour the more frequent these became, yet once he was home for more than a couple of months the urge to get back out there became irresistible. This last tour had been very arduous and Roger was in the "I've had it with touring" mode.

The tapes from eager keyboard players flooded into Thames Talent once it was common knowledge that the seat was vacant. David Rosenthal was from New Jersey and his tape certainly impressed, even to the point of Ritchie saying he was almost too good, such was his classical background. However we brought him to a rehearsal and after quite a few hours of jamming he was offered the job. David was only twenty-one years old and looked it. It was quite sobering to think that we three - Roger, Ritchie and myself were thirteen years older and way more experienced in this business. David would have to have a 'handle with care' sign on him at least for the first few months (okay, weeks!)

Come November, we journeyed up to Vermont to rehearse in a rented house for the album 'Straight Between The Eyes'. It went well with 'Little Joe' demonstrating once more that he was more than a foil for Ritchie, interpreting his riffs and music structure with strong lyrics. Joe's voice was exceptionally adaptable and he kept himself in shape too, so he was always 'on the money' at rehearsals and recording, which matched perfectly Ritchie's ideals of professionalism and dedication. The Judy Garland tag didn't get mentioned anymore, so Joe had got his spurs. It was a good time to be around them. Rehearsals done we moved on to a snow bound Montreal, Canada to Le Studio (how do they come up with these imaginative names, those innovative French Canadians!) to start the album.

The studio had been recommended to Roger by Nazareth, who he was producing. It was very picturesque overlooking a large frozen lake and we were up to our 'small bits' in two to three feet of snow. "What was wrong with Montserrat?" was a thought that briefly flitted through my frozen head. At least Ritchie would lay off playing soccer for a while, which unfortunately meant his little pranks would get more of an airing. On arrival, set for a reasonably long stay I unpacked my gear to discover I had left my accessory bag of toiletries, adapters and essential electrical 'gear' behind in New Canaan. I was seriously angry with myself and could 'see' the damn bag back in the bathroom at home. The more I thought, the clearer the picture seemed to be of it sitting in my bathroom. How could I be so careless and moreover how was I going to replace the various essentials way out here in the back of beyond in snow bound Canada?

As was usual, on the first evening of recording, Ritchie summoned everyone for drinks and a meal. I was still livid at myself, and Ritchie enquired as to why I was in such a bad mood? Typically he laughed out loud at my misfortune. After three or four 'libations', the talk got argumentative about, ridiculously, the longest river in America. I said it was the Mississippi, Ritchie said it was the Allegheny. I told him he was talking out of his arse, Ritchie revved it up and a discussion, fuelled by my bad humour became a full-scale shouting match. To settle it I stormed off to the lounge where the amused barman had said there was a set of maps or a reference book, anything to get the last word over that argumentative git. I found a bookcase, opened it and there was my accessory bag! Behind me I heard the hysterical laughter of Richard Blackmore - I'd been got at last. Seems on check in he had rifled my bag and removed the object of his mirth and my anger. He lived off his triumph for days, as many as it took for me to forgive him. Not very rock 'n' roll either in the accepted sense either, as in chicks and drugs, exceptionally childish looking back on it now really, but kinda sums up Ritchie at times.

The actual recording of the album took only five weeks thanks to the rehearsal time in Vermont. The atmosphere was good and for Ritchie it was prank- heaven, a sure indication that all was well with him. I had still not forgiven him for the opening prank of the 'lost' accessory bag. Downtime was spent ice-skating and David taught those interested enough, to ski. Ritchie ordered the now big yawn of 'room emptying' for David, who, when asked to look out of the window to the patio at dinner one night, saw the entire contents of his room replicating the positions of that room, complete with his clothes and shoes neatly by the bed, covered in a thick layer of snow. The road crew and I had been ordered to do it by his lordship and frankly it had become boring, boring, boring, as well as, this time, a cold useless thing to do.

The list thought by our leader went on and on. The old cellophane on the toilet routine, the cranking up of the room heater to tropical temperatures whilst occupant is asleep trick, and of course we mustn't forget the snow-drift over the door gag, rigged to drop as the unsuspecting victim, this time Joe, emerged. The latter could well have killed Joe as he was small, though well made, whereas the snowdrift was very large and not. It all amused Ritchie greatly as the arch orchestrator, but my age was thirty-five, and now beginning to show as I now found these pranks a tad tedious.

I always listened to the album charts, as a fan mostly, and to see how our contemporaries, rivals if you like, were getting on. I was in this business because I loved it and what better way to live your life than being right in the epicentre of everything you loved AND get paid for it. I considered myself a very lucky guy. I was particularly pleased to see AC/DC, after their tragedy with Bon Scott, topping the US Album charts, as the year closed, with 'For Those About To Rock, We Salute You'. My old mate Brian Johnson had made the big time at last. I never discussed these triumphs of former support acts with Ritchie as he always seemed disinterested, but I nevertheless got the impression that it rankled him when he was alone with his thoughts in his candle-lit dressing room.

As the cold harsh light of January 1982 dawned, it found me back in Connecticut at my house in New Canaan. Bruce and the agency were planning the next attack on the US market with the release of 'Straight Between The Eyes' and the inevitable tour to promote it. Rainbow were now very mainstream rock, but for all that, still considered THE band to support to get on the rickety ladder to rock stardom. The American leg would be a mind numbing 105 days long starting on May 10th in London, Ontario, Canada supported by Iron Maiden and country rockers .38 Special. Ritchie decided we would travel by tour bus rather than flying, which made life a lot easier for me as we were not constricted by airline timetables or have the fuss of checking in to airports. Travelling was now far more flexible.

This was not the first time we had elected to tour by bus, but now Ritchie had his 'special' bus, a black Silver Eagle with its master bedroom for him, of course, and bunks for the rest of us complete with a special driver, one Bill Miller. He was an ex-Vietnam Vet, quiet, sometimes shy, but above all a great driver. Ritchie loved him! One drawback was Ritchie's erratic decision-making concerning when and if to drive overnight to the next gig. That meant Bill could never plan his sleep schedule to fit the requirement of 'safe driving'. One day Bill said to me; "Can you drive one of these things?" "Of course" said I. You see, I had previously driven a tour bus when one of our drivers needed a rest even though it was a much older version of this magnificent machine and, of course, I had driven trucks. Buses, man? It would be a breeze! Well, almost. You just had to go careful round the corners at speed otherwise you tended to tip all the bed and bunk residents on their arse! Hmmm, revenge and Ritchie were two words that flitted playfully through my brain. Bill and I became firm friends. He even perceived that I could more or less control Ritchie. I did not disavow him of this ridiculous idea. Supervision of a super hero is superficial!

Touring now fell into a pattern. Bill long hauled us to the hotel and then I would take the wheel of this glorious monster and take Ritchie and the band to the sound check and back. Sometimes it would be just Ritchie and I - two big overgrown kids driving a big arse bus through big cities. Ha, ha, ha. I'd drive everyone to the show too and back again. That way Bill got his rest in case Ritchie wanted to up sticks and away through the night to the next gig. I first got the respect of the entire band when, one morning in Rochester New York, Bill awoke sick as a dog and I had to drive the whole cast to Binghamton. Now the band looked at me as a 'do anything kinda guy'. Maybe that proved to be to my detriment in the long run. Over the tours, Bill would become the most rested bus driver in the history of rock 'n' roll and with all this rest we got the cleanest and best maintained bus in rock 'n' roll.

On this tour, Bruce Dickinson, who had joined Iron Maiden three months before, once their set was finished, would sit beside the stage watching our show, ever the faithful fan. The relationship with .38 Special was, for some reason, less cordial although I really enjoyed their music. Perhaps they felt they were a little too country and shouldn't have been on a tour with heavy rockers Rainbow and Iron Maiden. On reflection it was a mismatch, but they didn't die, they were too good. They would later go on to huge success in the country charts, their albums selling by the bucket load. Even mismatches got successful supporting Rainbow!

As we were travelling by road the itinerary was by necessity logical in its planning and it allowed us to play smaller cities like Flint, Kalmazoo, Fort Wayne, Toledo, Merrillville, Davenport, and just about Anywhereville. On June 5th, we played The Alpine Valley Music Theatre in Milwaukee and it was freezing despite being early summer. It was the wind, you see, which must have been from the north straight from the Arctic sweeping across the lake. Ritchie stood it for thirty minutes then did the old 'guitar off / lay on top of amp / switch off / exit stage left silently' routine and we were done much to the disgust of the locals who were obviously made of far hardier stuff.

This was the last we saw of our support bands who then split off to tour together whilst we were joined by those merry German chaps, The Scorpions, who by now were becoming a force to be reckoned with. Ah well, it made Ritchie happy as backstage took on the atmosphere of a German bierkeller. The tour quickly fell into the routine of hotel / gig / bus / the road / hotel / gig yada, yada, yada. No point in listing the cities, just get an American A-Z and if its there, we played it.

In mid August we played two big sold-out stadium shows in St. Louis at The Busch Memorial Stadium and The Kansas City Arrowhead Stadium, not headlining, but as special guests to REO Speedwagon who were massive at the time having had a number one album, 'Hi Fidelity', in the US charts the year before. Also on the bill were Ted Nugent and John Cougar Mellencamp who had by now become his own man, playing his brand of music and not one dictated to him by well meaning, but misguided management. He was number one in the album charts with 'American Fool' and number one in the singles charts with 'Jack And Diane'.

In San Antonio, the show was filmed for the video release 'Live Between The Eyes'. This tour was, of course without the now long-gone, famous rainbow arch. The 'centre piece' was now two giant blood shot eyes mimicking the 'Straight Between The Eyes' album cover with two huge spotlights acting as the iris of each eye. Another great idea badly executed as some nights, when the eyes descended from behind the curtain up on the rig, the 'eyes', (which were supposed to be synchronised to look left then right and beam straight out into the audience as one and look as if they were ripping out your soul), got an independent life of their own. Alas, they, hilariously, became 'cross-eyed'; one would not work or would start winking. Ooooh, scary! Not quite the effect we were hoping for!

UFO joined us on some dates too, but as Ian Broad had left Ritchie to be replaced by one Barry Ambrosio, the expected tension was not there with Phil Mogg. Despite the relationship with Broad going back to the early sixties, the pair had an on again, off again kind of friendship, which led to the untimely split. Ambrosio was yet another in a long line of personal roadies for Ritchie who had no experience or qualification whatsoever for the job other than a willingness to play soccer, seemingly the only necessary attribute for Ritchie, but which made everybody else's job that much harder. Those faithful football fools! By mid August, we returned home to Connecticut to prepare for the next part of the tour, Japan and Europe.

It was nice to get these breaks in the tour as life on the road, whilst enjoyable, was mixed with large measures of tedium. To outsiders, it seems to be an endless 'pleasurefest', but the reality is large expanses of boredom like an endless becalmed sea, with you and the band either sitting in an airport lounge, on a plane, in a tour bus, dressing room, hotel room or a hotel bar interspersed by one daily two-hour dose of high octane, adrenalin rush action called the show. If you don't keep in shape health wise, then tours take their toll on you. I felt okay, but was conscious that I was getting a widening girth, which just would not shrink despite the compulsory weekly, if not daily, soccer workouts with RB. I was now a mid field sweeper as opposed to a nippy winger of a few years before. Would goalkeeping be the sad option in the years to come?

My day would start around 10am when Thames Talent opened up, a swift libation to kick start the system and I'd be into my routine of setting up the next leg of the tour with visas for all the band and crew which by now was forty strong, sorting hotels choice and all travel, be it 'train, plane or automobile' and liasing with my production manager on his requirements. The personal requests of each member of the band took the longest as; after all, this tour would only be successful if they and especially Ritchie got my individual service and attention. It was like looking after five spoilt kids in a way. No wonder I had none of my own! Yet I wouldn't have had it any other way. You're either born to this life or your not.

I took this break from the road as an opportunity to get mam and dad out to America whilst their health was still reasonable, especially as dad had now retired. I rang them up and told them to get their passports in order as I was sending them two round trip tickets to New York. They were over the moon. They flew into Newark where I had arranged a stretch limo to pick them up and whisk them to my place in New Canaan. Well, the kick for me was as equal if not more so than the kick they got. The King and Queen of South Shields, yer bugger! However just to bring them down to earth I took 'em back after the holiday in my truck! Well, can't spoil them too much!

They had a great time although my ma looked in too many cupboards and ran her finger over too many surfaces for dust, but that's mam's. I had of course dusted, shoved stuff under beds and thrown away a few dishes, but she knew, naturally. Dad just drank it all in, the sites, the smells, the cars, and the people. I took them up to the top of the Twin Towers too: Hard to imagine now the tragedy that would unfold years later. We talked a lot too, more so than ever before and I know they were happy for me, a feeling that would stay with me to this day. I was pleased that I could do a little something to repay them for all their love and freedom that I had been granted to follow my dreams. I 'm sure I had worried them beyond measure at times. I'm glad now that they had such a great time as sadly for them and all the family, they were not to see many more years.

We arrived in Japan on October 10th, two days prior to playing three nights at the Festival Hall in Osaka as a prelude to a tramp round the country ending on 22nd with the obligatory two nights at The Budokan in Tokyo. Seven days and five thousand miles later we started the European leg in Oslo, Norway at the Drammenshalen supported by those infamous female rockers Girlschool. In 2005 they reunited and toured and included me on their mailing list, although why and how, I have no idea! They were lots of fun, those gals, who could play some mean rock as well as enter into the extra-curricula activities of the road with enthusiasm such as drinking, pranks and general mayhem. We played with them, if you'll pardon the expression, right through November in Denmark, Finland, Sweden, Germany, Holland and finally Spain where, you guessed it, UFO joined us. Moggie and the boys certainly enjoyed certain fame and notoriety with Spanish fans, which livened up the boredom of an endless trek no end.

The tour over, with surprisingly no British dates, those band members and crew who were US residents, returned home to Connecticut for Christmas and an uncertain future for some. The tour, though on the surface successful, had not pushed Rainbow to the super group stature that Ritchie expected and demanded. He was very quiet on the return flight, deep in private conversation with Bruce. Would the inevitable Yuletide team changes be made once more, I asked myself, as 1983 approached? Ritchie, in a rare moment of indecision decided to come off the road while he thought his future through. Bruce, having no short term plan for the band decided to 'lay off' Joe, David and Bobby indefinitely which didn't go down too well, but it was better that way than giving them false hope.

Bruce had always kept in touch with Phil Banfield, Ian Gillan's personal manager and more than once I heard the rumour around the office that the two of them were 'in a huddle' over, if not a complete reunion of Deep Purple, at least a one off concert with the fabled line-up. Whilst the gods conferred, I settled into a life of domesticity in New Canaan. I still got my wages as a member of the inner sanctum of permanent employees of Rainbow /Blackmore / Thames Talent. This, of course, included turning out for weekly soccer games as well as the daily routine of running errands for Ritchie, Thames Talent or whoever, while Roger, by this time was in the studios working on his solo album 'The Mask', with David Rosenthal.

My personal life was no better on the girlfriend front as whenever a relationship looked like it would go somewhere we would disappear on tour for half the year and the closeness would evaporate as the physical distance increased. The rumours of a Purple reunion persisted until March when Ritchie told me he would have one last attempt at breaking Rainbow. I was mystified as we were a massive draw in most markets, were we not already 'broken'? Just what was he after? The albums, although not triple platinum, still sold in considerable number and the tours were always pretty much sold out in most venues. He had the respect of virtually every musician you could shake a stick at and Bruce had ensured his personal wealth was not only intact, but also expanding. In truth, he was not exactly unhappy, more restless and ill at ease. I guess the word was 'unfulfilled'. The "crossroads" feel must have been catching. Our old 'sparring' partners UFO had now decided to knock it on the head with Phil Mogg apparently having had a nervous breakdown, which was, I thought, very unlike Moggie. The band had, he was quoted, gone as far as they could. Maybe Ritchie felt the same way?

David, Joe and Bobby were returned to the payroll although the latter's tenure was short-lived and a new drummer was on the shopping list. The search did not take long as Roger had been using one of Joe's mates from way back, one Chuck Bürgi of Hall and Oates fame, on his solo album and recommended him. A case of being in the right place at the right time or perhaps Joe had had a hand in getting Bobby the boot too - a little whisper here, a whisper there as to the drummers unsuitability and whadya know, I've got this mate who'd be great. That Joe was quietly empire building. Chuck, an experienced session drummer, was good however and, as Ritchie rated him, it was a done deal.

The writing for the album began in earnest with Joe increasingly Ritchie's collaborator. We hoofed it up to Vermont in May for the two of them to kick them into shape with the rest of the band and then rocked over to the Sweet Silence Studios in Copenhagen to record the 'Bent Out Of Shape' album with engineer Fleming Rasmussen. By now the recording procedure was a well oiled machine from a financial perspective, due now to Ritchie's insistence that the writing process took place prior to expensive studio time, which had by now been brought down to a very economic five weeks.

'The Bent Out Of Shape' tour started in England in September supported by ex Runaway Lita Ford. We had not toured here for two years, as Ritchie believed we had played the venues too frequently and feared over exposure. The two opening shows at the Royal Court Theatre, Liverpool were sell-outs, however, and Ritchie visibly relaxed. The next night was to be a huge nostalgia trip for me as we were to play Whitley Bay Ice Rink, to which I had walked, ferried and bussed as a lad eighteen years previously, and where I had first caught the incurable virus called rock 'n' roll. All the vivid memories of skating around to Paul Anka, Cliff Richard and The Shadows and the early Liverpool sounds flooded in on me as I walked through the familiar doors and a huge disappointment burst that rose tinted bubble.

The ice palace had become a shit hole! It was a rundown, paint peeling, pigeon shit encrusted corpse, masquerading as my teenage memory and I was devastated. It was a sharp lesson in never looking back because you can't go back, only forward. I spent the entire show on automatic, getting it done as quickly as possible. Mam and dad came by, as was usual when we played the North East and they had their traditional tête-à-tête with Ritchie. We all went back to our hotel in Newcastle where we had a meal and many drinks. Part of me, however, was ten miles away in a frozen memory and a realization that I was now thirty-six and not eighteen. Where had all the years gone?

The tour continued for ten more nights and it became apparent that our Joe and Lita had become an item. Tour romances are a rare occurrence because of the almost exclusive 'boys club' atmosphere, so this was odd, but somehow romantic to see the two making goo goo eyes at each other at every meeting, quite touching in an innocent way really. Not very rock 'n' roll though! Whatever happened to 'wham, bam, thank you mam'!

All was not well with Ritchie, however. His soccer playing through the summer had taken its toll when he began to develop a stiff neck, which in turn gave him a tingling sensation in his fingers. Not what you need in his line of work really! It turned out he had tweaked a nerve in his neck (doubtless scoring that all important winning goal - cue slow motion replay to our hero, resplendent in German strip, out-jumping a static English defence to head the winning goal in the 1982 World Cup for the homeland. Ah, those Blackmore dreams!) A physio was added to the extensive crew list plus very heavily padded guitar straps and the old trouper, well, trouped!

I had always prided myself that our crew were the best, but once in a while problems occurred that were beyond even their cunning savvy. At the beginning of the European leg we were due to play a basketball hall in Odense in Denmark. As usual, Raymond D'Addario had sent out the equipment specs stating how much room we needed to rig back line, PA and lighting. You can never entirely trust venue owners to know their own venues, which is pretty tragic when you think about it. I don't know one tour manager that will, hand on heart, trust a venue. It's always a nervous voyage of discovery, even if you've played them countless times, 'cos they forget to tell you about alterations, additions and deletions to the hall specifications since you were there last. Oh well!

Anyway, the hall confirmed they could comply with his requests. When the rigging started it was apparent that the lighting rig was too high for the proscenium of the stage, so the lads decided to 'free stand' it in front of the stage on the auditorium floor. That brought the lights themselves so low that they were burning the band at the sound check. But this was the only solution to the problem and the show went ahead. Half way through, some of the more enthusiastic fans found out they could climb the lighting rig to get a better view and it began to rock and then sway alarmingly the more fans climbed onto it. I ran to the security chief, which isn't easy in a packed hall, to get him to protect the rig and get those crazy

Danes off it. Too late the whole deal toppled over into the crowd as if in slow motion.

The band stopped playing in shock as fans ran for their lives. Lighting rigs are heavy and seriously hot. Death by crushing or burning to death would be a probability. Miraculously, neither of these became realities although there were a couple of broken legs and many cuts and bruises. The local promoter, working for our old friend Erik Thomsen, was in deep trouble and the next five dates under his company had to be cancelled while the authorities had a chat with him. We moved on, but I'm sure Bruce and Erik were in a huddle to sort out the liability. The tour reconvened on October 5th in Copenhagen at The Falconer Teatret for one night followed by the last night, forty-eight hours later, in Helsinki, Finland. An odd European tour - short and no German dates?

Three weeks later, America and twenty-three shows in thirty-seven days lay ahead. This was probably the shortest US tour ever for us, so there was obviously something wrong. The mood in the office was not good either. I heard tales of cancelled dates due to poor ticket sales and Ritchie was certainly not a happy guy to be around. Over the last year, he had introduced Deep Purple classics into the show because the fans undoubtedly wanted to hear them, but they were slightly beyond Joe's singing talent. Don't get me wrong, Joe was a great singer, but not of heavy rock. He was a master at melodic rock, AOR and classic rock, but he wasn't a screamer in the Gillan mould and if you're doing 'Smoke On The Water', or 'Child In Time', well, 'nuff said. The tour kicked off in Worcester, Mass at The Centrum Auditorium on October 28th and travelled the Eastern States supported on occasions by Chuck's former band Aldo Nova, but once we hit the Mid West, we teamed up with Blue Oyster Cult. The tour was not a happy one.

There was an all-pervading sense of the 'end of term', the final and last term of Rainbow. Nothing was said, but then it perhaps was not necessary. When you live 24/7 with guys, you get to read the body language pretty accurately and it said 'OVER' in big shiny letters. We then broke for Christmas, as was the tradition. Bruce Payne, as ever was prepared. He had seen that the writing on the wall too for Rainbow for some months and had contacted Phil Banfield in the early winter of 1983 to test the water as to Ian's feelings about a Deep Purple reunion. After all, Ian's career, post Purple had not been the glory trail he wanted and he was currently making a complete arse of himself with Black Sabbath, as to this day, he still doesn't know any of the lyrics he sang, whilst Ritchie with Rainbow had arguably been far more successful. Jon Lord was with David in Whitesnake, but that was totally David's gig, so Jon would have been no more than an extremely competent sideman with little say in musical policy. Paicey was back home, happy in his domestic bliss and being a much sought after session drummer.

As they say, it's all in the timing and Bruce always had his perfect. I asked him to clarify the situation and to be fair, he was honest and up front in telling me of his plans and reassured me that I would be running the show on the road if the deals could be done to reform Deep Purple. He intimated that any reunion would be on Ritchie's terms and he, Bruce, would be in the jump seat as the overall manager. Relieved and excited by the prospect, I enjoyed that Christmas of 1983.

CHAPTER TWELVE
THE WINNING TEAM UNITED

In late January, Mr. Paice, Mr. Lord and Mr. Gillan were set to arrive at JFK Airport, New York and I was dispatched to pick them up and take them to a waterfront Hotel in Greenwich, Connecticut to meet up with Mr. Glover and Mr. Blackmore and of course Bruce. They arrived separately. No hidden agenda, no mystery, they just lived in separate places, although they all flew from the same airport, to the same destination, but at different times: Nothing new there. For some reason I was really nervous about seeing them again under these circumstances. After all I'd seen Paicey and Jon on a sparse few occasions over the last eight years when they had turned up at Rainbow shows and of course I'd been with Ritchie and Roger throughout most of that time. With Ian, it was different. I had not seen or heard from him since we departed in Tokyo all those years ago. Some guys just never phone or write, although I did get and have had a Christmas card from him and his missus, Bron every year to this day. He had just kept himself apart as if any contact with his old band mates would have scuppered any chance of solo success. Something similar to bumping into an old much-loved girl friend would hinder any new romance.

I booked them separate rooms and kept it all under wraps. No one knew what was planned except the five musicians, Bruce, myself and, of course, Phil Banfield, Ian's manager. Initially only Bruce and the former band mates met for dinner and drinks in a private dining room. I was asked to wait in the lobby either to take them all back from whence they came or to celebrate. This was not cut and dried by any means. At 11pm, I got a call to go up to the room. I entered with a certain amount of trepidation. Would it be smiles or glum faces? I looked at Ritchie and Ian first. If they were not happy bunnies, then the deal was off. They were chatting away like old school chums and I knew Deep Purple were to be back together.

With the deal seemingly done, everyone returned home to quietly tie up their current situations and get ready to reconvene in early summer to start writing and rehearse for the new Deep Purple album. Bruce had to tell Joe Lynn Turner who, I think, was initially told that Rainbow was to be put on ice, rather than disbanded and that Bruce would get him a solo album deal in the interim. Whether this was Bruce's way of letting Joe down easy or just hedging his bets to keep Joe close in case the Purple reunion was short lived, only Bruce knows.

Whatever, Purple did stay together and Rainbow did not rise again for another ten years, alas without Joe. Jon said his goodbyes to Whitesnake and Rainbow had one last contract for three shows to fulfil in Japan in mid March. At the last show at the Budokan in Tokyo, Ritchie got his wish and 'Difficult to Cure' was performed with an orchestra, all the parts being written by David Rosenthal, much to his credit and musical ability and taped for video release. Was this Bruce wringing one last drop of blood from Rainbow or fulfilling a wish for his client? Tough call!

By May, Bruce asked me to scout out a suitable rehearsal location and studio in the general Massachusetts, Maine or Vermont area of Eastern America. I still had my doubts that this 'reunion' would last long knowing the personalities involved, but I went with the flow (like what else would I do?) Roger and I found a place in Massachusetts called Bass Lodge. The good folks there sent down a private plane and we flew up to look the place over. It was perfect; it had a house with a live-in chef, separate accommodation for both crew and band and, of course, a studio. We did the deal and made arrangements for the band and crew to assemble.

After only a few days the main drawback to this 'ideal spot' manifested itself. It was absolutely miles from anywhere, which left the band with nothing to amuse themselves with during downtime, no restaurants or bars for miles in any direction. It had a feeling of total isolation from the outside world. Purple were social animals and this 'sleepy hollow' was driving them crazy. I was ordered immediately to find somewhere else a bit closer to civilisation. Stowe in Vermont immediately came to mind where we had rehearsed Rainbow so successfully. I drove up there alone and met with Ian Broad, (yes, that crazy lad was back in the fold as Ritchie's fetch 'n carry guy) and had meetings with realtors to look at suitable properties to rent. Ian had made some good contacts for properties there. We spent almost the whole of the next day looking at everything from closed hotels to small houses, too small for the project. Then a house called Horizons, found courtesy of a local British pub owner Richard Hughes, seemed like a place well worthy of a look and through the real estate agent, I approached the property, which consisted of two houses in their own grounds overlooking a valley, I knew it would be perfect. The main house had a massive basement that stretched the full area of the house with full height ceilings - excellent.

The band accepted my word and we uprooted and transferred there without delay. We booked Le Mobile, from Montreal and Guy Charbaneau, a really lovely guy, and the owner, showed up with it himself and parked up outside. Then we encountered the first of a few minor problems. There wasn't sufficient power to run the mobile, the house and all our equipment, but then in all honesty, why would there be? A local electrician was immediately contacted and he showed up with remarkable speed. He hard-wired the mobile directly to the power pole down the driveway and installed extra breakers so we wouldn't burn the place down which wouldn't have gone down too well!

The recording of 'Perfect Strangers' began in earnest. Richard's Pub, uniquely named 'The Pub at Stowe' so one could get confused, became our social club and he did rather well for the time we were there, probably increasing his turnover tenfold. He offered a friendly ear and chat, but not much in the way of discounts! After several weeks we were done and Ritchie with Roger flew off to Hamburg to mix it. Another more pleasant aspect of Richard's Pub was a lady called Michele who worked behind the bar. Over the course of the weeks we were there, we struck up a close friendship; a very close friendship and I invited her back to Connecticut. She and I visited each other over the coming months and eventually, I bought a house in Trumbull, Connecticut, and in she moved with daughters Christina and Jennifer, who were four and six years old respectively. Suddenly I had a family and responsibilities and, you know, I liked it. I was becoming a sad old fart who came home from these long tours to nobody, to an empty house whilst virtually everybody else had someone there. All right some of the guys wish they hadn't and envied me like crazy, but on balance it was time to settle down and this felt, well, right.

It was also in that pub where I met one of my best friends to this day, in one Roger Marcoux Jr. He was the local beat cop, a sergeant at the time. He wandered in to chat with Richard and see how things were, part of his daily routine. Richard introduced me and as it turned out, he was a huge fan of both Rainbow and Deep Purple and had quite some knowledge of their music. He was a bit of a musician himself, playing keyboards and guitar, mostly for himself but occasionally for his local church in nearby Morrisville. He's a fantastic bloke, who went on to do D.E.A. work and be head of his unit. He later went to Haiti as part of a program that President Clinton had set up to oust anti government and anti police extremists. That, I would say, was his most dangerous of all assignments. He is currently the Sheriff of Lamoille County in Vermont and was elected in absentia while in Haiti. Just shows how highly regarded he was in the local community.

He asked me one day if it would be okay to drop by Horizons just to see the band at work to which I agreed. It couldn't hurt to have the police check out the vicinity anyway. He was in uniform when he called by. He knocked on the back door, which led into the kitchen. This was reasonably common, someone casually yelled, "Come on in". Imagine the scene when the kitchen door opened and the shadow of a policeman in full uniform, baton and holstered gun fell across the kitchen table where a couple of crew were casually rolling some weed for the days consumption. They instantly shot into high-speed action clearing the table like two demented waiters, even whistling as they did it. It drew attention rather than deflected it, but Roger just didn't notice or pretended to. He smiled and politely asked if he could watch the band recording. Never was a wish more readily or politely granted. I nearly pissed my pants with laughter. He very quickly became part of the scenery, getting along really well with everyone and even joining us on the soccer field from time to time. A one of a kind guy indeed and I'm proud our friendship has survived the years since.

Whilst Ian Broad is fresh in my mind, I just have to tell you of yet another call above and beyond that of duty by this stalwart of the personal roadie fraternity. It was around this time with Ian back as Ritchie's 'personal' that they were playing pool at a Tavern close to Ritchie's house in Connecticut: Nothing remotely out of the ordinary about that you say and you're right. Then a rather large guy comes into the bar, orders a beer and places a couple of quarters on the edge of the pool table and says he'll play the winner. For those who play pool, it's the tradition. Well, not for Ritchie. He tells Ian to tell the guy that they are going to play again (and again and again). The guy says politely that that isn't how it goes and he WILL play the winner next. "Sort him out, Ian" says Ritchie.

If you've ever watched Laurel and Hardy films where Hardy turns to the camera and stoically accepts with resignation what is about to unfold, then Ian must have had his Hardy moment right there. "Now don't be a fool" said the big guy to Ian. "Just hit him, Ian" Ritchie urged. The big guy then reached into his pocket, took out his cop badge and said, putting it on the bar top; "Now I'm off duty, so it goes no further if you fancy your chances". Ian looked at Ritchie who obviously didn't want Ian to back down; after all it wouldn't look good (for Ritchie, to hell with Ian!) The guy made a grab for Ritchie quite rightly recognising who was the real aggressor. Missed, but grabbed hair, which came right out in his hand: Bet that surprised him! Well, so much for that hair weave too! Ritchie yelped and legged it out of the bar with Ian now grappling with the long arm (sorry!) of the law. Our guitar hero sped home leaving the faithful Ian to mete out retribution.

Some hours later, an embarrassed Ian limped back to his master. "Did you beat him up good?" said an optimistic Ritchie. Another Hardy look to camera as Ian trudged silently off to clean up, blood leaking everywhere. Ian was such a faithful person to Ritchie. It was at that moment that Ritchie realised that Ian had returned without the "piece" and the ever-faithful personal roadie was despatched immediately to the scene of the crime to retrieve it. He just did whatever Ritchie asked him to do.

In the Rainbow days, at his master's request he even drove, a rented XJ6 Jaguar right through the front glass doors of The Glasgow Marriott Hotel right up to the reception desk in order to avoid the fans waiting outside! I'm sure Ritchie had said drive me right up to the front door, not the front desk, but who knows for sure, only the man in black. When the car finally screeched to a halt in a shower of brick dust and broken ornaments, Ritchie just got out, asked for his room key and proceeded to the elevator whilst Ian reversed back out again in front of the speechless reception staff. Ian obviously misheard; at least I think that's what happened! Yet again it was left to me to explain. How? Compensate and strike the hotel off my long list of those available to the band in Glasgow.

Anyway, I digress - back to Horizons, the end of recording and our Mr Gillan. He felt in need of some R and R after the long hours, days and weeks closeted in the studios and fancied scuba diving for some reason. Now I had done some diving on the various short vacations I had taken with Cozy, Bruce and Barbara Fucigna from Thames Talent over the years in St. Thomas, St. Croix and Grand Cayman in the Caribbean. (Come to think of it, that was were I had spent most of my hard earned money, damn it!), so Ian asked me where I could recommend for him to take up the sport. I did not hesitate in telling him that Grand Cayman was the spot. He told me to book it and that I was to go with him and his family. Ah, those perks of the job, great weren't they!

I booked it up at the same place I had been with Cozy, Bruce and Barbara - beachfront condos and arranged diving lessons with a guy named Chet King who had an instant rapport with the singer and they became close buddies and remain so to this day, which is easy with Ian as, to his credit, he is one of the most gregarious guys you'll meet in a days march - so easy to talk to. In fact when he packs up rock 'n' roll he would make a great living as a TV chat show host, although it would have to be set in a bar! Chet is also one of my life long buddies to this day too, great guy, great job - lives in Albany, New York now, having given up instructing some years back, to flee the island with a lady friend. Ian's holiday was a great success. I say Ian's because although I was there too, I was expected to be at his beck and call, although in truth that wasn't a stretch. I could think of a ton of worse places to be at someone's beck and call!

We returned to America to rehearse for what would be a long, massively successful world tour. As per usual I got the entire rough itinerary from the office and spent most of the early summer weeks setting every detail up from hotels to visas to crew to travel. All tweaked to suit my charges. It really was great to have them all back together. The tour was set to start in New Zealand and Australia, but I did not go!

As I have intimated over the years, 'socialising' had been a major part of Deep Purple's and Rainbow's way of letting off steam after a show. Imperceptibly, but surely, alcohol had become part of my everyday life. Lately, even when we were not touring I had taken to having a beer to start the day. In my eyes it was harmless, just something I fancied rather than needed, but gradually it became something I did have to have and if I couldn't then the day went to hell and I could not get the work started until that first beer. Well, that doesn't go unnoticed, even if you think you cover it well. Bruce came to me and said that the band thought it best if I missed the first part of the tour in Australia and New Zealand and get myself sorted out and then I could rejoin the tour in America.

We were already in L.A. at the time, rehearsing at S.I.R. (Studio Instrument Rentals) and staying at the Sunset Marquis, my old home. I was devastated and angry at myself for 'fucking up', although in truth I had not done so with the band, but with myself and I feared that once I had been replaced, albeit on a temporary basis, it would be the thin end of the wedge and my future would be in jeopardy. How could I have been so dumb? I had always been just a beer man, but then with the success of first Purple and then Rainbow, money had ceased to be an issue, as I'd become pretty well paid. I graduated first to scotch, then vodka as my drink of the moment. I'd get pissed pretty often, only after the show I must add, but we all did. For me alas it became an addiction. It was the first thing I thought about when I woke up. I had one and within half an hour I felt terrible and had to have another. The vicious circle! Realising I had a problem, I returned to drinking beer, but that's still alcohol so I stayed on the roundabout of booze.

The band flew off to New Zealand and I flew back to Connecticut, very much alone and down as far as I thought possible. With that wake up call from Bruce, I booked myself into a rehab clinic not far from my house in New Canaan, called the Silver Hill Foundation on a twenty-eight day course. Thinking back, Deep Purple and Bruce had been pretty tolerant of the situation especially as so much was at stake. I like to think it was a measure of how much they valued me. Their message, however, was clear. Clean up or leave! Bruce explained that they wanted me to be well and were aware that I could not do it on my own. Rehab was clearly the only option and if I was prepared to put myself through the programme, my job would be open when I returned. They, the band, were even prepared to pay for it, but I was insured and the treatment was fully covered. I had got myself into this mess and I alone would get myself out.

The night before I spoke with Ian Gillan, and he was totally sympathetic and assured me I would get over it as he had. Had he been there? I had no recollection. Maybe it had been while I was with Rainbow; maybe Old Ian was just being kind. I have never asked him to this day, why should I? I got totally shit faced that night, listening to Def Leppard's album 'Pyromania' which had given my pals from Sheffield a seven million selling album and they had been voted the most popular band in America. No more press-ganged soccer games for them I thought drunkenly to myself.

The next morning, Don Bernstein, Bruce's "record pusher", drove me in to the centre totally out of it, which I'm told is a very common occurrence with alcoholics getting on the program. One last monumental bender eh! I even gave up smoking as well that day. Talk about adding to the pressure, but I thought I might as well exorcise all my demons in one fell swoop. I sat down in reception and somehow completed all the entry paperwork. You see, I was never 'blackout' pissed, there was always a small part of me that stayed sober enough to know how pissed I was, so, when asked, I could still perform short term tasks like form filling or signing bar bills! The writing was a bit wobbly, mind.

Silver Hill had different units for different addictions like booze, pills, cocaine, and whatever had taken your addictive fancy. I was assigned to Grey House where they explained I would stay for three to four days to go through detox. This could be unpleasant, they said, so they would monitor my hourly progress and had pills to counteract the worst ramifications. These were Librium tablets, known in the rehab business as 'a drink in a pill' and I got as many as I wanted to keep me comfortable, which I thought odd at the time… still do! I told the nurse that that was no good; as I had to recover to keep my job, not swap one addiction for another, as I saw it. She said that recovery had no short cut and that I should take the Librium at least for the first booze free twenty-four hours. I reluctantly agreed and went to my room where a doctor soon came to assess my overall physical fitness. I was passed A1 and the long journey back to sobriety began.

It hurt, physically hurt and, my God, I needed that Librium. After three days of pain and snatched sleep, I moved on to the next stage where I started to have meetings and teachings with other boozers and why we had become the way we were. You know, the famous "I'm Colin and I'm an Alcoholic". I have to say I learned a lot about drink and a lot about myself. The problem was I did not fit the pattern; no one can from the business of rock 'n' roll. I was in there with accountants, bankers, and Manhattan socialites, even someone from the executive ranks of Kodak. In their world, to be at work with a few bevies inside you would be a hanging offence, so their booze pattern involved a lot of secrecy. In rock 'n' roll and especially on the road, it's expected that you'll have had a few drinks, almost mandatory - damn suspicious if you hadn't. So I was out of the loop really on a lot of the 'talking' sessions, just sat there and listened, fascinated, at these high rollers and their 'daily dance with drink and drugs'. They were from all walks of life; addiction is not selective.

We had all our meals together, breakfast, lunch and dinner, all together under a common bond. I'd listen to all the stories of how they had got from there to here and if I fitted in anywhere to those stories, did I have any commonality with them. Well, some of the tales were just awful.

Shootings, beatings, stabbings: Degradation, all for the sake of that next drink. With a lot of them it was depression, stress or unemployment that had driven them to addiction. Well, that had nowt to do with me. I was happy, carefree and had a great job! Family problems? No, everything was hunky dory!

I tried to explain to them that being in the bar at noon with a few Bloody Mary's inside me talking to my employers and record company exec's was commonplace and that they would be doing the same, if not more so! It had just got out of hand, that was all. I blamed no one but myself. Sure there were days on the road when I had horrendous hangovers, but my cure was not to suffer them and take aspirin, but to have another drink. I got better way quicker! Roger Glover wouldn't and he had hangovers for England. 'The hair of the dog' was not for our Rog; Auntie Aspirin was always the first hand he reached for. Now I was in rehab and he wasn't, who was the mug?

I was aghast at the fact that some of these people were on their third visit and that scared the shit out of me. I dumped the Librium pretty quickly, scared of another problem and decided to ride it out 'cold turkey' under the watchful eyes of the doctors. I stayed in touch with the band by email, (we used Tandy computers with huge modems. State of the art, then!) mainly with Jon Lord who kept me up to date with the bands progress and he asked as to my mine. This was generally a banned activity in there, but I begged and pleaded and was given five minutes or so each day to send and receive. Barbara, from Thames Talent came over a few times with sympathy and a smile, which meant a lot.

I did however tell Eddie and Betty. I mean, that's me Mam and Dad, I just couldn't leave them out of it. I would never have forgiven myself if they had found out from someone else. They were sad and I know upset, but tried not to show it saying soothing words over the phone that only parents say to wayward sons. No anger, of course, not their style. Three weeks in and I felt so much better, so much so that the Foundation asked me to take seven of my brother and sister 'inmates' out for the day! Not on a walk, but to a bar to eat! Were they outta their minds? Well, apparently not. This was part of the program of getting back into the community. How come me? I guess I had "Mother Hen" (Lordy's phrase) written all over me, God damn it! Off we went, me driving a people carrier and where do they send us? To my local bar! I walk in and everybody knows me, the bar tender pulls a vodka and tonic. "Hi Colin,

Roger and Ian writing at Stowe, Vermont for the first reunion album, *Perfect Strangers. (Hart)*

Above:
L to R; Charlie Lewis, Ian Gillan, Raymond D'addario (behind shoulder) Ian Paice and Jon Lord
in the driveway at Horizons in Stowe, Vermont, 22nd May 1984.
The scene of the first reunion recording for the album *Perfect Strangers*.

Below:
Engineer Nick Blagona with Ian Paice and Roger in Le Mobile truck. *(Hart)*

Left: Jon Lord in full rock 'n' roll regalia, warming up during the recording sessions for the *Perfect Strangers* album in Stowe, Vermont, 23rd May 1984.

Below: Jon with Roger, part of the winning team re-united... for a game of darts!
(Hart)

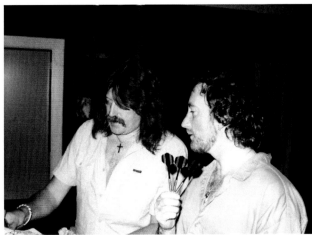

Below: After a charter flight during the *Perfect Strangers Tour*.
R. Ian Paice (partial) John "Magnet" Ward, Roger, Jon, Ian Gillan, Christophe Roth, Nick Cua, our tour accountant at the time and myself.

Right:
Roger continuing to practice for
the World Darts Championship,
7th May 1986.

Below:
Ian and Roger at a party in
Stowe, Vermont, 4th July 1986.
(Hart)

Right:
Ian Gillan after a football game on a day off between shows in Budapest and Oldenburg, during the *House Of Blue Light Tour*, 30th January 1987.

Below:
Ian Paice and Jon Lord backstage in Berlin, 3rd February 1987 with Mick Ralphs of Bad Company, whose band was the support act for the tour. *(Hart)*

Above left: With George Harrison at Ian Paice's house in Henley. George wouldn't let me stand up, as I made him look too short! Above right: Roger in the studio, 3rd March 1988.

Below: Roger outside George Harrison's gates at Friar Park, Henley, chatting to whoever answered the bell, 16th March 1988. *(Hart)*

Above: The launch party for the *Nobody's Perfect* album in Germany, 13th June 1988. Roger and Ian in the foreground. Ritchie and Paicey can be seen over Ian's left shoulder.

Below: Ian and Roger getting some well-earned rest
on the *Nobody's Perfect Tour* in Italy, 16th September 1988. *(Hart)*

Back to Vermont for rehearsals with Joe Lynn Turner who was finally drafted in to replace the departed Ian Gillan after several others had been considered including,
Jimmy Barnes, Ronnie James Dio, Brian Howe and Jimi Jamison.
Joe was the consummate professional and was not fazed at all.
He stepped right up to the plate and strutted his stuff.
(Hart)

Above:
Ritchie in an airport lounge in Brazil, 24th August 1991 during the *Slaves And Masters Tour*, dressed in the appropriate German national team tracksuit top! *(Fodder)*

Left:
By the end of September 1991, The *Slaves And Masters* trek stuttered to a halt with one-off shows in Poland, Athens and Israel. The feeling in the band was awful. Only Ritchie seemed happy with the current line-up as appears evident here alongside his assistants Jim Manngard and Rob Fodder, just after the last show of the tour in Tel Aviv, 29th September.
(Hart)

Above:
Ian Gillan back in Purple once again, for the twenty-fifth anniversary tour, appropriately named
The Battle Rages On, sharing a thoughtful moment with his wife Bron. *(Hart)*

Below:
Al Dutton (I.G's assistant), me & Ian G in a hotel bar in Austria, 30th September 1993. *(Fodder)*

ght:
ᴧ Paice, also in the hotel bar in
ᴧstria, 30th September 1993,
ɔking happy to have Ian Gillan
 ck in the fold.
odder)

Left:
R.B. in one of his favourite
"disguises" for wandering through
airports and leaving hotels. This
was taken in the car in Germany,
going to the airport during the
1993 tour.

Below:
A more typical R.B. look,
backstage in France,
18th October 1993
(Fodder)

Right: Backstage in Birmingham before the infamous camera incident. Ritchie's leg is strapped up following a slip on dry ice at the previous show in London, which prompted a doctor to advise him not to perform, although he went ahead with the show, albeit with some controversy. *(Fodder)*

Below: Jim Manngard, Ritchie and Rob Fodder, backstage in Scandinavia towards the end o Ritchie's time in Purple, with his name for the recently recorded album. (Hart)

Top:
L-R: Bruce Payne, Roger, his wife Les and myself, the day he renewed his vows in a temple in India, April 1995.

Middle:
Ian G, Willie Fyffe (Ronnie Dio's assistant) and myself, having a laugh in the bar after a show.

Bottom:
Ian Paice on our tour bus in Europe
(Hart)

Right: Joe Satriani came in at short
notice to complete the *Battle Rages
On Tour* in Japan, after Ritchie quit.
He also did one European tour with us
the following year before returning to
his solo career. Here I am backstage
with him at one of his solo shows on
5th May 2000.

Above: With Joe Eilliot at a Def Leppa
show in West Palm Beac

Left: Reunited with Ronnie James Dio wh
accompanied Purple for the "Albert" to
as we dubbed it, performing Jon
Concerto For Group & Orchestr

Below: The crew and band in Riga, Latvia, 8th
November 2000 at the end of yet another European
tour. As it happened, it turned out to be my last one.
(Hart)

Abov
With my life-long friend an
co-author Dick Alli

you're usual?" "No, errr mines a Coca Cola and these folk will have the same" I said tight-lipped. He cracks up - he's so funny, that Colin. "No seriously, eight cokes and the menu, ta".

I took them to a corner table and to be frank we had a really good time. Well, as good as I've ever had sober with a banker, an accountant, a socialite, a butcher, a baker and a candlestick maker. I eventually get them all back to the Foundation and we had to immediately take a urine test. We all pissed and passed. For me it was surprisingly easy, others I know found it a huge strain. (Being in the pub, not taking the test!) I was ecstatic, felt great, probably because I now knew I had a wonderful future with a bunch of guys I had the utmost respect for and with whom I had the time of my life. I was not about to fuck that up. As they had allowed me to bring a computer into my room, I had managed to set up the American part of the tour whilst in rehab, how cool was that? Mind you, a nurse stood shotgun over me while I sent the emails, vetting them, just in case I was ordering booze or worse.

My twenty-eight days were up and I prepared to leave. The Foundation made me promise that whenever I was home from my travels I would drop in so they could keep me monitored and I did for all the time I lived in Connecticut. They were good folks and I've never had to go back for the wrong reasons. Have I had a drink since? Why yes. Have I been pissed since? Yes to that too. Have I a problem now? No, I have not, although I did slip back, but that's running ahead of this tale. I went home for my first alcohol free Christmas for as long as I could remember, except for my childhood years. I spent Christmas with Bruce and we even went to a movie together on New Years Eve, another first for me... a sober New Years Eve 1984!

****

January 1985 and I was back, raring to go with the band for the start of the US leg of the 'Perfect Strangers' tour. I had to admit to a little nervousness. How would they be? Would they not drink in my presence? Would they treat me with kid gloves? Did they think I wasn't up to it? Nah, nothing changed. I kissed my new family goodbye and flew to Texas to join the band in Odessa where we would rehearse for three days prior to the start of a forty-six date US leg of the world tour, which would end on April 9th in Seattle. First night at The Ector County Coliseum in Odessa, Texas, Paicey asked me to whip up his 'Jack and Coke' like nothing had happened and really that was how it had to be. There was no point in me being employed if I did not fully function as the tour manager of one of the greatest rock bands of all time and that categorically meant being around booze pretty much 24/7. I wouldn't mind betting Bruce told them to do it as a test, to see if I flinched and if I had, I know I would have been history. I didn't and wasn't! It really was not that difficult, even though I fancied a drink, really I did, but I stayed firmly on the wagon.

We continued on to Amarillo, Wichita, and Houston with all the dates run by Pace Concerts who had assigned a production manager, Gary Becker, to look after the local promoters. He was brilliant and really looked after the ground transportation and hotels, so much so that he helped make my re-entry onto the road easy. I owe him. He went ahead of the band alongside Ray D'Addario and the crew, while I continued to travel with the band. We continued on to Dallas, San Antonio, El Paso and all points everywhere for weeks. We did two dates at the Arena, Long Beach, California, where Ozzy Osborne and Sharon turned up back stage. Ozzy had, of course, long departed from Black Sabbath and was enjoying a successful solo career guided by Sharon. He spent a while talking to Ian who had recently fronted Sabbath too. Wouldn't have minded being a fly on the wall to that little chat.

Meanwhile, an assistant for me, in the shape of John Ward, augmented the crew. Ian and Ritchie too had their own personal assistants in Christophe Roth and John Murphy respectively. Yet, as the tour moved forward Christophe eventually left the line up and John Murphy ended up becoming my assistant, and we were left to run the show unaided, which included the personal side for each member of the band. Maybe I was still being tested that I could cope in a boozeless world. I guess I passed! John and I became a great team and his presence was priceless. He knew Ritchie inside out, so that was half the battle right there.

The cities became a blur - Phoenix, San Diego, Denver, St Louis, Kansas, Chicago (two nights at The ULC Pavilion), Detroit, Cleveland (two nights again - Richfield Coliseum) and into the Eastern States. On March 5th at The Civic Center, Providence, Rhode Island, the band celebrated my thirty eighth birthday by presenting me with two strippers. What a fine gesture and greatly appreciated and enjoyed by all. Wasn't it wonderful when you could share your presents, Mam and Dad would have been so proud! I was raised properly, me.

Three days later we headlined at the Meadowlands Arena in New Jersey. Whenever we returned to this great city I would often spend a few minutes thinking back to my first visit all those years ago when I arrived with Matthews Southern Comfort on what I thought then was a one off chance of a lifetime jolly. On through the Mid West and down to Florida and back up to Pennsylvania until by April we were in Canada with shows in Ottawa, Montreal, Toronto, and a drop back to St. Paul in the States and back to Vancouver. The band was brilliant, just like the old days and we were drawing massive crowds. We were even written up in Billboard as one of the highest grossing US rock tours of 1985 amassing some $7 million dollars and change! That's small by today's standards, but huge then.*

We took a breather for a month while I sorted out the visas, tickets and itinerary with our travel manager Diane Murphy. She had fast become an essential part of the backroom staff from 1983 when she had come onboard to arrange the 'Bent Out Of Shape' tour for Rainbow. When I first met her back then I was in need of someone who "knew the world and knew everything" (her modest words) in the sense of someone who had been most places, worn the hat and got the T-shirt. Diane fitted the bill and wanted the job. British, but living in Connecticut, she had lived in Singapore and several other exotic locations around the globe before settling stateside. She was working with a local travel agency, doing IBM accounts, but it was her enthusiasm, her 'worldliness' and ability to cut a great deal without lowering the standard expected by our boys that impressed everybody, with the possible exception of Bruce who always believed he could better the deals. It's a man thing! Over the years Diane has been at a lot of our shows all over the world, often at her own expense. I used to have to almost plead with Bruce to cover her hotel rooms, as he never felt he should have to, despite her having saved the band thousands of dollars over the years. Go figure! We have also remained friends to this day, but more of Diane later.

By May 3rd we were ready once more to hit the road with a one off show in Honolulu as a stepping-stone into Japan with dates for the inscrutable Mr. Udo. Such was the success of the reunion, we did four sold out shows at the Budokan in Tokyo plus two in Osaka and one in Nagoya. On the third day in Tokyo, Ritchie called to demand my presence at yet another soccer game, this time against the Japanese crew. Now Japan in the mid eighties was a baseball crazy country. Soccer had not yet

---

* It was the second biggest grossing American tour that year after Bruce Springsteen, who was at his commercial peak.

gained a foothold to any large degree like it would within another fifteen years when it staged the World Cup. In 1985, they were barely able to kick a ball, let alone understand all the nuances of the game. We won by a net full and our Ritchie scored, bless him. No surprises there then!

On arriving back in Connecticut mid May, I prepared for the final European leg. It was a pleasure to be able to plan this tour properly with a chance to rest up and catch your breath before setting off again or maybe it was a tangible sign that we were all getting older and unending dates would only serve to fatigue the band and the crew so much that tempers would fray and performances would flag. That would only serve to burst the bubble of this current success long before it would naturally happen (for I was sure it would). The band was getting on fine, but I was always conscious that Ritchie and Ian were a volatile mix, like nitro glycerine. All would be fine, but you didn't want to be around when it got shaken up too much. Better to take it nice and steady.

June 14th and Stockholm, Sweden for three shows for our old pal Erik Thomsen and local promoter Thomas of EMA Telstar: A real gentleman in the business, as were all who worked for him. How nice and a refreshing change to do dates in Scandinavia in the summer, I thought! I never realised Sweden didn't have wall-to-wall snow twelve months of the year!

A week later, we flew back to England to headline the Knebworth Fayre festival held on Saturday June 22nd. The supporting cast was, wait for it... yes, The Scorpions closely followed by Ritchie's best pals, reformed UFO, plus the very heavy presence (in every sense of the word) of Leslie West and Mountain, Blackfoot and Mama's Boys (who?) Last but not in any way least, Meat Loaf. I didn't really get to see any of them, no time, as looking after my lot took every second there was and all my attention. All I got to hear was obviously the music which was kind of distorted 'cos it was all directed away from back stage, so no proper observation was possible, either audio or visual.

Anyway, headlining had its responsibilities and creating an impression was right up there. Ritchie, his lady, Bruce, Roger, Nick Cua (tour accountant) and myself stayed in London whilst Ian, Paicey and Jon Lord were home with their families. Ritchie wanted to arrive in style by helicopter (like you do!), so the others had to arrive similarly with their wives and children. It always seemed to be that way. If RB was to arrive in style, then everyone else should do the same. This entailed us now arranging said modes of transport, which was reasonably easy providing you ignored the price, but as they say, if you needed to know you couldn't afford it. Come the day, a helicopter was dispatched to pick up the family Gillan whilst another flew down near Henley, west of London, to pick up the Lord's and the Paice's. Thank God they lived close to each other, else it would have been four! Two cars came to our hotel in London and took us to the London heliport on the Thames from whence we winged it (maybe that should be rotored it?) to Knebworth.

I have to say it was dead impressive to fly over a packed festival site and see the assembled multitude all look and point skyward as if the gods were about to descend from heaven, but that would've been too egotistical, wouldn't it? The show went fantastically well, but as it drew to a close I looked apprehensively at the gathering clouds and rain. The show over, encores done, the applause abating, the family Gillan immediately climbed aboard their 'chopper' as the rains came down and ascended into the gathering gloom and sped home to Milton Keynes, maybe a fine pub and a rather tasty meal. The rest of us, I'm afraid, dallied too long and our friendly pilots nixed the departure for reasons of safety as it was now raining in biblical style, the clouds so low you could almost touch 'em. We were all up to our ears in mud at this point anyway, as it had pissed down for a while.

At times like these all eyes and seekers of immediate solutions turn to mother. That would be me. "Okay, Colin. How are you going to get us home? Didn't you check the weather? No back up plan?" "Well, yes to the weather and no to the plan as you all wanted to fly whatever, would've made no difference" I muttered under my breath. "I'm on it," I said out loud confidently. I tried everywhere for immediate transportation which I finally did obtain in the form of a battered Ford Transit minibus. It just managed to accommodate the very pissed off Lord and Paice party along with John Ward, to travel, not quite in the manner of our arrival, but hey, it could've been worse, could've been the trucks! Ritchie, Bruce, Nick Cua and myself managed to secure a ride in two rather nice Mercedes back to London, but the Transit, having deposited its first consignment, had to do a quick turn around and head back for more stranded musicians, some of whom had also helicoptered in. The receptionists at the Sheraton Towers Hotel had a private snigger, or may have been horrified, I'm not sure, as this rock star headlining entourage slurped and squelched to the elevator in very damp clothes and extremely muddy wellies. The great impresario in the sky sure had a sense of humour that day.

The following day we flew to Genk in Belgium to continue the tour and then whistle stopped to Vienna, Mannheim, Nurnberg, Paris and Nice. This was supposed to be the end of the tour, but Bruce, true to form just had to take more dates, such was the demand back in America. There would be six shows in ten days starting on August 14th in Columbia, Maryland. As all the dates were reasonably close geographically, it was decided that the best plan would be to hire a plane and fly each day to the shows and back again each night. No checking in and out of hotels and thus, hopefully, no frayed tempers. Diane Murphy found and chartered us a 'Short 360' from Allegheny Commuter Airlines and our pilot was Don Beyers. We flew to Niagara Falls, Alpine Valley, Wichita and Rochester, New York. The final show on August 24th needed a far bigger aircraft as it was way over in Dallas, Texas where we were to headline The Texas Jam in the Cotton Bowl Stadium. This was a big, big show and was a fitting finale to the world tour. The supporting bands were impressive and in no particular order were - every bodies favourite vegetarian Ted Nugent, our German chums The Scorpions again (I'm sure they were stalking us) and soon to be massive and beautifully formed Bon Jovi ('Slippery When Wet' was over a year in the future), plus Night Ranger, Grim Reaper and Victory.

The tour wound to a halt and everyone headed to their respective homes for a long but well-earned rest through autumn and Christmas. For me, it would be a family Christmas with Michele and the girls. Purple were back bigger than ever and all was well in the world. Yet it would be another seventeen months before the band would play live again.

CHAPTER THIRTEEN
CALL OF THE WILD

By the end of January 1986, plans were hatched to begin the follow up to 'Perfect Strangers' and once again I was asked by Bruce and Roger to fix Stowe in Vermont. This time they wanted something different from Horizons, so I went off on a search mission again to check out a few suggestions from our friends up there, including Richard Hughes, Roger, the cop and the local Century 21 Real Estate rental specialists. After looking over what seemed like hundreds, but in reality, were only a handful of properties, one of the suggestions was the Stowe Playhouse, temporarily closed due to lack of any local action. This became the chosen site and once again, Le Mobile was booked and scheduled for arrival. Guy once again behind the wheel and our trusty engineer Nick Blagona scheduled to fly in later.

This time it would be a little more difficult, as I had to also secure separate accommodations for each band member and their respective families and girlfriends de jour. Roger and Ian would go ahead of the others to write the material. The two of them put together some reasonably impressive songs, but there was trouble a-brewin'. Ritchie not only didn't like them, but from the moment the band reunited he had also wanted a change in the song writing royalty agreement. Traditionally all Purple songs had been credited equally to the 'band'. Ritchie wanted this changed to the individual writers responsible for each song, irrespective of the collective work that was done on them to knock them into shape. This was as welcome as a fart in a spacesuit. These guys were a collective song writing partnership in every sense of the word. I was there and saw the process evolve. Ian was always writing lyrics, always had a book with him where he constantly wrote down ideas based on his daily observations of his and life in general. Roger never stopped arranging in his head, thinking about how songs could always be improved. No Purple song would be the same without the input and musical brilliance of Jon and Paicey either. They were the energy that breathed life into them. Of course Ritchie was important, pivotal even to those stunning riffs that were the very essence of the band. In short, they were a BAND.

A lot of these problems occurred because nobody, apart from Ian, would ever directly confront Ritchie over such issues. Jon, Roger and Paicey could be unhappy with some aspects of the songs, but they would privately bitch to Ian and he would then confront Ritchie, so it wasn't always Ian's bitch, so to speak. The others preferred to load the gun, so long as Ian would fire it, which of course he was more than happy to do. They'd even go to Bruce with their problems who, in turn, would tell the guitarist that they were unhappy. Ritchie would reply truthfully that they had not told him there was a problem to which Bruce would just shrug and say, "Well, they wouldn't". However, the royalty question was Ritchie being Captain Chaos again. He just loved it. Peace and tranquillity were just there for him to gleefully disrupt and he never missed an opportunity.

The recording was slow and not unlike pulling teeth. The tension was palpable. Why? They'd just come off a record-breaking tour; they were by any standard in the rock business, staggeringly successful. Yet the demons were still there. It was as if Ritchie wanted out, but to what he did not know, so until he did, he would be obnoxious. Roger and Ian took themselves off to a quiet corner of the Playhouse to continue writing. Ritchie kept himself to himself and Paicey and Jon were, as ever, interested but non-confrontational observers. Me? I was bored!

By the end of June, everyone went their separate ways, the record more or less finished, but not with any enthusiasm. This would not be a blockbuster. The mobile was driven south to the back of Roger's house in Greenwich, Connecticut where he and Ian finished off the album, adding and improving some vocal tracks. That suited me as I lived no more than ten or so miles away and could be with them all the time and get to sleep in my own bed - bliss!

Once the album was finished, Ian and Roger accompanied by Charlie Lewis and our Canadian engineer Nick Blagona went off to Montserrat in the Caribbean to do their own album 'Accidentally On Purpose', leaving me to the tender mercy of Ritchie and mandatory games of soccer! It was a long lay off, apart from the soccer, a time, which was filled by doing up my house, being a father to the two girls and having a happy domestic time with Michele. It was a good time, one that I savoured. I was conscious that I would be forty next birthday and that milestone kinda made me reflect on where I was, where I'd come from and more importantly where

I was headed. I hoped that it could mean a move into management and a more permanent post within Thames Talent. I had paid my dues on the road and knew the business better than most. Would Bruce make the move or would I have to drop bigger hints? I kept in constant touch with the office and would often pop in to see what plans were being made for the inevitable tour to coincide with the release of 'The House Of Blue Light' which was scheduled for January 1987.

By autumn, plans were put in place and I began the now familiar routine of setting up the tour. I talked constantly with Raymond D'Addario with regard to production and Diane Murphy for all our travel needs. It was going to be a long tour running from January to the beginning of September. The objective was to surpass the success of the last record-breaking tour in 1985. The plans were meticulously thought out with new territories to conquer as the eastern block of Europe began to open up to rock bands.

With the tour set and all plans agreed, I set off from JFK to fly to Frankfurt, Germany for rehearsals at the MTV Studios where Ray had gathered together the crew and production staff. Ritchie had gone out a day earlier no doubt to get into German mode, with the rest of the bands arrival coinciding with mine, except for Roger who got delayed back home in Connecticut which was very unlike him. Domestic strife? The band and I stayed out at the airport at the seriously expensive Hotel Gravenbruch Kempinski (doesn't that trip off the tongue as Monica Lewinsky would say way in the future, in a galaxy far, far away!) whilst the crew stayed downtown at The Holiday Inn City Tower. This necessitated us hiring four Mercedes to take us to and fro from the studios. Why four? Because we could, silly! The whole production staff would be over thirty strong - Lighting, sound, riggers, truck and bus drivers, catering, wardrobe, accountants, and personal roadies. Oh yeah, the band too plus Bruce from time to time, and of course me.

The show sounded and looked good and Ritchie and Ian were being civil to each other; Jon Lord had his separate case full of his reading matter for the tour, which would, over the next nine months, become the tour library and Ian had his Daily Telegraph crosswords, which, as he would assure a puzzled Steve Morse years later, was how he practised his craft of lyrics. Roger just took it all in, glad to be back on the road away from domesticity which, I think, he found stifling. Easy to be a rock god on the road, way harder at home with the wife, eh Rog!

The tour kicked off in Budapest, Hungary for three sell out nights at the Sportcsarnok. New country, new language, same reaction except these folk had been starved of decadent Western rock 'live' since, well, rock had started. There were still a few wrinkles to iron out in the show, but the fans knew no different or cared. The feeling was good as we went on to more familiar territory in Germany, Italy, Switzerland, France Belgium, Holland and Sweden where we finished at The Scandinavium in Gothenburg on 28th February. Without pause for breath, we went on to play two rammed full nights at Wembley Arena and Ritchie, yes, did the encore, one of the two nights anyway! (Maybe he feared Cozy was lurking backstage). The Playhouse, Edinburgh and two nights at the NEC, Birmingham, followed these shows. No chance to see mam and dad in Newcastle, but I did get them down to London for the Wembley shows. They were as always glad to see me and me them. The concern in their faces as to my drink 'problem' was there to see, but it was hardly mentioned. After all I was visibly sober. Ritchie, as always, greeted them with genuine warmth for which I will always be grateful. He was and is an enigma.

Next was America, which was scheduled to stretch right through the summer months. We broke to recharge batteries for six weeks and to give me time to get back to base to finalise all the travel and production schedules. The first show was, crazily, Portland, Oregon followed by Rochester, New York! West to East Coast! Raymond and I played merry fuck with Thames for such crazy routing. Bruce, of course just shrugged. Thankfully it then settled down to shows on the East Coast - Worcester, Mass; Providence, Philadelphia and out to the mid west to Pittsburgh, Chicago, Indianapolis and so on. Joan Jett and The Blackhearts supported us throughout.

Most of the time, dates end up as a blur in your consciousness, but Richfield Coliseum, Cleveland on May 11th stood out as a day lifted from the mundane. Ritchie squished a plate of Spaghetti into Ian's face on the pretext that the singer had somehow 'spiked' it. Cool! Now Ian is not a small guy and I fully expected World War III to instantly break out as did Ritchie who put up his fists Queensbury rules style, which on reflection now was hilarious as Ian would just have kicked him in the bollocks. No, Ian, seriously pissed off, but in wonderful and surprising control, got up imperiously, told the guitarist that fighting was not happening and disappeared into the bathroom to clean up, shutting the door behind him.

Ritchie just stood there with all us just looking at him stony-faced. I half expected someone to say that he should have had the carbonara instead. He went back to his room. The following show, understandably, was not the best they'd done.

Then it happened and it was going so well, (apart from Cleveland). We had broken the tour on May 18th for a five-day break after the traditional stop at Alpine Valley. I had gone back to Connecticut for no other particular reason than to stock up on clean laundry and see Michele and the girls. I then flew out to California to hook up with the tour, which was to restart with two sold out shows at the Irvine Meadows Amphitheatre in The City of Angels. From there we played Mountain View, Sacramento, San Diego and then to Phoenix where Ritchie broke his finger!

The original stunt was, of course, well planned each night. Ritchie would throw his Stratocaster up in the air and catch it. Fairly simple stuff, eh? As the guitar came down it would be accompanied by amp 'crashes' caused by a roadie kicking a small Marshall reverb unit behind the scenes: Simple, but effective you might say. This time Ritchie threw the Strat way up, higher than usual, looked up to catch it and lost sight of it in the lights. He should have let it go in hindsight, but grabbed for where he thought it was in its downward flight. The guitar landed right on the end of middle finger of his left hand, rather crucial for a right-handed guitarist. I was watching from the wings and thought. "Fucking hell, that must have hurt". Ritchie carried on in obvious discomfort, but did not do the encore which by now could have meant he was hurt or just being Ritchie, how could you tell! Alas, the initial numbness was gone and our boy was now in great pain and he was taken to hospital where the digit was diagnosed as broken - no shit!

I'm sure I caught the glimmer of a smile on Ian's face at the news, but then of course I could've been wrong and it had been a touch of wind! The tour was over, naturally. I phoned Bruce with the bad news and then spent half the night re-arranging with Diane, for the flights for everyone out of Phoenix back to wherever. The crew were informed and all dates postponed until further notice and I'd only got to the first layer of fresh clothes in my case. When this occurs (the cancelled tour, not my clothes), you hope the promoters who are now going to have to cancel, have some sort of cancellation insurance to cover the loss, but in my experience, this type of insurance can be prohibitive, the premium often close to the hoped for profit. Many 'wing it' and take the loss knowing that they will get the rescheduled show if there is one. Joan Jett too had to take the hit of a cancelled tour, which was a shame as they had done well and were proving to be increasingly popular as we went on. The loss of income to them was far more damaging in the short term.

So, six weeks later, the digit mended, we found ourselves back in Europe in Helsinki, Finland to be exact and on time for these ten shows which would culminate in Verona, Italy on September 7th. You couldn't escape the fact that a bunch of American promoters were now consulting their brokers and the small print of their policies while we rolled on. Only these shows to do and it was over. No Australia and New Zealand and more puzzling, no Japan which was always a given on any tour - odd! I didn't ask why, as it was not my place, and the tour had been nine months with the enforced break anyway. We all went home and the band went on vacation.

Rock star vacations are usually somewhere exotic, expensive and hot, you would think. Ritchie asked me to set him and Tammi Williams, his current lady, with a tour of German Castles! Eh right, German Castles? Okay? I got Diane on the case, she'd know. However it was not just him and Tammi. No, a couple of soccer proficient roadies went too, just for that relaxing game or two of five a side soccer with local opposition with the insurance that Ritchie's side were above average. It was quite common too for the castles to have no electricity or hot and cold running water - exquisite. I bet Tammi had a blast!

****

Back in Connecticut with time to think, I had the distinct feeling that it was all about to go 'tits up' again. The camaraderie had just melted away, the five band chums had retired to their separate worlds keeping their own counsel and 'phoning in' the show. The audiences didn't seem to notice and why would they? They get to see the band once every two years and, so high is the expectation, they forgive or indeed don't even notice a below par effort. I, on the other hand, saw the show every night and could compare the enthusiasm of the first shows of the tour to the 'going through the motions' of the last. At times on the tour we had brought in recording facilities to tape parts of the show for inclusion in the next album which to me seemed a bit throwaway, but I understood it was done to complete a three album deal with the record company, Polydor. Who knew on what Machiavellian scheme Bruce was working? Far more worrying was the decision to allow French TV to video the whole Cologne show and take sound from our board. I wonder if that subsequently turned up as a bootleg DVD and video years later?

'Nobody's Perfect' the resulting live album, was, according to Ian, the worst Purple album ever and he was ashamed to be associated with it. Easy, Ian! Well, I'd heard better for sure. I personally don't like live or even part live albums, but a lot do, yet the inclusion of 'Hush' was a puzzler, I'll admit, especially as it was done in the studios at Hook End Manor in Checkendon, England, as a jam in the February of '88. Taking the piss, really. The arguments went on as to where it should be mixed, especially between Ian and Bruce, the former plumping for New York, which naturally got my vote, as Roger, Ritchie and the management were based near there and, of course, me.

The arguments carried on as to where to record future stuff. The thought of New York appalled Jon, however. A heated argument then took place fuelled in part by Ian's frustration with the way things were starting to fall apart and the fact that he was drinking quite heavily again, something which I could immediately identify with as I, too, had had the odd libation on this tour, but in my defence I knew how to handle it, (or so I told myself). No, I had not slipped back. I knew the signs of addiction and could always step back from the brink. I had a family to consider now and a job that I knew would be history should I lapse completely. Whenever the booze really flowed, I made my excuses and went to bed. To stay would have been a disaster and when the voice in my head said go to bed, this time I listened.

We went back to Horizons in Stowe to do the album as the snow began to fall. Things were by now spiralling out of control where Ian was concerned with his alcohol intake and his relationship with Ritchie and Bruce whose expertise, Ian had publicly ridiculed. The rest of us were concerned spectators on the one hand, trying to finish an uninspired album and on the other trying to keep the peace between the two camps and hoping that relationships would mend.

Horizons, as described earlier was a big house with a huge basement, with five master suites and a separate house a short walk away. I was staying in the "little" house this time, with Roger and Nick Blagona the engineer. In this unit was a separate hot tub room in which Ian had taken to relax at every opportunity. On this particular night Ritchie had come over in a rage to remonstrate with Tammi, who had come to me to fix her a flight home, as she'd had a serious tiff with his nibs.

However, he wasn't having her take off and wanted to drag her back to his suite. I was acting as referee when Ian hammered on the door. He had gone back to the main house, found it locked and came back to me to get a key or whatever. He was seriously drunk for a change, (as was Ritchie to be fair) and as the guitarist whipped open the door, no doubt to tell Ian to fuck off, we were met by this apparition of the naked singer, gently steaming from the recently vacated hot tub with two bin bags on his feet to protect them from the snow, like you would, his clothes under his arm, obviously expecting free passage back into the night and to his quarters with the key.

Only he came up short when he saw this domestic scene of Ritchie, Tammi and myself. Not what he expected at all and, unable to stop his forward momentum, he fell into the room, in front of Ritchie, Tammi and I. I stood him up and he fell out backwards into the snow. Ah well, that broke the spell! The three of us didn't know whether to laugh, cry or in Ritchie's case take a swing at him, but it did calm things down and Tammi forgot her flight into the night and returned with Ritchie to his suite. You know, I bet Ritchie never even thanked Ian either for inadvertently saving the moment for him. I just sat there, patted the singer on the head escorted him back to the main house, then went to my bed, chuckling.

CHAPTER FOURTEEN
NOBODY'S PERFECT

With Christmas and New Year gone by cosily at home with Michele and the girls, 1988 dawned to, well, not a lot. 'Nobody's Perfect' was being mixed ready for a July release and the band were at rest or working on personal projects. I had no money problems, existing quite nicely thank you on a good retainer. I would ring or go to the office to discuss with Bruce what the long terms plans were for the year ahead and then await any calls from Ritchie or Roger who were the only members who lived in America. Regular weekly soccer games occurred with Ritchie. They were mandatory of course, and even the weather was not a deterrent as he would always ask me to find an indoor facility if the condition dictated it. Good job, I loved to play. It would have been hell otherwise.

My young nephew, Stephen, Carol's younger son was now twenty and living with his Mam and Dad in Fraserburgh in the wild and woolly North of Scotland where they still ran the Mission. He was unemployed and rang me to ask for a job on the road crew. He was a good bass player as well and was into rock music with a vengeance. In an odd slightly embarrassing way, I was his hero being with Purple and Rainbow, mixing with the consigenti of the rock world. I did not know what to do. Carol wrote to me and asked that I either put him off the idea or encourage him, but to do nothing was not an option.

Sisters really cut to the chase, don't they? I wrote to him spelling out what a precarious industry this was and that road crew were freelancers mostly and not employed like me fifty-two weeks per year. I added that when they did work, they would sleep infrequently, work physically exhausting, stupidly long hours, eat dull unappetising food, get acne, bad breath and be considered the lowest of the low. They might get laid a few times, but would risk a visit to the clinic as a consequence. Relationships with girls back home would go down the tubes too, because they believed all of the above. Did I lay it on too thick? Was it a balanced considered letter to a kid desperate to break in? Hell no, this was my nephew and my sister would kill me if anything happened to the lad! Stephen backed off and I know he was deeply disappointed. My hero status lay in the dust. In truth, I had not overstated the situation. I was lucky; many aren't who are attracted to this 'profession'. Stephen would later go on to marry, have kids and have a happy stable life, still plays a mean bass though!

It was late May when Bruce called to say that the band were to headline a major concert in August at the Giants Stadium, East Rutherford, New Jersey, home of the New York Jets and Giants. A venue I knew well, as I had attended many a New York Cosmos soccer game there in the past. The touring machine had to be made ready. At last, action stations! I called Raymond D'Addario to muster the crew together and discussed with Bruce the question of a warm up date prior to the stadium show as, patently, the band would be rusty, having not played together since Verona the September before, some eight months ago. It was decided to play a small club in Baltimore, Maryland named Hammerjacks two days before the big show. The trouble with clubs this size is they fail to rehearse the crew, even though the band may well have had a good work out - it's a question of size as the art mistress said to the gardener! This club was very small and the band had the novelty of coming into a venue through the front door and sharing one dressing room - way too much contact.

The club thought they'd done well to supply free bottled beer, bless 'em, so, muttering under my breath, I sent out for the customary Jack Daniels, Johnnie Walker Black and other favourites of the moment. The band actually seemed to enjoy the intimacy of the club, took them back to when they were aspiring to glory. What's the expression, 'the journey is better than the eventual destination' or something like that. This summer of '88 was a good time for heavy rock. Van Halen and Def Leppard had number one albums in the American charts with 'OU812' and 'Hysteria' respectively in July, and now Guns 'N Roses were number one in August with 'Appetite For Destruction' and would soon have the number one single with 'Sweet Child Of Mine'. They were to be with us at Giants Stadium along with Aerosmith who had topped the singles chart the previous December with 'Dude, Look Like A Lady' - some bill.

The day before the show was set aside for sound checks and we were kept to a tight schedule to accommodate a G 'N R video shoot at the stadium. The film production company laid down camera rail tracks, lighting and all manner of additional equipment to complete the shoot. As would be the theme of their career, Axl Rose was a 'no show' and the band was filmed 'sans Axl'. They would be forced to film the Gunner's performance the following day and edit Axl's performance from that into the video. It's pretty obvious too when you see it and I'm sure most have. Aerosmith were still in their toxic period and I will never forget Steven Tyler's limo arriving backstage where the singer emerged, very pharmaceutically challenged, and turned the wrong way proceeding to wobble down a darkened hall way in completely the wrong direction to the stage, very 'Spinal Tap'. I ran after him and gently turned him around, directing him to the dressing rooms. He then amazed me by transforming into a more or less coherent rock star and turned in a wonderful performance only to revert to a mumbling fool once it was all over. You know, the human body is a wonderful machine with awesome powers of recovery and repair.

Purple had to pull out all the stops to prevent being overwhelmed by the competition which, lets face it, were two of the best live rock bands worthy of the name. The longevity and high level of success of Purple and it has to be said of Ritchie with Rainbow, saved their arse that day. They delivered big time and showed that, when it mattered, they were still one of the best rock bands ever with songs that would stand the test of time, classics of their genre. The show, in theory, was a triple-header of "Deep Purple and Aerosmith with special guests, Guns 'N Roses". The latter opened with Aerosmith closing which suited us as we reckoned being in the middle would mean that we'd get the best audience reaction, which proved to be the case, late comers and early leavers would still be 'in the house'.

The euphoria of Giants Stadium dissipated pretty quickly and the atmosphere in the band deteriorated once more. The office had fixed some dates in Europe starting that September, but no others, which was very odd as I fully expected to be out on the road for our customary nine months to promote the album, no matter how mediocre. As we arrived in Florence, Italy to start the tour I was contacted by Bad Company's management asking if I would fancy jumping ship to look after them for their upcoming tour of America. It was very flattering and I sat in my hotel room, thinking about the current unease and uncertainty in our camp. The thought of a fresh start with a totally different band and management set up was very appealing, but I'm a loyal sorta chap and I believed I had unfinished business with Deep Purple. They were at a low ebb and to take flight at this point wouldn't have been right. They had, after all, kept my job open when I had fallen off the wagon, so it was, if you will, my way of paying back that loyalty. I stayed.

That same evening at a press conference, Ian confirmed his lack of confidence in Bruce. When asked why the tour was so illogically routed, he replied that it was because the bands manager was a 'dick head'. I winced and thought then that Ian was signing his own death warrant. The tour ended at the end of the month in Bremen with everyone heading to their various homes. By late November, Ian returned to Stowe with the rest of the band to work on some tracks, but his mood had not changed, or his frustration with Bruce's management style. The band and Bruce met quietly away from Ian, which wasn't hard considering he was now chugging the booze unrelentingly and decided that enough was enough and he would be sacked.

I took him to the airport for the Christmas break, bade him farewell knowing it was over, but sworn to secrecy. Bruce had told Phil Banfield, who had agreed to tell Ian once he got back to England. As soon as I knew that he was aware, I phoned him up expressing my personal sorrow at the parting and how it had been handled. He wrote me a letter a week or so later. Had Ian got a raw deal? Yes, he had, merely for saying what everybody else felt. Bruce would always side with the strongest member of the band, which at that moment was Ritchie. That would change, and then, predictably, would Bruce. At the end of the day his agenda was to keep the money making machine doing just that. Personalities took second place and anyway he was and is a very egotistical man and being ridiculed in public was never going to go unpunished and a public apology wasn't Ian's style either. Something had to give and did.

******

So, who would replace Ian in this spring of 1989? Would the fans accept Deep Purple without Ian Gillan? It was hard to imagine. Would Ritchie continue to be Captain Chaos? Meanwhile we continued to play football. One night in Long Island at one of these soccer gatherings, at a charity game for radio station WBAB-FM, Ritchie, who still lived with Tammi, was smitten, no other word for it, by a young lady called Candice Isralow (soon to become Candice Night). At nineteen, Ritchie was twenty-five years her senior, but he cared not. There was a connection from the get-go. Ritchie's personal roadie at the time, Artie, became the go between and began to fix up clandestine meetings between the two. It was for a long time pretty un-rock-like in that the meetings were pretty innocent and Ritchie was a' courting the young lady in the old fashioned way. He was in love.

It was late summer and as the band began to regroup and think about the next album and the crucial decision of a new singer, they decided to give me a permanent assistant, something, for which I had been lobbying for years. I opted to keep John Murphy, as he was a very funny American guy from Staten Island, an ex-drummer and we had already become firm friends, while he was Ritchie's personal. He was a friend of Ritchie's and made him laugh, so he had a great chance of staying the course. Ritchie loves his 'court jesters' - I should know! However, John was a very quick learner so he was in. We shared some of my best times on the road together, as we made each other laugh and could easily take the bad and turn it into a hysterical hour or two. Much later he would leave us to go back to college and eventually became a correctional officer on Rykers Island! See what this business drove some poor guys to do!

I took this opportunity of inactivity to fly home to England for Eddie and Betty's Golden Wedding Anniversary bash in South Shields. Home, a nice word and this town held so many memories, but my home was also in Connecticut with Michele and the girls. I was used to American culture now, I paid its taxes and listened to its news rather than that of England, not that I could have got it that easily. America was and still is a very insular society. The town seemed smaller than I remember, the buildings had changed, and folk had got older. People I hadn't seen for ages, in my mind, hadn't aged so it was hard to keep the mild shock off my face when I saw them in the flesh and they were so different. Hell, I'm sure it was the same for them with me. The party was held at the Four Seasons restaurant on the beachfront and I spent my time kissing and cuddling aunts, uncles and friends.

Thankfully, Carol, David, Paul and Stephen, and Dick and Diane were there too and to whose company I could retreat if the prodigal son syndrome became too overpowering. The speeches were made and mam and dad looked happy, proud, but tired. Well, they weren't spring chickens anymore. The next day, as Carol and David had to get back to Fraserburgh in Scotland, mam and dad elected to take me to Newcastle Airport to catch a flight to Heathrow and onwards to New York. Having made our farewells, mam and dad drove back to Shields.

It was the last time I was to see my mam. On the way home, she collapsed in the car and dad drove her straight to hospital from where they tried to transfer her to the bigger hospital in Newcastle. Alas, she died in the ambulance. She had had an abdominal aortic aneurism, which had ruptured in her stomach and nothing really could have been done to save her. I was unaware of this tragedy unfolding as I was mid Atlantic. On arrival at Kennedy Airport, I rang Barbara at Thames Talent to get my messages to be told the devastating news. Seemingly, Dick, who knew by now, had telexed them, as he guessed they would be my first port of call on landing. I went home to dump clothes and book an immediate return flight home. My answering machine blinked as I came through the door. It was David with the sad news. I called him. He had tried to get me paged at Heathrow to catch me before my flight left for New York, but missed me and had left the message as the next best thing.

For whatever the reason, I just could not get on a flight that day or any day that week. I got back home eventually nine days later, but missed the funeral, as dad in his shocked state had just rushed everything through. He didn't even think to get David, his son-in-law to take the funeral, leaving it instead to an anonymous vicar who neither knew or took the time to find out about my mam. I'm told his eulogy upset more folk than it helped as a consequence. I stayed with dad and Carol, feeling a tad inadequate, as you do at times like these. Carol and I drew closer. When it appeared dad would be okay, I left him once more to fly home. Dad, at this time was not well as he had a major kidney problem, which required him taking increasing trips to Sunderland Royal Hospital for dialysis. My mam's death just knocked the stuffing out of him. After all, he had been married to Betty for fifty years. Her passing did not leave a simple hole in his life; it was a massive crater, which he knew he would never fill. The enormity of it overwhelmed him.

CHAPTER FIFTEEN
TRUTH HURTS

O nce back in America the months rolled by as many names were thrown into the ring for the singer's seat, Australians John Farnham and Jimmy Barnes being right up front with dear old Ronnie James Dio and Bad Company's Brian Howe. Ritchie called me up and said that the decision over a new singer would have to wait and I should go and find a new place to rehearse and record. Now this was late November and as per usual the location specification was "Vermont, near a pub with a place where I can make a lot of noise close by to a condo complex, which we can all call home". "Don't forget the regulation ghosts and ghoulies," I thought as I set off northwards.

I eventually found a mothballed golf clubhouse in a remote part of Vermont in Stratton. "This is winter and golf itself is not an option, so why not hire the place out to us fine English musicians" I proposed to the owners. They accepted, quite bemused. The nearest airport worthy of the name was Albany in upstate New York, a hundred mile or so round trip, which was fine in the summer, but this was the depths of winter in arse-high snow. The band assembled, we began in earnest to contact singers and, where necessary, flew them in. Yup, to Albany which meant me driving back and forth through all weathers to pick 'em up and bring 'em in.

Three such singers were American Terry Brock from a band called Strangeways, Jimi Jamison from Survivor and Kal Swann from British Rockers Lion. None made the grade except perhaps Jimi who, on his management advice, turned us down in favour of a solo career. Well, you've all heard the theme tune to 'Baywatch' whilst you watched Jasmine Bleeth run across the beach in slow motion, oh yeah! Good choice, Jimi! Finally, Ritchie suggested Joe Lynn Turner, who was contacted and agreed to fly up. I met him at Albany and in atrocious weather took him to golf! It took hours and on arrival I asked him if he minded going straight in to meet the band and go through a few numbers. Joe, as I've said earlier, was and still is the consummate professional, and was not fazed by this at all. He stepped right up to the plate and strutted his stuff. Smiles all round, one singer delivered. The scene was surreal. Here was the band muffled up in winter gear in this bar overlooking rolling hills of deep snow with a tennis court just visible in a large drift outside. The heating was struggling to be worthy of the name, but at least the bar was open. Naturally, Bruce was back in Connecticut in a warm office.

To celebrate we did a gig in the local pub, the Red Fox Inn, but without Jon Lord who declined to play in such cramped surroundings. It was just to let off steam really, so nobody minded him being absent. We all went back to our various homes for Christmas. When I reached mine, I was met with the news that my dad had been taken into hospital. I feared the worst.

As 1990 dawned, dad was still in hospital and I kept in close contact with Carol as to his condition. Two weeks in, his condition worsened and Carol moved down from Fraserburgh to be by his side. The hospital asked her if they could stop his, by now, daily dialysis as it was causing him much distress and wasn't really having the desired effect anyway. She rang me to discuss it and said that we had a terrible decision to make right there right then to give permission for the machine to be turned off. "What do we do? It's just you and me to make this decision," she said. 'Let me sleep on it" I said, but in truth I did not have an answer, nor did I sleep.

If they stopped he would have about a week, they said. What an awful situation. As per usual, my dear old dad sorted out my problem for me, like he always did when I was living at home. He died the next morning. I think he believed it was time to leave the stage. In truth I believe he died of a broken heart. I flew home. After the funeral on 31st January 1990, where David did, this time, thankfully officiate; I stayed at their empty memory-filled apartment with Carol where we began to pack everything up. Diane came up from Yorkshire, ever my best pal, to help out. When it was done, Di dropped me off once more at Newcastle Airport and I headed home to America and I've never been back to Shields since.

****

With Deep Purple once again settled (well, for now at least. I never considered anything permanent), writing and rehearsals began for the next album, which would become 'Slaves And Masters'. When they had reformed six years earlier, At one time or another they had all said that if one was to go they would call it a day, but when it came down to it, they wanted to carry on. The snow of Vermont had at last got to the band as they decided that a warmer climate would be a far better option and Ritchie could get to play soccer on a more regular basis. To say the band decided is perhaps stretching reality a bit. In truth, Mr. B. decided and the others went along with it, as that was the line of least resistance. As long as he was happy, everybody was. Familiar eh!

I found the ideal place, Greg Rike Productions in Altamonte Springs, north of Orlando in Florida. After having seen places in Miami and Tampa, we plumped for Altamonte. It had everything: Great studio, great living quarters close by at Sable Point Apartments, pool, plenty of bars and wonderful weather. What was not to like! The studios also had a great girl working for them called Doree Rice who was of immeasurable help in sourcing stuff and generally making my life way easier. I mean she knew how to get hold of absolutely everything. If you've got good folk on the ground, life's a ball and if you haven't, yeuch! I'm glad to say Doree, her husband Greg (Rice, not Rike) and family are still close friends today.

The band assembled and Paicey brought his whole family too. Roger was to produce the album and it consisted of working up new and existing material, which Ian had done demos for with Roger. The atmosphere was relaxed and the recording one of a series of jams. The result was, over the six months it took to record with a break midway, err okay, which was borne out by the reviews. Would it sell? Yes to the hardcore fans, of which there were, thankfully tens if not hundreds of thousands. Would it win new ones? The jury was out on that. As was usual, it was tweeked by Roger at Soundtec and Power Station Studios in New York a little later, once the dust had settled and Roger could hear it all afresh. Nick Blagona assisted him.

The album was released in September 1990, which involved the band flying to Hamburg a couple of weeks later to do some promo work for our record label BMG. Ritchie took this as an opportunity to have a 'castle cruise 'n romp' dragging along the ever-patient Tammi, (who by now still had no idea of the existence of Candice) and faithful roadie Artie Hoar.

With Christmas and New Year done, the entire band assembled in London in January to rehearse and record the video, 'King Of Dreams'. As was usual at these affairs Ritchie was awkward, nervous and slow to respond to direction. It was at times like these that he tried the patience of saints; mine in particular. I mean, why be fucking awkward? It only delays the process (video) it doesn't make it go away. Surely common sense (ah!) dictated that if he gave a great performance with the minimum of fuss, then the finished item would be that much better and he would gain from it. A no brainer or what? Roger, Ritchie, Joe, myself and most of the non UK resident crew stayed at the Sheraton in Knightsbridge where, on Superbowl Sunday, we stayed up to the early hours watching the Giants play the Bills. The next day, there was an early photo call, with photographer Didi Zill. Look at them, can you tell we'd had a great night?

Rehearsals done, we set off for Europe to open the tour in the Czech Republic in Ostrava, where we rehearsed for a couple of days more. Ray D'Addario, our stalwart production manager now had the comfort of a stage manager, David Keighley to assist him. David would come and go in various guises throughout the next ten years on the road as his career in rock progressed. We were supported on the tour by one of Bruce's new signings, the all girl band Vixen led by Janet Gardner on guitar and vocals, Jan Kuehnemund on lead, Share Pederson on bass and Roxy Petrucci on drums. They would stay with us throughout Europe and America. The question begged however - why did we start here in a remake scene from Napoleons retreat from Moscow? Ah yes, the Thames Talent bookers struck again. "Lets see, mmmm, its winter, snow on the ground, big arse semi truck trailers, full of gear on nice Eastern European, poorly maintained, ice covered little roads - sounds like a fuck of a good plan! Lets do it".

The weather outside the rehearsal rooms was atrocious, unbelievably cold, so much so that the diesel fuel line froze in one of the trucks, causing quite a delay in getting to the first show. The drivers cursed those wonderful tour planners, I can tell you, as did I. We all stayed at the wonderfully named Hotel Atom, where the suites were $57 per night and one could enjoy a good steak dinner with wine and a couple of Budvars (original Budweiser) for the princely sum of $7 including a tip. These dubious benefits, which in fact only highlighted the financial plight of the locals (borne out by the fact that one of the cars left outside the hotel front door was minus all its wheels one morning, sitting on bricks), did not, however, make up for the physical discomfort of the weather. The show at the Palace of Culture and Sport went well, exceedingly well, filmed by Czech TV and the locals lapped it up.

The tour continued to Budapest in Hungary and the band could not wait to get out of Ostrava to, hopefully, more comfortable and warmer surroundings. The journey by car would take six hours. I followed the rest of the band in the last car with Ritchie, tour accountant, Chris Patterson and Ritchie's personal assistant, Artie Hoar. Poor Chris had to suffer the whole journey with Ritchie's acoustic guitar stuck between his legs as our maestro wanted to play on the way. Well, he never did, and Chris, new to the job, didn't feel like protesting. It was a very uncomfortable six hours with an oblivious Ritchie asleep behind us. Artie, whose soccer skills far out weighed his roadie skills, which wasn't hard, had an amazing sense of humour which of course he needed a-plenty for the staggering amount of crazy requests his employer would put him through that would push his patience and good humour to the limit. Artie had first met Ritchie back in 1986 in a bar back in his hometown quite near where Artie lived. Ritchie needed a partner for a game of Foosball, you know, that daft little table soccer game with plastic men strung together on rods, which you twirl back and forth to hit a small ball into a 'goal'. It kept Ritchie amused for hours. Anyway, not unusually it ended in a fight where Artie demonstrated his, then unknown, black belt karate skills. Our Man In Black, suitably impressed had an instant new best friend!

Initially Artie was Ritchie's 'house sitter' while he was on tour, but on the departures of firstly Ian Broad and then one Frank 'The Bass' Morgan, Artie Hoar joined our merry band for this tour. Lets pause a little here. Now Frank Morgan was unbelievable. Once again he was the typical Blackmore assistant, no roadie skills, but a keen, if not good soccer player with an added impediment. He had ambitions way above his station in the music department. He insisted on taking a bass guitar on tour with him. When I asked him why, he said, "To keep my chops up?" "Why" I repeated. "Well, if anything happens to Rog on tour, I'm there, I know all the parts, would not be problem" he said eagerly and with admirable, though misplaced enthusiasm. "Well, if that day ever dawned, pal, we would not be coming to you" I thought as I smiled and walked away, shaking my head in sheer disbelief.

Unhappily, Frank thought this was a distinct possibility and would continue to leave his bass out for either Murphy or me to organise onto the luggage breakout at hotel departures. This pissed us both off big time, so we'd get a bit clumsy with the bass guitar. Murphy had the uncanny habit of throwing it to me, right at the moment I got distracted and was looking the other way or it would drop off the luggage cart just as it would pass a flight of descending stairs. Old Frank just carried on oblivious to the mishaps to his instrument. Surely he noticed how out of tune it became at the very least?

Nothing is forever, especially assisting Mr. B. and Frank 'The Bass' was replaced by the Karate Kid, Artie Hoar, once he realised that Roger wasn't ever going to get that sick. Alas Artie would not last either although he really, really tried to stay the pace. You see, Ritchie had a hairdresser, Cindy Drucker, who would fly in on various points of any tour to give Ritchie's 'hair' a tune up so to speak. Anyway on one of the early European dates she was getting on his nerves, which wasn't that hard in the scheme of things as I'm sure you've all come to realise, and he says to Artie the immortal line (for Ritchie). "Get rid of her". This meant get her out of the dressing room and back to the hotel (not permanently, just thought I'd clear that up).

This gave Artie a problem, as there was only one limo left at the venue at the bands disposal, the rest of the band including me having already gone back to the hotel. Artie explained this to Ritchie who, losing patience now with Artie told him that Cindy was to go NOW. Artie sent her off in the last remaining car. "Has she gone?" said the guitarist. "Yeah" replied the relieved Artie. "Well, lets go then," said Ritchie to which the bemused Artie points out that "there's no cars left, Cindy just took the last one, but it will be back in ten or so minutes!" Ritchie then launched into a tirade of abuse at this turn of events. Artie was dumb struck and turned away mumbling to himself and went outside to wait for the return of the limo. Ritchie then emerged from the stage door, hailed a passing car, which he then persuaded probably with promises of untold riches to take him to the hotel and disappeared into the night with Artie left standing on the pavement cursing the day he walked into that bar to play Foosball.

Zagreb followed Budapest and then to civilised France. The straw finally broke Artie's broad back after that show in Metz when he came to my room in tears, saying he could take no more. Seemingly Ritchie had balled him out for leaving, to Artie, a non-existent soccer ball back at the venue and had ordered him to go back and get it as he had deliberately left it there! Artie was beside himself. How could he go back on a mission that was doomed to fail, as the soccer ball was not there in the first place? He begged to be flown out of there. I tried to convince him to stay, but poor Artie had cracked, so I phoned the ever-reliable Diane and got him a flight. He was so happy, a smile as big as the Brooklyn Bridge split his face. Ritchie was less than happy when it was apparent that he had a hole in his entourage, but in truth he didn't care. Artie was disposable. Chris

Patterson filled some of the gap assisting me to assist the Dark One who stayed more or less happy. Rob Fodder replaced Artie when we got to Japan.

The tour was going okay despite a less than enthusiastic reaction to the album, but calls for Gillan could be heard in those little quite interludes in the show. Annoying, especially for Joe who was giving 110%. On to eight shows in Germany followed by a short trip to Scandinavia where Erik Thomsen was his playful self. The European section finished mid-March with seven UK shows including four sold out nights at Hammersmith Odeon in London where the band held court with old friends and family. Carol and David came to the show and it was good to hear the news from home first hand.

My nephew Paul, now twenty-six, had fulfilled all his early promise in music. He had progressed from Chethams in Manchester to York University where he obtained a first in music, became Conductor of York Symphony Orchestra and then the Northern Ballet Theatre and that was all before his tea! He was clearly headed for stardom in that field of music. Mam and dad had been very proud, as, of course were Carol and David. It made me very happy, too. Stephen was still trying various things and at times I began to regret my decision to put him off our business. Still what was done was done. He's now happily married to Marianne with beautiful kids, son Angus and daughter Mara.

The tour headed to America for a March 17th start in Burlington, Vermont, but it would only run for eight shows, a sure indication that the public just wasn't accepting Joe or that it had had it with Deep Purple. The shows were confined to the East Coast with the only stand out date being at Radio City Music Hall in Manhattan, New York City. The mood within the band was not good. We said farewell to Vixen at this point. Well, the band did, Bruce had got close to Janet and indeed they became an item and she soon moved into his home in Rowayton, Connecticut. Way to go, Bruce.

May was taken off whilst I set up the visas and permits for the band and crew to hit Japan. This too was disappointing. Only four shows, of which three were at the Budokan in Tokyo. Mr Udo was apologetic, but didn't really come out with what was wrong. Too much of a gentleman, I guess. We then did a show each in Bangkok and Singapore on the way back west. Nice if you were a tourist, we weren't. It was getting tedious as we went home for July to rest and, of course, play more football.

The following month Brazil welcomed us, yes welcomed. The shows went great, probably as we hadn't played there before and the country was waking up to touring rock acts. Bruce brought along his best friend Bill Dill, (actual name, trust me) who spoke fluent Portuguese. The reason was so that Bill could spy on our promoters to see if and how we were getting screwed, which we undoubtedly were, it's the national pastime after-all. We played seven shows in nine days to ecstatic reactions. Bruce instructed me to take as much cash as I could from the tour from every source, the box office, the merchandising, everywhere so that he could try to keep up with the shortfall and excuses from the promoters for late payments on fees.

Edson da Costa was the promoters tour manager and I knew he sympathised with my plight and helped a lot in making sure I could bag all the Cruzeiros I could, despite blistering abuse from Bruce who I tried to get to chill out, as Edson was helping our cause, not hindering, probably to the great annoyance of his employers. I had cash stuffed everywhere. To any outsider I had steadily put on weight and in fact this was the first version of 'The Fat Sumo Suit" so popular at parties these days! The band, oblivious to these daily cash raids, visibly stirred from its slumber and played an accurate facsimile of the Deep Purple I knew and loved. Funny what a good crowd does to the standard of the concert. It was hard to keep up with the revolving door that was the crew at these times, which was borne out by a curious fax I got from Barbara at the Thames Talent Office. She asked me to let Chris, our tour accountant, know that he was to pay Rob Fodder his per diems, as she had just noticed he was on the pay roll. Odd, really as Rob had been with us since Japan and Chris had been paying him anyway. Eh duh!

Of course, as we were in Brazil, Ritchie just had to organise some games of soccer being in the country that boasted the second best national side in the world... next to Germany? Well, according to the Ober Gruppen Führer anyway. I remember we were set to play a record company team one day and of course Ritchie had to win at any cost, so he got me to go out and recruit four or five junior members of some really hot local side. I was aided and abetted by the local promoter who knew to where and who I should call. I was to pass them off as local crew.

Ritchie, enthusiasm personified, bought brand new kit and prior to the match, he and I went through our team list and he carefully replaced key positions with those 'crew' who had suddenly appeared at our side. Poor old Charlie, for years our stalwart goalkeeper, found himself on the bench and he was not amused. His replacement? The Brazilian under 19's goalie! No contest really. Needless to say we won by a hatful and of course Ritchie scored, like you doubted that. With that heavy dose of euphoria, Ritchie played a magical set that night, but that was the exception rather than the rule on that tour. By the end of September 1991, The 'Slaves And Masters' trek stuttered to a halt with one-off shows in Poland, Athens and Israel. The feeling in the band was awful. No energy, no bright eyes, any future?

CHAPTER SIXTEEN
TIME TO KILL

Bruce always knew when to orchestrate the changes. Whether it was the mood of the band this time, the dwindling tour receipts, the lack of interest of promoters (borne out by the lack of dates) or a combination of all of them, whatever, a change was in the wind and I privately agreed. This version of Purple was too 'poppy'; it just wasn't the same band or importantly the same sound. A lot of the press reviews said it was more like a Rainbow show than a hard rock Purple show. There were, of course, the more obvious signs to me, the vigilant observer, like Bruce and Ritchie going off into animated huddles and covert meetings. Then Bruce getting each of the other members on the phone to judge reaction. Yup, no big prizes for what was being cooked up. Bruce wanted to go back for Ian Gillan, but was obviously finding Ritchie a tough one to convince. I don't think he had any argument from Roger, Paicey or Jon.

Christmas passed into the spring of 1992 and still nothing was resolved. By late spring, Bruce and the band asked me to book Bearsville Studios in upstate New York in Woodstock, to begin rehearsals and writing for the new album. Bearsville was about a two-hour drive from Connecticut and was built by Bob Dylan's legendary manager Albert Grossman. It's in the heart of the Catskill Mountains and minutes from the bars, shops and restaurants that had sprung up in Woodstock, yes, that Woodstock. It was the typical Purple recording location. As I booked the studio time, I thought to myself, "why with Joe?" This cajoling of Ritchie to let Ian back was sure taking its time. Midway through rehearsals, it happened and Joe was told what in truth was common knowledge to the rest of the band, Bruce, probably Barbara and of course myself.

I think it had all been apparent that another album and tour with Joe was a non-starter commercially for both band and record company. Joe, I knew felt the change in atmosphere. He judged rightly that he was going to be replaced. He sensed from Paicey and Jon, oddly, as they never betrayed their feelings, that they wanted their Ian back, when he (Joe) had done nothing wrong, given his all in fact, but he was no Gillan or Coverdale. That's not a criticism; Joe just had a great, but different voice, not quite suited to the sound of Purple. Ritchie stayed silent on the subject. Roger, as always, wanted to get on with the writing, staying away from any controversy. Hard call for him as he was one of Ian's best chums, but had also served time in Rainbow with Joe very successfully. Better to keep the old bandana head down.

Bruce needed to bring in reinforcements to finally convince Ritchie that his nemesis Ian should be recalled - The record company. They, I believe, pointed out to him that 'Slaves and Masters' had been a relative flop and if there was to be a renewed enthusiasm for the band from within BMG then it would be more forthcoming if Gillan was back in the 'acceptable' line-up. (Were they reading from Bruce's script?). Ritchie felt that some sort of blame was being placed at his door for the album's failure, never accepting that one of the prime reasons for Ian's departure in the first place, was himself. He reluctantly agreed and Bruce contacted Phil Banfield, who was still Ian's personal manager.

On the personal front, whilst we were away at Bearsville, Michele, who had come up for a very brief visit without the girls, when she could have stayed for weeks, only to tell me she was leaving to find happiness allegedly with someone else. Turns out, the girls were staying with her new love. Later, reflecting on the failed relationship, I had missed every damned sign that she was seeing someone else. It was the manager of her work place, a two faced asshole, who always shook my hand when he saw me. He later in turn left Michele for a younger, more blonde version, while away working on a ship. So now she would feel what I had felt. Justice? I thought about it for many months and whilst I understood, as I was forever away with the band, I found it hard to take. Coming from a seafaring community, I was used to the 'men folk' being away for months at a time and the wives keeping the home fires burning, so to speak, ever faithful. Rose tinted glasses? Yes, I suppose so. Was I equally to blame? Maybe. It didn't stop it hurting, alone again, naturally.

Back to the plot: Apparently, Ian had not had a good time of it away from Purple from a financial point of view, although his latest band Repo Depo was, in his estimation the real deal and would make it. He told me much later that his decision to tour with Black Sabbath a decade before had been purely financial and he had never taken the trouble to learn the lyrics that he couldn't understand anyway. Surely not, hardly Proust, were they? Al Dutton, Ian's personal, who would accompany Ian as part of this package, told me unbelievable horror stories of touring with Ian to unmentionable places with unpronounceable names on buses where the locals lit fires in the back to cook and keep warm. Not quite what Ian had been used to, but to his eternal credit he just laughed about it over a beer or three recounting those tales of deprivation back safe in the warm bosom of Purple once again.

Once Ian agreed to return in principle, the band dispatched Roger to England with some of the tapes we had recently recorded with Joe for the new album, just to confirm that Ian could still hack it vocally. Nothing could be left to chance whatever the history. He could and despite, I believe, his annoyance at having been 'auditioned' in this way, he confirmed that he would return. Whilst I was really pleased, I wondered how long it would take for tensions to fire up between Ian and Ritchie, would there be mutual respect or animosity?

Tutzing in Germany was chosen as the reunion location at Red Rooster Studios. The cast assembled and whilst all welcomed Ian with enthusiasm, there was just the barest nod of recognition between the two egos. After a minimum of rehearsal and composition, we would move firstly back to the Bearsville Studios in New York and then to Orlando to Greg Rike Studios. The location in Tutzing gave me a lot of problems because it was one side of Munich whereas the new airport was totally the other side. Pretty much like Heathrow is to say London City Docks or New York JFK is to South New Jersey. Basically an awful, time-consuming schlep, picking up various members of the band who predictably all arrived on different days. The recording took up, with mixing, the whole of the winter of 1992. The tensions soon surfaced, probably earlier than even I thought. Not overt, just little niggly things. Ritchie would show up at the studios two hours late one day, so Ian wouldn't show at all the next just to show him.

Right from the start there was trouble. The studio had living quarters like a mini motel, very comfortable, with one large apartment with two bedrooms over the studio itself, which the owner called "home" when recording there himself. They would need to spend hours together, writing and tweaking lyrics and melodies. Well, I went to the airport a few days later to get the Maestro and gave him a rundown on who was where and what was happening. His main concern was as usual, "I hope there's somewhere to play football?" Shit, this was winter! We did get in a couple of games in the mud nearby, before I was ordered to find a more suitable solution. With all the local help I could muster, I found an Astroturf pitch that we got permission to use. It was quite some distance away, so getting games organised was a major task.

Well, back to Red Rooster and I showed Ritchie to the biggest of the suites in the main guesthouse. His first and only question was, "I want to see where Ian and Roger are!" "Shit, here we go," I thought. I took him over and his facial expression said it all. "Get them out, I want this." I was quaking at the thought of Ian's reaction. However, Ian and Roger seemed to have expected it and with a little shuffling, I allowed them to take their choices from the other accommodations. I got bumped out of mine by Ian as a consequence, but just wanted them to be happy. Seems like it was going to be a hard road. Nothing more was said on the matter or Ritchie's late arrivals, but I'd known these two characters for twenty years back then and I could read 'em like a book. The album would be called 'The Battle Rages On' - very apt!

****

The new album was scheduled for a July '93 release and by April I was back in Connecticut working with Thames Talent to make sense out of the touring detail based on a schedule of the tour, which was due to start on July 27th in Binghamton in upstate New York. It would finish some six months later in Japan. That meant long meetings with Diane Murphy, our trusty travel manager, for all our travel requirements, both crew and band, but always allowing the latter their personal quirks in the best hotels as to room style, position, floor and other, ahem, personal services. With the band still domicile on two separate continents, the location of rehearsals had to be arranged to suit everyone, but rarely did. We eventually brought everyone to Long Island to rehearse at the Veterans Lodge in Hauppauge, which was a short drive from Ritchie's house (just to show who was pulling the strings).

Finally, I had the big 'sit down' with Ray D'Addario the production manager, to choose, fix and arrange the providers of sound, light and transport of equipment, crew, band and attendant personnel such as caterers, wardrobe, drivers, accountants and personal roadies for each member of the band. Ah, mustn't forget Bruce. That's a fair number of folk to be traipsing half way around the world, all of who would need visas in those countries that required 'em. Our crew had stabilised somewhat now in terms of key personnel. They are worth a mention. Drum tech was Scott "porno" Porterfield; bass tech - Richard Marchesani; keyboards - Stuart Wickes; guitars - Jim Manngard; Samuelson Concert Productions did the lighting and varilites, Laserlite F/X did, well, lasers and sound was provided by Showco of Dallas. TransAm did the trucks whilst Wharfdale did the crew coaches in Europe. Finally catering was done so wonderfully by Eat To The Beat. This was now the nineties, so we were also now bound by some laws on the road (that just didn't exist in the early years) such as having to provide this location catering that MUST be able to offer a choice of dishes, one of which must be vegetarian. Sure beat a soggy pizza or a cold burger on the run in my early days. Little did I know that this tour would be one of the most memorable of my life with Deep Purple for a host of bizarre and absurd reasons. Things were about to go a little crazy!

As I said the tour was scheduled to start in America in July for a month of shows, but Bruce suddenly, without explanation, pulled them. The reasons were blurred according to whose rumour you believed. The first was that the album needed a remix seemingly on the orders of BMG; the other was that Ritchie had booked a holiday in Germany and was not going to cancel it. That Ritchie went on holiday on the same dates as the American shows, was true, but did he only go because they'd been cancelled anyway due to the remix? I preferred to think the latter was true, but you never really knew! In any event, as things would turn out, American fans were never to see this latest reformation of the classic line-up.

Having geared myself up and all the band and crew to start late July, this false dawn meant everybody kicking their heels until September. With no relationship and my property in Trumbull threatened by development, I decided I'd had enough of snow in winter and moved to Florida to Altamonte Springs, north of Orlando. I rented an apartment in Club Esprit for a year but stayed two, finally buying a house in Apopka in March 1995. It wasn't without tears as I lost around $45,000 in the move. I hadn't realised quick enough that the development around my house had adversely affected its value, so that I was forced to sell way under what I'd paid. I was not a happy bunny, but I had to cut my loss and to me it made sense as I was where the band preferred to record and in these massively improving ways of communication, I did not feel I had to be on top of Bruce and everyone at Thames Talent. More importantly, I could have a life away from the band, just too far away to be at the beck and call of specifically Ritchie. The house in Trumbull had too many ghosts anyhow. I had given up long ago on the notion that Bruce would take me on inside his organisation. "Colin, lad, if ever your days come to an end with the band you'll be discarded like yesterdays junk," I thought to myself, prophetically, as it would turn out.

Rehearsals were reconvened for Bregenz in Austria, where I arrived mid September to ensure all was well for the arrival of the band. Bregenz had a problem in that its nearest international airport was Zurich, some 120 miles away over the border in Switzerland. Picking the band up was, therefore, a nightmare as, despite my protestations and pleadings they mostly decided predictably to arrive separately and on different days. The round trip, though not difficult, was long and over a border, which of course, had guards. All went well as I zipped back and forth past this small, indifferent border post so many times that they had taken to waving at me like an old friend until the morning came to pick up Ritchie who had flown in from New York.

As I approached I was waived unusually into the stop zone behind a line of cars, instead of the customary wave through. I looked at my watch careful to be sure I didn't miss his arrival. Well, the customs guys obviously thought that today of all days I looked like the master drug runner. I asked them what the problem was? "Ve haf zeen you driving zees mercedeez zis vay und zat vay several times a day... und vy voud zat be, vee ask ourzelvez?" As I tried to explain, they shredded the car to bits and, after two hours having then not quite so neatly put it back together, they had the cheek to ask for T-shirts and any other Purple swag I could give them. I quickly obliged as time was evaporating fast. They then smugly waived me through probably thinking, "vell, zat fucked up your day, but tanks for the T-shirts and photos".

And it did and Ritchie's too. I tore down the Autobahn to the airport breaking every speed limit. I had allowed plenty of time for hold-ups when I left Bregenz, but not two hours. Praying the flight was delayed, I screeched to a halt at arrivals, ran into the terminal to see that for once not only was his flight on time, it had been early. No Ritchie and, of course, he didn't have a mobile phone with universal pick up to track him down. The airline had no clue as to his whereabouts, I searched every bar and restaurant, paged him many times, but all to no avail. I daren't leave the airport just in case he showed up so I called the hotel asking them to call me if he arrived. I waited an hour before I got the message that he had indeed got to the hotel.

Driving back at full speed, the guards gave me a merry wave as I sped once more over the border like I was their best fucking mate. They must have wondered why I returned alone, having given them this long drawn out reason why I needed to hurry to pick up "the boss" at the airport. I returned their greeting in the customary way with one digit aloft. When I got back to the Best Western Hotel, Ritchie's room had "do not disturb" outside and I had to wait all day to be on the wrong end of a tongue lashing before he arose calmly in the evening to rehearse. I winced as he asked me what had happened, knowing that he normally would not accept any excuses for things going wrong especially when they directly affected him. He must have had an extraordinarily good sleep in an exceptional room as he just nodded when I explained, and said that he had taken a taxi when it was apparent that I was absent, and that he had also been stopped at the border where he had signed autographs. That was it. One of the very rare understanding moments from RB, especially as the taxi would have been a fortune. It would, however be his last on this tour. Two days later we moved on to Rome to rehearse with the full sound and light show at The Palaghiaccio where we were due to open the tour the next day. The old feeling and sound was still there. Goose bump time!

We stayed in Italy for four dates, and then moved on to Austria and Germany for thirteen shows in sixteen days where Ritchie visibly brightened. Being back in his adopted Fatherland had that effect, conversing with the natives in their own language gave him a sense of power, (like he needed any more). France followed, then we made it to Switzerland, where Ritchie summoned me to his dressing room after the show and announced that he would not be doing the two shows in Spain the following two days. He said, "pull the shows, ring Bruce and tell him I'm not going. Tell him I never agreed to do dates in Spain on this tour. They've been thrown in against my wishes and I'm not doing them". (Stamp of foot and toss of hair).

It goes without saying that they weren't thrown in; they had been there from the start. What to do? First of all, I went to Raymond and told him to pack everything away, but not to let any of the trucks, buses or crew leave until he'd heard further from me. I went to the rest of the band, packed them off to the hotel saying that I didn't think Spain would be on as Blackmore had just announced that he wouldn't be doing it. They collectively raised their eyes to the heavens, muttering expletives. I then phoned Bruce in Connecticut. I explained that Ritchie was adamant he would not do Spain, said they had been sprung on him and he was off to the south of France for two days with Candice (Surprised? Yes, she, by now, had officially replaced Tammi).

Bruce, well used to Ritchie's pronouncements said that if that was what he was set to do, then little could be done. He then told me to phone the Spanish promoter and explain that Blackmore was too ill to perform and that he (Bruce) would produce the necessary legal documents like medical certificates, but I should get Ritchie to a friendly doctor to support the claim. Wonderful! I went to Ritchie who of course flatly refused to see a doctor, telling me to get Roger to do it. I went to Roger, who being Roger, agreed. Whaaaat! Sounds simple eh? Well the aftermath of this little tantrum cost the band $75,000 in cancellation fees plus whatever it cost to keep band and extensive crew in hotels along the way. Makes sense, of course not, this is rock 'n' roll.

Ritchie couldn't care less and swanned off to the South of France with his girlfriend and the ever faithful Rob Fodder trailing along behind. The band though, were determined that the cost would come out of Ritchie's take from the tour, not theirs and told Bruce who subsequently approached Ritchie explaining that the band would not foot the bill, he simply replied "whatever" with a shrug, as if he'd been asked to pay for a simple round of drinks.

The two days off were welcome and we went on to Austria and took our unexpected break there. Rest over, we played Innsbruck, Vienna and Wels, and then continued to Prague in the Czech Republic where the old maestro threw another curve ball. After the show we all returned to The Hyatt Hotel, which had a huge atrium lobby where I parked myself with a relaxing après show drinkie. I happened to glance up at Ritchie's room and saw the curtain twitch as Ritchie scoped who was about. Sure enough, the bar called me over to say I had a call. Well, no surprises who this was. "Come up to my room now" - never one to beat about the bush, our Ritchie. He opened the door with the chain on and stuck an envelope in my hand and instructed me to, "Take this to the band and read it to them individually, don't give it to them, sit them down and read it to them. Got that?"

The door closed and, clamping my palm over my mouth, I suppressed a giggle, it was so bizarre. What was he up to now? I immediately ripped open the envelope on the way to the elevator and it was a five-page resignation letter setting out the reasons for leaving the band. In it he agreed to play through to Helsinki, the last date on the European leg, but wouldn't do Japan as, once more, this had been sprung upon him without his knowledge, let alone his permission. This was odd, as he had already surrendered his passport to me in order to fix his Japanese visa. How did I wheedle this out of him if he didn't know where he was going? Okay, this was Ritchie, so I made allowances.

The letter went on to say that the band was a joke and he could no longer work with this clown, Ian Gillan. This was apparently a reference to how Ian dressed and pranced around on stage. Well, Ian had taken to wearing pyjama type pants with drawstring waist and red sneakers, but so what. Ritchie, however, did not think it was very "rock 'n' roll" whatever that is. Really this was Ritchie flexing his presumed muscle to show who was the boss and who was to blame for this problem. I think this was his attempt to finally destroy Purple once and for all. He probably thought that once this was done, Bruce would side with him as in the past and he could either form a brand new Purple or resurrect Rainbow with Bruce orchestrating everything.

This time, however, he had not talked it through with Bruce before making his statement. Was he now that sure of Bruce? Apparently, and he got it wrong, so wrong. I went to my room and phoned Bruce back in Connecticut. "What's up?" said a very sleepy Bruce. "Ritchie's resigned, he'll do the tour up to Helsinki, but not Japan. I've got a five pager from him that I need to read to you. He wants me to read it to the band individually". "Do me a favour, fax it right over to me now and we can then read it together. Tell the band quietly and I'll ring them once I've read the letter and thought about it. Don't do what Ritchie said". "Well, I wasn't going to do that anyway, they're not schoolboys".

So I faxed the letter and we read it together digesting the contents. I then called the others relating what had occurred and telling them that Bruce would call them individually later, so be prepared for a late night. Jon just laughed, Paicey cursed and Roger, being Roger was sad and said he'd go and talk Ritchie round. Well, Mr. B. wouldn't even open his door to Roger, so that got him even more dejected. The phone calls between Bruce and the band went on all night. Finally Bruce phoned me and told me that the band would carry on and he would find a replacement for Japan. If Ritchie was to leave, then so be it. The rest of the European tour should continue as if nothing had happened. He would fly out to catch the last day in Helsinki; meanwhile he had a lot to do. "Well", I thought. "Bruce has finally had enough too. This is going to be very interesting".

The next morning I got up, put the wake up calls through to the band with the luggage pull time and went, as was my routine, to checkout to settle the accounts. At the appointed time Ritchie and Candice came into the hotel lobby expecting, I'm sure, utter chaos. All was normal. The rest of the band nodded their "good mornings" to each other and to Ritchie, who was resplendent in a long leather overcoat and a big pointy Tyrolean type hat. Candy was dressed the same and they both wore dark glasses just to maintain their anonymity, I suppose. Who mentioned clowns? Actually they looked more like Spy vs Spy from Mad magazine. Ritchie could not understand what was going on or rather what was not going on. He visibly fumed. There should be turmoil, but the band was just laughing it up as I got them to pay their incidentals. Nobody said a word to him about the letter or his resignation, they just carried on as if nothing had happened which, of course, burned him up. He just couldn't bring himself to broach the subject either, so we just went on to the next show, which was at the Zabrze Sport Hall in Katowice, Poland where it was bloody, freezing.

At the airport, he pulled me to one side and said "What's everyone so fucking happy about, didn't you read them the letter?" "Oh Yeh, they all had a look at it". "But you read it to them, right". "Well, they know what's in it and Bruce has a copy too". "He has?" he snapped back. "Yeh, it's a done deal". "I'm not going to Japan, you know". "Okay, that's fine" I said as I carried on checking everyone in. He wandered away bemused at my nonchalance. The tour continued to Brussels and then to the Ahoy Stadium, Rotterdam.

I was sitting in the production office backstage, busy filling in Japanese visa forms for the crew and making plans for Japan, which was due to start in three weeks on 2nd December. Ritchie stepped into the office, something he had never done before, as you went to Ritchie, never the other way around. "I told you I ain't going to fucking Japan" he said as he saw the pile of Japanese visa forms and photos and me working on the computer, punching in names for the crew and band to go to there. Yeah, I know," I said without looking up, thinking that I knew we were going, but hadn't a clue who would replace the gentleman who stood before me.

He spun round and stormed back to his dressing room, ripped his visa out of his passport, tore the offending page into little bits of confetti, stormed back and dropped them into my outstretched hand. "Thanks" I said, as I carried on with my work. "I told you I'm not fucking going and I mean it," he screamed. "Yeah, I know," I said quietly, as I tossed the shredded visa into the bin beside me. He was fucking livid, not quite understanding why there was no reaction. When was it going to dawn on him that he had pressed too many buttons too many times, especially with Bruce who had bent over backwards in the past to make things run Ritchie's way? Too many times Bruce and I had concocted white lies to the rest of the band as to why certain things had to be when all along it was just Ritchie exerting his power. I'm sure they probably guessed, but if they didn't, sorry lads! It was just to keep the peace and to keep things rolling.

The mood was now miserable as we got set to play four dates in England. Ritchie's interaction with Ian was obstructive, not constructive as if he was trying his best to make the singer look a fool on stage. Ian, in turn would repay the guitarist in a similar fashion. Kids! Blackmore would now start to show up late and turn things around once he got there. He'd demand that the show be put back despite me telling him of the financial consequences. He didn't care, the others just wanted to get through it. Behind the scenes, things were progressing. Bruce phoned Mr. Udo in Japan, explained the problem and asked him if we could pull off the tour without Ritchie and which guitarists, if any, would be acceptable to Japanese fans. Mr. Udo said he would get back to him, which he did and said that if Ritchie was definitely not coming then the solution would be that only Steve Vai or Joe Satriani would placate the Japanese. No shit!

Bruce contacted Bill Graham Management for Joe and amazingly he was free and after sleeping on it, enthusiastically agreed to join for Japan. The band were quietly told and only the crew who were to go to Japan, but on the pain of instant dismissal if they told Ritchie, Rob Fodder or Jim Manngard the guitar tech, both of whom would not be going for obvious reasons. Thankfully, confidentiality was maintained. Roger later contacted Joe and asked if he was familiar with Purple's stuff. He said that Roger must be joking; he loved the band. Roger then sent him the live tapes of this show and said a silent prayer. Back on stage, the fans must have sensed the tension, but the sound was still great, better than ever, maybe driven on by that very atmosphere of danger, mistrust and electricity you can feel sometimes in a large crowd and you sense its going to boil over into mayhem. Maybe that's the essence of great live heavy rock. We were supported on this European leg of the tour in the main by a band called Culture Cross, who were just… well, unmemorable.

On to England for four dates supported by The Storm, the shows being at Manchester Apollo, two nights at London's Brixton Academy with the last at the NEC, Birmingham, which was to be videoed for later release, a decision to which the entire band had agreed. Please keep that in mind for what then unfolded. The Brixton and Manchester shows had gone really well and the NEC, Birmingham would be the last for the band in England with the famous line-up. Here I must clear up an often reported and widely argued mess, over what happened at the video taping of the show. It had been decided by the record company, that Manchester Apollo would be the chosen site of the video and audio recording. Ritchie baulked at this suggestion and said that if anywhere it should be Birmingham, but definitely not the Apollo. His reasons were solid. Too small for all the cameras and we would have fans sightlines blocked by platforms etc. and so it was agreed that it would be re-arranged to do it at the NEC.

Now, this was all agreed before the tour began, as Ritchie wanted to know where the cameras would be and how many. He had discussed it with Bruce, but he wanted to see the plans and be sure the venue had been changed. I was dispatched to see Mr. B. and sat in his kitchen with him, he still in his pyjamas where he was shown the plot and said okay to all of it, even down to the four cameras on stage, two behind the P.A and two handheld. And so, to the show: Ritchie, as ever, was late on stage, so I went to his dressing room to see what was up. The door was locked of course, as he intended to be late. Rob Fodder emerged and said he would be ready in a few minutes. I waited for the word and then Rob gave me the thumbs up, so I got the rest of the band and gave the okay to the producers, directors, et al, that we were ready and gave the okay for the crew to kill the lights and start the intro tape.

So out comes Ritchie, walks up the ramp, takes one look at the cameras on the stage and turns and locks himself back in his dressing room. I rush down to find out what was wrong and his reaction was, "Get those fucking cameras off the stage now!" I tried to tell him that he had agreed to this weeks ago, but he wasn't coming on until they were gone. Rob Fodder cleared Ritchie's side of the stage of one such offending cameraman. Ritchie walked slowly to join the already started concert. The intro tape was never stopped and the rest of the band had started without him, as can be seen on the video.

We got the cameras moved, but not to Ritchie's satisfaction. He was looking for trouble now and grabbed a water jug that was behind the amps, ran across to Jon's side of the stage and threw it at one of the remaining cameramen. Alas, he missed and the water went a bit to the left of him right on to Bron, Ian Gillan's wife. Roger's wife, Les also took a hit, but Bron was drenched. Well, the almighty sure had a sense of drama, not to say very bad aim. Could have been any number of twenty people who were in the VIP area, but no, his eventual target had to be Mrs. Bron Gillan. Why? Gillan naturally saw red and probably would have strung Ritchie up there and then but for Bron's calming influence. Whether she considered it a genuine mistake or not, who's to know? Like most top ladies, I think she summed up a potential disaster in an instant and worked out that the coolest thing to do was actually nothing. This would defuse both Ritchie's evil action (if it indeed had been one, which I doubt) and stopped Ian reacting the way any red-blooded male like Ian was apt to do. The show carried on, but no encore. Ritchie left the arena later, pointing his finger at me, he growled, "this is all your fault, Colin". Well, wasn't everything?

And so to Scandinavia and Helsinki for the last four shows supported by Finland's, Royal Tramps and the last day of the Blackmore era. Bruce rang me to say he would definitely be there, but not to tell Ritchie. He arrived at the hotel the morning of the show, with his lady, Janet. Later in the day, around noon, the phone rang and it was Ritchie. "Here's one for you, Colin. If you don't get Bruce Payne here by show time, there will be no show" he said, obviously believing that Bruce was back in America and I had got the unsolvable problem, the last kick in the balls, the parting gift to the band. "Okay" I said unconcerned. "I'm serious. If I don't see Bruce at my door before I leave the hotel, there will be no show tonight". "Yeah, okay, no problem". "I'm dead serious, you know that". At 6.30pm, Ritchie made one last desperate call. "You remember what I said about Bruce?" "Yeah, I know". At that moment Bruce knocked on Ritchie's door. "I understand you want to see me," said Bruce, loving every minute of the look on Ritchie's face. "Ah, yeah errrr, what you doing here?" said Ritchie, never one for the snappy killer reply, desperately trying not to say, "How the fuck did you get here?" He was so pissed off as, once again, things had not turned to chaos as he had planned. "Surely the light must come on now," I thought. "Can't you see that things are happening around you now that you are unaware of, over which you have no control?" This was not a nice place for him to be now.

We got to the show and Ritchie went to his dressing room, locking the door behind him. I knew he would make the show run as late as possible, one last defiant attempt to piss everybody else off. I took the band to the foot of the stairs three times before he emerged and played the show of his life. (Well what did you expect?) Hard to figure, eh. Back at the hotel, I expected him to have checked out and disappeared, but, no, there he was in the bar, his arm around Candice, glass of wine in hand. Did he think this was his ultimate moment to gloat?

The rest of the band and crew filtered into the bar, the other end to Ritchie, but after about an hour both factions intermingled like nothing was wrong, but no one mentioned Japan or Satriani. Bruce, unbeknownst to the guitarist, had already decided that he no longer wanted to be his manager anymore. He had been worn down to the point of no return. The next day I made sure that everyone got off onto their respective flights as this was the end of this part of the tour. It would be two weeks before we met up again in Tokyo.

I took Ritchie and Candice to the departure gate and gave them their boarding passes. "Well, this is it, Ritchie" I said not knowing what else to say, a bit lame really after the years I had worked for him. Should I hug him, although he wasn't a tactile sorta guy? I just shook his hand. "Yeah... see you" he replied, slowly looking into my eyes for something else, anything else. I had a lump as big as a golf ball in my throat and I know he did too, despite it all. We had been together over twenty years, through Purple and Rainbow. Some of the most exciting and exasperating days of my life, yet despite his crazy ways, he was and still is a guitar genius. I love him to bits (in a manly way, of course, ahem). He showed complete unconditional kindness and gentle caring for my folks. How could I ever repay him that? I felt like slapping him and hugging him all at once. As he stood there all his ego, lust for power and chaos in tandem with his wonderful creativity seemed to evaporate leaving this almost sad, lost figure, the ultimate 'Billy no mates". We just shook hands again almost not wanting to let go, the silence screaming. He turned away. I wouldn't speak to him again for twelve years.

His departure had a postscript. Once everybody had returned home, Bruce was in his office in Connecticut when he got a call from Ritchie. "So, Bruce, where do we go from here?" enquired Ritchie. "What's this 'we'? I really think you and I should meet, Ritchie". So Ritchie came in to Thames Talent and Bruce explained quietly and sympathetically that he'd had enough of the association, had enough of the tantrums and tears. He would release Ritchie from his contract and, once he had found new representation, do all he could to make the transition as smooth as possible. Ritchie was stunned that it had all backfired so badly. He thought, I believe, that he could bring Purple to its knees. He allegedly told this to Bruce, told him he wanted a clean sweep, a total clear out of band, crew, just everybody and now it had totally flip flopped on him. He was devastated. After time he found a New York lawyer to handle his affairs and, with Bruce's help, he severed that last connection to Deep Purple.

CHAPTER SEVENTEEN
SOON FORGOTTEN

I returned to my new apartment in Orlando, blessing the warm climate and made the final arrangements for Japan. I spoke at times to the band on official matters, but the conversation would often turn to Ritchie. It was a mixture of elation at the prospect of a future freed from his controlling ways; yet full of apprehension and of course nostalgia. Not so much for Ian as there was a complete breakdown of trust and friendship, yet Ian never trashed Ritchie's reputation as a guitarist supreme, it's just that the rest didn't match up. Jon adored Ritchie despite him being one of the most impossible people to deal with. Paicey, never one to voice his opinions out loud, felt that if Ritchie was on top of his game and in a good mood then the whole band became unstoppable, but when he wasn't, everybody suffered. Roger, just felt the same exasperation that I did. Both of us had been around him the longest. We both agreed he has a deep trouble within him that maybe even he can't get quite get a handle on. That's what makes him want to destroy the very things he's taken so much time and effort to construct.

So we got to Japan, where we had scheduled three full days of rehearsals with Joe. The band was set up in a studio and I spoke to Joe before he left the States saying I would pick him up at the airport. He declined saying he had his own guy, Kevin Burns and to meet them at the hotel. When he and Kevin arrived, the rest of the band were in the lobby to greet him. The niceties taken care of, I asked him what he wanted to do (as in rest, shower, eat) to which he replied, "Well let's go and do it". We got to the studios and waited for Joe, who had stopped back at the hotel to shower away the long flight. The band assembled along with me, Mr. Udo and Bruce in the control room, Jon asked Joe, "Where do you want to start?" "At the beginning?"

Joe knew the set as he'd had the tapes from Roger. They began and it was stunning. It was as if he had been with Deep Purple from the very beginning. He went almost flawlessly through the complete show, aping

Ritchie exactly, adding nothing of his own prodigious talent. Jon was awestruck as Joe played off Jon's licks and riffs as if it was the most natural thing in the world. At the end of the session, not only did we know that it would be all right, but we felt the next two days of rehearsals were completely unnecessary. We could have done a show that night, nobody could doubt that. You know, added to his great talent he was a gentleman, a really good guy. What a difference! You know what was extraordinary? Joe was just as chuffed to be playing with Deep Purple as they were with him.

The first show was in Nagoya at the Rainbow Hall. How apt! Prior to the show I waited to see how Joe would look, accepting that his playing was up to muster and some. He appeared in black jeans, black work boots, a black and white polka dot shirt with his long hair part tied back in a ponytail and part tied up on top, Samurai style. He looked the absolute dog's bollocks! Sheer presence and the Japanese crowd were bowled over by what they saw as reverence to their ancient culture. Game, set and match to Joe. The show was fantastic. Whenever it came to the celebrated guitar breaks, the crowd almost held its breath waiting to see if Joe would put his slant on it or do it like it was meant to be. This was especially noticeable in the immortal guitar solo in 'Highway Star'. He didn't disappoint and, if you looked away it could've been Ritchie, but the time honoured lick done, Joe would add his own brilliance. Hey, two for one, what a bargain! We floated on through Japan on a cloud of euphoria.

****

Home to Florida for Christmas. Alone? Yes. Lonely? No. I kinda liked my own company and space now and with mam and dad gone, there was precious little to take me back to England. I kept in contact with Carol and David, though probably not as often as she would have liked. I also kept in touch with Stephen and Paul who was now a busy and successful conductor. Joe agreed to stay for another European tour scheduled for June '94, which would run for a month. Bruce and the band tried to persuade him to join permanently, but he had his own projects, his obligations to Sony Records and Bill Graham Management. He saw, I'm sure, that his future lay on a different path. No hard feelings, just a little disappointment. Joe liberated the band. They now realised again that being in Deep Purple was just about the most fun you could have without getting naked. The vibe put a smile back on the faces of the crew too. Me? I couldn't wipe the smile off my face for months. Alas, we now had the hard, hard job of finding a replacement for Joe. However, we had the tour and his company to look forward to for one more month. It went in an enjoyable flash from June 3rd in Berlin, saying our goodbyes in Austria on 5th July.

Back home, the discussions for the replacement began in earnest. Bruce was pencilling in dates for November, forever confident that a top guy would be found. Steve Morse's name appeared very early, as he was a 'known' name who had been winning guitar polls seemingly forever. Roger went to see him in Atlanta. (Like who else would? Always the Ambassador, our Rog). He liked what he saw and, after chatting with Steve who was a big fan of the band, got him to agree to join, saying he would send on tapes. Steve had some dates to finish with his band The Dixie Dregs in Australia and agreed to rendezvous with us in Mexico City in November to rehearse and play two to three dates just to ensure there was social compatibility, rather than musical.

Come November, I picked him up at the airport two days before we were due to open at the Palacio De Los Deportes. It was a re-run of Joe Satriani. He did the whole show right off the bat, note for note. I turned to Charlie, jokingly and said, "I thought Blackmore said this was hard? Looks a piece of piss to me". Of course, Joe and Steve are masters of their craft as is Ritchie, so no offence intended to any of the aforementioned, but it was remarkable to see Steve effortlessly sail through the set. We did the first show of this latest era on 23rd November followed by two more shows in Monterey and in Corpus Christi, Texas. I could see the creative gleam in everyone's eye as sails were set for home and Christmas. Here again the audiences would hold their breath as the celebrated solos approached, just waiting for Steve to fuck 'em up and at the same time praying he didn't. Of course he didn't and the ovation was deafening. The air guitarist's had orgasms too!

It seemed odd, but very pleasant, to spend Christmas in warm weather, lazing by the pool and socialising with my new friends in Altamonte. Life was good. I played soccer, but now it was my choice of the where and when, not Ritchie's and it wasn't a problem if I was on the losing team - no recriminations.

I started to book studio time at Greg Rike Studios for the writing and recording of the next record. It was to be a long drawn out process starting in February and ending nine months later. The album 'Purpendicular' was a welcome return of the energy of old. We didn't stay in the studios the whole time however. Through March and early April we hit the road, firstly with two warm up dates in Florida and then to Korea, followed by South Africa for eight shows in nine days. We then went on to a brief hello and goodbye to India with a date each in Bombay and New Delhi. Good to see the good old boys at Thames Talent hadn't lost their touch for humour, even though they'd obviously lost their atlas! In fairness, these three countries were now viable propositions as they had always been off the tour agenda all the while Ritchie was in the band. For some illogical reason, they were on the old Blackmore black list. Whenever Bruce brought up the subject, Old Rich would shake his head and just mutter, "nah, not going there" with no reason given or for that matter expected.

The dates in Korea at the Olympic Park Gymnasium stand out as they were sponsored and titled "Something Special with Deep Purple", which on the face of it looked innocent enough on the flyers and tickets. The morning of the first show I was in my hotel room fielding calls from India and South Africa, our next ports of call on the tour. India wanted to know everything from "can the band come to dinner, come to a club, come paint my house?" Just every sort of crazy request from the mundane to the outrageous. Then I got a call from a very nervous Raymond asking me to get my butt over to the hall double quick. I smelled trouble. When I got to the show, I saw this massive backdrop behind the equipment with tour name, a huge whisky bottle and the penny dropped, gadoinnnng! "Something Special" was a brand of whisky!

The massive banner was brightly lit effectively trashing most of our mood lighting. I thought to myself, "the band is going to just freak at this". I rang Bruce back at the hotel and told him what I thought. He calmly told me to get onto the promoter and tell him that if the banner stayed, the show would be off. The promoter went ballistic and summoned me back to the hotel, the Sheraton, for a showdown with Bruce. At the hotel, Bruce took me to one side and said, "look, you sort this out. Tell them they can have the banner to the side unlit, but not behind the band and I want more money for it to be anywhere in the arena anyway, but you sort it out". Was this some sort of test? Me sort it out? I met the promoter in the lobby and suggested we went back to the arena together. Getting the visas for Korea had been a nightmare in the first place and now to be faced with this problem rather made the day of departure somewhat attractive.

Koreans, it has to be said, are very pleasant, efficient and polite, not to Japanese standards which are unequalled, but still right up there so it was disconcerting to see the promoter on the edge of an anger moment. Once there, I explained as nicely as I could that the banner had to go from where it was. They (the promoter had by this time been joined by colleagues) talked excitedly amongst themselves and it didn't seem to be going my way until I played the "show's off" card. Always does the trick with the promoters seeing their investment, house and cars disappearing into the nearest river.

I pulled Raymond at the same time and asked him how the fuck did he let them put it up in the first place. He protested innocence saying it was the name of the tour and he assumed it had been okay'd. I took the now very agitated promoter to one side and purred in my kindest deal making voice that I could give him two banners, stage left and right beside the PA stacks, but unlit as a gesture of goodwill. He muttered, consulted with his colleagues and agreed, probably reckoning he was getting two for one. I also told him it would cost an extra $10,000US cash. His inscrutability visibly slipped momentarily, but faced with a no show and my cheery, but unbending demeanour (seriously!), he agreed.

Back at the hotel, I handed over the cash to Bruce who, for once, seemed to be impressed and told the band. The show went down a storm and honour was satisfied all round. A few days later, while on a stopover on the way to South Africa, at The Mandarin Hotel in Singapore, I sat at the bar with Bruce. He told me that the band had decided to give me $1,000 as thanks for my success in securing the extra cash in Korea. That was the first and last time I had that type of acknowledgment from Bruce or the band for going the extra yard for them. This was at a time when I was averaging around $40,000 a year from the band as a basic wage, which was then supplemented by per diems (daily expense's) and bonuses if we were on tour or in the studios. Not bad, but not great in relation to what some tour managers got then and certainly get now. As an industry norm it was probably well below par, but all in all, I had no regrets, well not many.

Looking back now, I didn't get what I was worth; didn't get proper pay for the hours, weeks and years that I put in over and above the call of duty. Yet, this was and is rock 'n' roll and there were a queue of guys waiting to take my place for a lot less. Not as good, mind, but I believe now in this business more than most others, that unless you stick up for yourself you will be mercilessly used, because they (the employers) trade on the fact that it is a 'glamour' gig and that is part of your payment. That applies to bands as well as crew! There was a post script to Korea - a bootleg entitled "Something Special" emerged six months later and was very successful - revenge?

After a 'whole' day off we flew to Johannesburg at the unearthly time of 1.15am on 22nd arriving at 5.30am local time. Now when I speak to promoters, I am at pains to explain the style of accommodation Purple expect, nay demand. Some listen, others well, they just don't. The Parktonian All Suite Hotel could not under any circumstances have been called luxurious, but given the time of day and travel fatigue, it was grudgingly accepted for one day. That evening we were to play a live "unplugged" performance on the local radio station. With Ian "pulling a sicky" claiming a sore throat and no drum kit (which allowed Paicey a day off), it was down to Jon, Roger and Steve to give wonderful renditions of 'Black Night', 'Child In Time', 'The Aviator', 'When A Blind Man Cries', and 'Woman From Tokyo'. The session took about an hour and was followed by a press call and a dinner hosted by the record company BMG. All very pleasant, no dramas, no primadonna moments and well, no Ritchie.

The tour started in Pretoria supported by Uriah Heep with four shows in Cape Town, where we stayed at the Peninsula Hotel, by far one of my favourite stops ever with ocean views over Robin Island where poor old Nelson Mandela served way too much time. We spent six days in all in Cape Town doing four shows at the Three Arts Theatre with the other days off. We then returned to Jo'burg for two more shows at the New Showstar Amphitheatre. In case you were a-wondering, yes, Mr. Van Wyk, the promoter had changed the hotel to the budget busting Carlton (now The Hyatt) prompted, I guess, by my telling him he was a dickhead when we left to fly to the first show in Durban. He had booked the band into economy saying business class was full which it plainly wasn't as, when we entered the aircraft, there were rows of empty seats in business class. He grudgingly upgraded everyone by "the magic of plastic", but I had to have my say with Mr. Van Wyk. He was deeply insulted apparently. Lets face it, I could have said far worse, quite restrained really. We did 'kiss and make up' by the end however.

The Showstar was adjacent to a fairground and at the sound check Steve Morse went AWOL for about an hour only to return elated and refreshed having just done several bungee jumps from a crane at the fair. Bruce was mortified as were the band. Bruce immediately rang Frank Solomon, Steve's manager to check on the insurance situation as, without a doubt, our intrepid 'flyer' would be back for more the next day. Steve holds a private pilots licence and revealed much later his love of stunt flying too. The band was less than amused, but Mr. Morse loves to live on the edge, its part of the package, so everyone had to get used to it. One of the other shows was in Durban where the truck carrying the back line got lost en route. Raymond wanted to cancel, the back line being somewhat crucial to proceedings, but Bruce for a change took it upon himself to calm down the tired crew and ask them to wait. His faith in the South African truck driver was mercifully not misplaced and it duly arrived albeit very late. The crew had been jeered and pelted with assorted crap by the audience for seemingly delaying everything for no good reason, but once it was visibly coming together the crowd lightened up. The show, of course, went up late and was foreshortened, but very few seemed to mind. This was after all the first time anyone in this neck of the worldly woods had seen Deep Purple on home soil. They would pretty much put up with anything except no performance at all. With South Africa over, my thoughts concentrated on India.

We flew from Johannesburg to Bombay on Air India, the 'red eye' departing at 4.45pm and flying through the night to arrive at a dusty, hot dawn of a day. The journey was interrupted by a fuel stop at Dar Es Salaam (on the coast of Tanzania, half way up the Indian Ocean side of West Africa for the geography scholars). Now this is 1995, six years before 9/11 and this is a seemingly innocent, terrorist ignorant world, yet even then I was amazed at the lack of security at the Jetway and how just anybody could come and go as the aircraft was cleaned and refuelled. Could have been a commuter flight in the midwest of America.

Before we left South Africa, I had sent literally hundreds of faxes and made countless phone calls to the Indian promoters named wonderfully 'Wizcraft Entertainments' of Bombay to try, desperately, to instil in them a sense of professionalism. I was getting that cramp in the guts feeling that always led the parade of a disaster. I hoped I was wrong, but I sort of had a hunch this trip would be interesting at the very least! I had implored the promoters to keep everything low key at the airport as anyone, let alone a high profile band, never looks its best after an overnight flight.

As we came through customs, the fans and the press were hanging from the rafters. I had also requested an air-conditioned luxury bus to take band and crew to the hotel. What I saw before me was just post war (First!) and was draped with a massive banner welcoming the band to India. Low key? This was just awful. The crew sniggered; the band did not as, to get to the seats, you had to climb into the drivers cab and then through a door to the passenger seats. The 'air conditioned' part consisted of whatever windows would open combined with an overhead fan at each double seat. Unfortunately only half of these worked. The promoter just smiled at me, honestly believing he had delivered the goods as ordered, assuring me this was the finest bus available. His little face fell when I ripped into him, telling him to remove the banner and get a better bus by tomorrow.

We set off for the hotel for the longest ride of our lives. The heat was unbearable and the unique smells of Bombay all pervading and only adding to everyone's discomfort. The traffic was a nightmare, no order, no sense of right of way and just too much of it. The hotel, The Taj Mahal Intercontinental was the saving grace even though there would be the customary room changes for the band. It's a knee jerk thing, whether it is necessary or just because they can, I suppose. Thankfully Wizcraft had listened when I faxed them that there were to be no interviews that day. Everyone settled in and crashed out.

The following day, Wizcraft had their revenge with a long list of visits, lunches and sightseeing, which was well meant, but unappreciated. They mostly fell by the wayside due the bands lack of interest and enthusiasm to venture out in the traffic once more. They did agree to a welcome dinner and of course a slew of press interviews, but only if it meant them taking place at The Intercontinental. On the third day, there was a romantic affair with Roger renewing his marriage vows with his wife Les in an Indian temple at what was supposed to be a quiet ceremony attended by Bruce, Janet Gardner of Vixen who was still an item with him, Steve Morse and myself. The place was packed, although not for Roger and Les. These were the daily worshippers! I was impressed. I'm not particularly religious; I have my own beliefs, but have a sneaking admiration for those who find such strength in being so devout. Perhaps it's a smidgeon of envy too. I wanted to capture the moment on film, but as I raised the video camera to eye level I felt a sharp stab in the back. Looking down and up I saw the impassive face of a guard and the muzzle of a very large rifle. The message was delivered - no cameras. Roger and Les looked happy, bless'em.

Back at the hotel, I continued to harangue the promoters for a better bus and demanded I inspect it before agreeing to use it to get to the gig. Well, it was a later model by about five minutes, but was a lot more comfortable and the aircon seemed to function properly. One thing you learn very early on in India is that the best-laid plans are just for the bin because nothing ever goes to plan. The first show on the 8th was at the spectacularly named 'Sharji Raje Bhosale Kreeda Sankul-Andheri Sports Complex' which naturally gave direction sign writers a bit of a problem, so they didn't do any. I was advised not to go to the venue in the afternoon to check all was well as, "you might not get back in time to return with the band for the show" due to the traffic mess. Wonderful country!

The new 'old' bus rocked up to the hotel and we departed for a journey that in any other part of the world would have taken thirty minutes max. This one took two long hours culminating in the thorny problem of the bus being too wide for the gates of the stadium. "This is just brilliant", I thought, a shade ironically as my heart thudded a new hole in my chest. The too cheery promoter said he would get some cars, but by then the band had had enough, got off the bus and walked the rest of the way. Oh, the show was of course first class and the sell out crowd were ecstatic, so starved of live rock music. We had arranged to do a runner from the stage to the cars, which would then be driven to board the magic bus, and on to the hotel. However only we could have a bus driver who would drive directly into a dead end street, only to then need help to reverse all the way back, by which time we had now merged with all the post concert traffic and were again facing a two hour run. I attempted to admonish our poor bewildered driver, only to be calmed by an unusually understanding band, who accepted it all as being a part of being where we were.

The next day we flew to Delhi to be met this time by very decent transport. We were then presented at the hotel, the Taj Palace, by two elephants forming an arch with their trunks. Not our usual greeting, quaint but charming nonetheless. Unfortunately a former prime minister died later that day, which put all plans totally out the window.* Three days

* Morarji Ranchhodji Desai (29 February 1896 – 10 April 1995) was an Indian independence activist and the fourth Prime Minister of India from 1977–79. He was the first Indian Prime Minister who did not belong to the Indian National Congress and the first to receive the highest civilian awards from both India and Pakistan, the Bharat Ratna and Nishaan-e-Pakistan.

of mourning are obligatory, so the show in the Jawaharlal Nehru Stadium was postponed until the 14th April, which meant five days of enforced leisure.

I had asked that every room have lots of bottled water to avoid the dreaded 'Delhi Belly' and my request was taken to its extreme where I had to remove some of it just to get my luggage in the damn room. Steve Morse, who is very hygienic and particular about cleanliness was horrified when, glancing out of the window he saw some local kids swimming in the water tank of an adjacent apartment block and one was taking a piss into it! We enjoyed the rest and sampled many of the local restaurants.

There were many interviews, but they were held in the hotel and were well organised and ran perfectly. Janet, Bruce's partner however, succumbed to the 'DB's' and was very ill spending the next three days in bed under medical supervision. She was vomiting and had appalling diarrhoea making her severely dehydrated. Sure made everyone very wary of any food we were to consume and really took the edge off the proceedings. The response to the show was similar to Bombay and Bruce promised to return in the near future.

The shows had a dark side however as they were billed as 'charity events' for expenses only, but there was a concern by the band as to just how big the expenses had been. There was a feeling that the 'charity' had an overtone of personal gain somewhere down the chain. The band did get paid for their performances however, in the form of a rather large "promotional fee" from the local telecommunications company. We left the next day for home with a horrendous routing of Delhi to Bombay to London to New York and, for me, Steve and Charlie Lewis to Orlando dropping band members and crew off along the way. It took me three days to get over that one.

CHAPTER EIGHTEEN
SOMETIMES I FEEL LIKE SCREAMING

The band did not tour again for nine months until February 1996 to coincide with the release of 'Purpendicular'. May to Christmas was spent at Greg Rike Studios completing the tracks, which seemed to be a tortuous and laborious process, the creativity being squeezed out, much like trying to get toothpaste out of a spent tube. The subsequent reviews turned out pretty well though and the album was snapped up by the mass of Purple fans, devoted to the end. The album cover proved to be very expensive. A British company, recommended by Ian Gillan, seemed to endlessly crisscross the Atlantic at the bands expense with many varied ideas for consideration to eventually come up with the idea of a broken match! I thought to myself "What a lovely life, in the wrong job here Harty my son!"

Toward the end of the time at Greg's, Raymond had been taking an awful lot of calls from overseas and he also asked Doree that she should tell everyone who called that he would call them back later, especially if the band was around. I rang The Agency in London, who were planning some Ritchie dates and they said they had Ray on his production schedule. They then rang Bruce to check if this was a mistake. Bruce immediately rang me to check it out and, sure enough, Ray had been hoping to work for Ritchie, and us on the side. Bruce's reaction was immediate and final. "Get rid of him today" (funny how that phrase keeps on reoccurring).

Now Bruce and Ray went back a long way, right back to Elf who Bruce managed and for whom Ray had been top banana roadie. Mattered not. Ray was instant history. He was told to clear his gear out of the apartments and be gone. Bruce asked me whom I thought should replace Ray and I proposed Charlie. Bruce was not keen, preferring instead a 'name' production manager that we could pinch from another top band. I insisted that Charlie was the man and wouldn't let us down. Bruce, a bit reluctantly, agreed, but I knew that if Charlie screwed up it would be my balls in the wringer. Thankfully they stayed intact. I digress.

I spent this time at 'home', not in a hotel and began to piece together a 'home' life away from the band, well as much as I could. Charlie now lived locally and we would often hook up in our leisure time in the local bars. My football playing returned to the fore and I began to play for a team from a local pub, St. Andrews Tavern, which was run by John Rowlands, his wife Dot and their sons Tom and Nick plus his wife, Jackie. John used to play pro soccer back in England for, most impressively Liverpool back in 1963, then on to lower league teams before ending up in America with The Seattle Sounders and San Jose. Having briefly returned to England, the lifestyle of America drew him back and into the pub trade. St. Andrews Tavern had four teams in the central Florida Soccer League and all were pretty successful, but if you wanted to play, John insisted you attended practice. He was as brutal a coach as he had been a player as many will painfully attest to, outplaying most opponents whose combined age equalled John's.

I also was a keen quiz captain, attending at every opportunity and gathering around me a mean bunch of specialists who won most weeks. They became my close chums - Irish Mike Dunne, Larry Schweitzer, Dave Duckworth, Neil McCormick and Rodrigo who all saved my sanity really because they were real people with real jobs who hadn't befriended me to get free tickets or to bask in my dubious reflected stardom. They didn't give a shit, which was wonderful. What was I doing? Well, on reflection, I was constructing a home life which I had basically never had since I'd left home in the early seventies. A home life that included a ring of pals, who were not in the business. It was what I needed in order to get some perspective on life. Being constantly on the road and only having any sort of social interaction with others in the same profession could and did make me seriously out of touch with 'normal' folk and normal 'standards'. Lets face it; life in rock is not your average way of life, not even for tour managers. When you get back from a long tour, its automatic to ring for room service, then stop yourself when you realise you're at home. That's scary!

I started to plan the new tour in the late fall (see how American I had become. I should be saying bloody autumn, my, how I'd changed). The office had planned it to run for pretty much a full year with brief breaks of two weeks at suitable and logical stops between continents and, naturally for Christmas. That tradition was absolutely unbreakable. The crew were assembled with Charlie as production manager and included

Mickey Lee Soule as Jon's keyboard tech. It was great to see Mickey again who, of course, had first crossed my path with Elf (just in case you'd all forgotten). The tenders for lights, sound, effects, and transport were agreed and contracted and Diane sat down with me to plan this monster from a hotel and airline perspective. We were good to go from January 1996.

The UK saw the first dates after we had rehearsed for four days. We kicked it off at Plymouth Pavilion on a cold forbidding February 15th. The mood inside, however, was very warm and upbeat, the old boys club atmosphere was back with nobody looking over their shoulder to see how a certain guitarist was feeling today. It was a blast and showed in the music, in its exuberance, in the obvious delight of the band to be doing the thing they knew they did so well. We did nineteen shows altogether in the UK, pretty much a record since the very early years when the band was starting out. We finished in London with two nights at the Brixton Academy to great acclaim and where the band could say their farewells to family and friends prior to the 'great trek'. I was very happy to see Carol and David who always turned out to see me despite the long journey from their home, which was now in Cornwall where they were still running the local fisherman's mission. Now we entered Europe for the first run of eighteen dates starting in Ulm, Germany and running on for a further six German shows; then to Rotterdam Ahoy Sportspalais, Brussels National Arena, Paris Zenith, and back into Germany and Austria.

Everything was going so well, too well! I began to feel ill; actually uneasy would be more accurate. I had this weird feeling that my heart had kicked out from its rhythm, its regular beat. I began to feel sweaty, clammy and light-headed. I knew something was wrong. I had not had an illness of any serious description in the last thirty years on the road, but knew instinctively that now something was wrong, terribly wrong. I called the tour accountant, Rick Taylor who came down to my room. He then called one of the German speaking crew who called an ambulance, which whisked me off to the local hospital. There they hooked me up to machines whilst the crew guy translated. The upshot of their diagnosis was 'atrial fibrillation' which basically was that one of the four chambers of my heart was playing up, causing the others to go out of time. I was not getting the full regular beat, more a three-quarter rapid beat which was the heart trying to catch up with itself. "Paicey would be appalled," I thought to myself trying to cheer the inner petrified self.

They gave me medication and suggested that it had been brought on by stress. Me? Stressed? I prided myself on being one of life's laid back ones, to the point of being almost horizontal. The mere fact of their diagnosis made me stressed even more. I sat down in my room to try to analyse the situation. Well, I had slipped back a tad with my drinking habits, maybe that was it? I vowed to go back on the wagon. I told Bruce, well I had to, and true to form he blamed it on the booze despite me protesting that the experts had said it was work related stress. Bruce, who was lawyer, doctor, dentist, banker and shrink all rolled into one, knew better of course. I reiterated that the doctors had confirmed that they had checked me out for booze problems and I had no liver or kidney damage and no high sugar levels, both indicators of a drink problem, but of course Bruce knew better. I didn't tell Bruce that the doctors had suggested I change jobs to which I said, "I can't, it's all I know". "Well, its what has brought you to us" they said softly.

I thought I heard a distant church bell toll mournfully at that point. I pushed it to the back of my mind and carried on, armed with my medication and a strong will to survive. Bruce's concern seemed to dissipate and all returned to normal. The tour continued. At the beginning of April we stopped for eight weeks after a show in Budapest. More a battery recharge break than anything else and I retreated back to the warmth, sunshine and security of Florida. I started taking vitamin pills by the bucket load and played soccer on a regular basis. My healthy glow restored, the tour reconvened in Esbjerg on 30th May to rehearse prior to the rock festival due to be staged over the weekend. Erik Thomsen arranged for us to play the Multihuset, a small private club via local promoter, Søren Holberg. Word soon got out and over 100 fans packed into his tiny club, which was so small the front rows could hand over beers to the band and chat to them in the breaks as they worked out the set list for the upcoming tour. Very intimate!

The next day, Friday, we played, supported by Suzi Quatro, and two other bands that meant little to me then let alone now, Shot Gone and Shu-bi-dua. We stayed at the Scandic Hotel who were a little overwhelmed by it all, but nevertheless treated us all very well. The next day we flew to Berlin on the way to Poznan, Poland. The Berlin Intercontinental is one of the nicest Hotels in the world and I've stayed in quite a few. It was in stark contrast to the Hotel Poznan where we ended up for the first of two shows in Poland on the following days. Life on the road, five star to no star in twenty-four hours - catch your luxury when you can! This run of dates would last two months playing Slovakia, Italy, Sweden, France, Finland and Russia where we played Dynamo Stadium. (Yes, I did resist the urge to run out on the pitch kicking a soccer ball just for the bragging rights). On July 10th we took a month off after playing the Stravinski Auditorium in Montreux. Ah what memories of arrest, love, life and smoke on the water.

Once again I rushed back to Orlando. Was this a subconscious reaction to the heart scare? Get home as quick as possible and return to a normal life with normal routines? Maybe it was just my age for I was now approaching my fiftieth birthday. I had never considered that before. After all being in the rock business allows you to officially be Peter Pan, though staying away from mirrors was always a good call.

With August over too soon, we returned once more to Europe, kicking off in Zurich on September 1st followed by Spain, Slovenia, Italy, the Central Stadium in Kiev in the Ukraine and back to Germany. The last shows were in France before a three-week preparation period for ten shows for Mr. Udo in Japan. We played the Paris Olympia on June 17th where the show was recorded for the 'Live At The Olympia' album. (Took ages to come up with that title!) I was feeling pretty good now. The nervousness about my health had faded and I felt reasonably optimistic that the Grim Reaper had merely tapped on my window and rattled the door, not actually demanded entry. Life on the road returned to our version of normal. The crew were in good shape as was the band. Why this mammoth tour? Well, we now had a guitarist who would work anywhere without question providing the pay cheque was right, he was comfortable and that the prospect of having fun with a great bunch of guys was pretty much guaranteed.

As winter beckoned, we started a short fifteen-date run through Canada and America, which included two shows at the Beacon Theatre in New York. We stayed at The Parker Meridian and after the show we, not unusually, all adjourned to the bar. Ian, who had some guests over, went to his room for 'just a minute'. This minute turned to forty and no Ian. The management came over and discreetly whispered in my ear that Mr. Gillan was stuck in the elevator between floors with a few other guests who numbered a lady, a couple and a room service guy with a tray full of drinks.

After some time the elevator was brought to the lobby where Ian berated me for not getting him down earlier, but his tantrum was short lived when it was pointed out that the tray of drinks, now unsurprisingly empty, would be complimentary. Just how I was responsible for a dodgy elevator was quite beyond me. A week after New York we appeared at the Palace in Auburn Hills, Detroit, Michigan at what can best be described as a rock v rap v metal showdown. We were up against seven other bands of which two were Corrosion Of Conformity and Danzig. It was amazing as we were totally out of place, yet we went down an absolute storm with most of the other bands in the wings watching. I let as many as was practical stand there and then did a rotation system. I just could not believe the admiration and respect there was for the band from these young 'punks'. As we drove the following morning to the airport to fly to Pittsburgh we heard a brilliant review on the radio, which lifted us all to a new level for the rest of the US dates.

Touring now was tiring, of that there was no doubt, but then the guys, apart from Steve, were all approaching fifty, and some had passed that milestone. Hard partying was a thing of the past. It was now a nice meal in the best restaurant followed by a quite drink and a cigar. There were kids to get through college and, for some, grandchildren to fuss over and be concerned for. Life had inevitably changed for them and their needs had perceptibly altered. It wasn't exactly wheelchairs and incontinent pants, but staying healthy was increasingly on the agenda including insuring all the guys little medical problems were addressed. Well, c'mon, everybody's got 'em to a large or lesser degree. Rock stars ain't no different. By this time, my assistant had been axed as, according to Bruce, he would be on tour and would share the load. Nice in theory, but in truth he added to the workload. I could always get more done when he was back in Connecticut. He just, well, meddled. Sorry, Bruce, you just did. The road was a tightly run ship and it ran exactly how I wanted.

This now all changed because, being another 'organiser', he wanted to change things to how he thought they should work, only for him to then disappear for a few days. Bruce's comfort standards were higher than anybodies, so when he was around, the hotel had to be the absolute best there was, despite it being on the wrong side of town to the venue or airport. Bruce's likes and dislikes were paramount, which meant chopping and changing plans that had been worked out and agreed months before. There can only be one 'gaffer' on the road and that was me. Information was everything and increasingly the office in Connecticut didn't give it, so

I had taken to talking to London, to The Agency, run by Neil Warnock, who was looking after us worldwide. There I had befriended Claire Stone and got her to give me the 'heads up' on any new dates and all information as soon as she got it, thus circumventing everyone at Thames Talent who, for whatever reason, just sat on it all. "Later" they would say. Well, "later" inevitably was too late.

Thames Talent was only a three person operation which could not handle all the work it had, so it ended up them doing it all in a, shall we say, less than an efficient manner and it was a Bruce policy to play all cards close to the chest. That was fine with outsiders, but I was an insider. Bruce wanted to break fresh new markets like Indonesia, but this took time with regard to visas and licences. Time I wasn't given until I jumped the loop to Claire, god bless her. When Bruce had his Agency in New York, there was always a secretary I could count on to do itineraries, visa prep and the like. Once it moved to Connecticut and the staff was reduced to just Bruce, Barbara Fucigna and a secretary, then I was saddled with all that work too. Thames just couldn't get their head round the fact that if we wanted the best truck, hotel, flight, lighting and sound deals, we needed time. Four weeks notice left us with whatever trucks were left, whatever sound and light company hadn't got any work which usually meant they weren't the best, whatever airline still had seats instead of the best airline and the hotel that still had rooms instead of the one of choice. It was immensely frustrating, not only for me but also for Diane Murphy, our long trusted and adored travel manager, too.

Eventually I hired the services of a visa agency in New York and London, which the band paid for, just to take the pressure off and ensure they got done properly and on time. Back stage passes were another bugbear. Bruce would nickel and dime these operations to the extent that I took a laminate machine on the road and we made them up ourselves when we ran out, in the production office hours before the next days show. Once again I farmed this out to Perry Passes in Nevada, who then shipped ahead to each location. It was efficient, slick and professional for just a few bucks relatively speaking. Bruce just did not get the plot. Once itineraries were complete, Bruce got a copy and turned them on their head. I always got a budget for hotels, say $150 each per day for the band and $75 each per day for crew. Not great, but with good planning Diane could find pretty good hotels. Bruce soon changed it all, with his much grander idea of the ideal hotel. The airline deals that Diane negotiated were top draw with a careful eye on budget. She always booked the band, Charlie and me on a round the world business ticket and invariably got us bumped to first, yet when Bruce was with us he insisted on a first class ticket regardless of cost. To no ones surprise, the budget went out of the window when Bruce was due on the tour and the band paid every time!

****

After the obligatory Christmas and New Year break, we started a set of dates in South America on 27th February 1997 at the Santa Laura Velodrome in Santiago, Chile followed by three in Buenos Aires, Argentina and eleven throughout Brazil finishing on 25th March in Lima, Peru at the Le Paz Stadium. South America was really opening up to rock bands now, a market forged by the likes of Queen and Elton John. I liked to think Rainbow had been one of the pioneers too.* As we went our separate ways to rest, it seemed that Bruce intended to squeeze the very last drop out of the band from a touring point of view as if he felt the dance would end very soon and someone would call for the last waltz.

Plans began to hatch for a new album and we all returned once more to Florida to Greg Rike Studios to begin the writing process. This was what I loved. Home in my own bed and the band close by recording - bliss. Unstressed, I began to formulate ideas to buy a house in subconscious recognition that I had found my way home. South Shields held nothing for me now other than far away memories. There was after all nobody there to go home to now. I felt I should look forward, not back. I settled back into my normal routine of playing soccer and checking in with the office (and secretly with Claire in London) to see what was being planned. Actually it wasn't much.

The next three months were clear before a couple of festival dates in Europe with a side trip to Beirut in the middle. Now I knew the old road map of most countries was an unknown publication to my office, they'd prove that time and time again, but how can doing three shows of our scale in Germany on July 6th, Lebanon on the 8th and back in Switzerland on the 12th be the move of sane people? Get your atlas out and take a look! Lets forget the expense, what about the logic, wear and tear on the band (forget the crew) and the inevitable lack of impact and a quality show for the fans because of the aforementioned. No, Bruce and doubtless the band, were after a home run money-wise. If the promoters were prepared

---

* In 1996, Blackmore had reactivated Rainbow and played in Chile, Argentina and Brazil.

to pay the big fee, the band would go anywhere, anytime. "Come back, Ritchie, all is forgiven" I thought wistfully, "You'd never have put up with this madness".

On July 5th, I arranged for us all to stay in Baden Baden, Germany and rehearse there in the deserted and disused Hans-Rosband Film Studios as it was sixty kilometres from the first show the next day, but farther enough away to avoid fans and other bands who were jamming up all the decent hotels in Lahr. At the rehearsals some very resourceful German fans managed to sneak in, which was just about acceptable, but then the buggers tried to tape everything, so eviction ensued. At times, they never learn when to stop pushing the envelope.

The first show was the Daytona Festival in Lahr, which had quite an impressive line-up including British rockers Thunder, oldies but goldies John Kay and Steppenwolf, Emerson, Lake and Palmer and a chance to chew the fat with dear old Bruce Dickinson sans Iron Maiden. As is normal in Germany the place was overrun with Hells Angels and other nasty bikers acting as "security". In order to, well, bring some order, I got hold of the promoter and with the help of a runner acquired several cases of Beck's finest ale and, iced down, presented them to the presumed leader of the 'Hitler Helmets'. After a case or three they were totally under my control and things went very smoothly, thank you. To all young aspiring tour managers, I highly recommend this method of getting the upper hand for your charges and sod the financial outlay, just put it down to tour expenses under 'security' although don't expect a receipt!

The whole event actually was a bit dire, as they can be. The dressing rooms were rather poor involving a long walk through an old aircraft hangar, which also included all the back stage catering. That establishment was constantly mobbed by all who had the right or who had blagged their way backstage, but thanks to my 'Becks Boys', Purple were swiftly moved through this melee to the stage and back again and, as a consequence of a virtual stress free warm up, did the business and stormed it as only bill toppers should. A good days work all round, hoorah!

Now for Beirut, which wasn't exactly around the next block. First off we flew Air France the very next day from Strasbourg to Paris which meant checking out of our hotel in Lahr at the crack of night for the 60 km drive to Strasbourg for a 9am check in. Nobody spoke much, who would or could? From Paris we flew direct to, lets face it, a war torn Beirut. Fair play to Bruce, he came too. Most managers would have taken a rain check. We arrived at 7pm and were met, sort of…? We had been promised that all formalities would have been done pre-arrival and that it would go seamlessly. "Just words, dear boy" as Jethro Tull's classy tour manager, Andy Truman, used to say to me many years before.

The immigration official demanded sternly that we "stand over there" whilst he dealt with our passports. As you can imagine that attitude was not popular with everyone, not rock star speak at all. Grudgingly, with much mumbling, the band and crew accepted it. I asked the official nicely not to stamp the passports, especially the American ones. Then I noticed he was about to do exactly that and shouted at him not to do it, shouting, "No, No, No". Bruce looked at me, shocked, and ran over to me asking that I calm down and not cause trouble. I turned on Bruce and nicely, but firmly, told him in a whisper to leave it alone, it was under control. The official, poised in mid stamp, asked if we were ashamed to be in his country. Looking him smack in the eye, I explained that it was not Lebanon that was a problem, it would be his neighbours in Israel as a Lebanese passport stamp would give us real problems getting in there in the future. Surprised, he burst out laughing! He agreed with me and understood my concern, handed back the passports without a stamp and, chuckling, welcomed us warmly to his country.

I learned later that Bruce had told the band, crew and anybody that would listen that he had told me to take the action I had. He sure pissed me off at times! As arranged, four stretch limo's awaited us outside the arrivals hall, all with a black suited armed guard in the front passenger seat and we set off to the city. This road divided the line of fighting, one side was bombed to oblivion whilst the other had neat apartments and banks, pretty much untouched - very surreal. We passed through checkpoints, passing units of marching troops as we headed to our hotel in the hills, the Printania Palace, which was a delight with really welcoming, nice hotel type folk, and no guns. We were, however, warned not to leave the hotel and wander out alone. No problem for me, thank you, although I did steal a glance in Ian's direction as orders not to do something became the irresistible urge to do the very thing he'd been asked not to do, boy's being boy's and Ian absolutely being Ian!

We had a press conference that night in a small club-cum-restaurant that was packed with lots of smiling faces. "This might be great" I mused, as we headed back to our hotel and the bar where we were politely informed that it did not shut for guests all the while there was a guest to serve. I groaned inwardly with the vision of a problem yet to come. The gig was at the Mont La Salle Arena, which was part of the university campus, a red clay outdoor sports field in truth.

The next day around mid morning, I got a call from an amused Charlie asking me to, "Hey, care to pop over and take a look?" I would do this anyway which Charlie well knew, so this intrigued me. It was as I expected and hoped - a free standing stage and some temporary walled, but not covered, dressing rooms. "Check out the bathroom" Charlie said, beaming. I was not too surprised at first glance. A standard toilet in a stall with a piece of cloth stapled over the front as the 'door'. "Look closer," said Charlie, barely suppressing a laugh. The bloody toilet was just standing on the ground connected to nothing at all, no waste pipe or even water tank to flush which, if it had, would have been bloody useless anyway. I summoned the promoters who couldn't really see the problem. I had asked for a toilet, which is what I had plainly got. Mmmmmmmm. I explained carefully the ways of the infidel and his toilet. Charlie went off to find somebody with a shovel who was instructed to at least dig a hole and trench into which a pipe should be inserted to the toilet at one end to take whatever to wherever and add an overhead tank with a running flush to aid said journey of whatever to wherever.

I informed the band of the toilet irregularity and said it would be wise to make themselves as 'comfortable' as possible before they came down for the show and that we would 'do a runner' back to the hotel right after the show. I got 100% agreement, which was an all time record. Funny that! Like all shows in these rock-starved outposts, the reception was amazing and the band reacted accordingly even though it was at least 80° in the moon shade. Back at the hotel the crew returned early as we had only brought a little backline and pretty soon the bar was 'steaming' with band, crew and fans, good beer and great food. Maybe these shows were okay after all. This is what is known in the trade as being lulled into a sense of false security.

The next morning, which would have been July 9th, saw us all up bright and early to fly either back to England for a couple of days at home or to Switzerland where we were due to play an open air festival on the 12th. Ian was going back to Liverpool to the Parr Studios to grab some more time to progress his solo album.* I had arranged, for security reasons that

* Dreamcatcher was released in September 1997 in Japan, October 1997 in the United Kingdom and in May 1998 in the USA.

we all got to Beirut airport at the same time to more or less coincide with the various flights. Having announced the night before the times of the baggage pull and departure, I was pleasantly surprised to see most of the crew at breakfast, although some were a little worse for wear. The band members were up too, as was the norm in the shape of Jon and Paicey who were both traditional early risers. It took quite a few rings to raise a very groggy Roger, but much to my distress, no answer from Mr. Gillan. Several attempts by phone, nothing. I went to his door and undertook much stout banging, still nothing. Now seriously worried, I went down to the front desk to get security to open up his room. As the door opened, there were Ian's cases neatly stacked by the door beside an empty bed, which had not been slept in. Oh shit! Then I remembered the fateful words of the barman the night before "We never close if there is..." Oh crap!

I ran to the bar and there he was along with two of the crew where they had spent the whole night putting the world to rights together with the bartender who also appeared to have invited half his family there too. They were all pretty hammered. I got hold of Charlie to get his wayward crew away to the airport whilst I attended to Ian. He was so shit-faced that nobody would ride with him to the airport except Rick Taylor, our trusty and beloved tour accountant, who would do anything to save the day for me. Ian swayed out to the first limo and got in whereupon two of the band then promptly got out and squashed into the second one. Way to go, Ian! Our singer then fell into a deep slumber.

As we neared the airport, Rick vainly tried to wake him. The limo pulled into 'departures' and Rick got out and walked off abandoning the sleeping passenger. I summoned the porters for the luggage and, on opening the door; Ian fell flat on the pavement, waking in mid descent. I picked him up, assured him all was well and to keep close to me as we went through the various checkpoints. Everyone else of course had made themselves scarce as if Ian was an unexploded bomb, which in a manner of speaking he potentially was. Ian has this capacity, rarely seen in others to pull himself together when it was really badly necessary. This was such an occasion. One deep breath and to the outside world he was as sober as a judge. We breezed through security, Ian smiling benignly at everyone. Once safely through, the strain too much, he reverted to a drunken wreck. Charlie and I separated all the baggage into Swiss bound and England bound. I asked Ian to stay there and not move while I completed check in and got his boarding pass from Louis Ball, our lighting tech who was on the same flight as Ian.

Louis had been detailed to ride shotgun on our boy and asked me where he was. We looked to the empty space that had once held Ian, then looked down to the array of luggage amidst which Ian and one of the crew were now gently snoring, borne on wings of alcohol to some deep, soft slumberland. I looked at Louis and smiling, whispered, "your problem now, old son and good luck". I walked, a relieved man, to the departure gate for Zurich. I learned later that, true to form, Ian pulled himself together enough to make it onto the plane where he promptly fell into a deep sleep once again for the whole journey back to England where he emerged fresh as a daisy eager to see what the brand new day had to offer. I don't know how he does it to this day, but only he seems to have that ability.

The Frauen Feld open air festival in Switzerland on July 12th was part of a three-day affair run by Good News Productions headed up by Andre Bechir who had always done our shows in Switzerland from day one. He's a stand up guy who always has a smile for everyone and never seems to panic. This is probably a testament to his attention to detail, great preparation and having fantastic staff. Lets be honest, rock bands can be a pain in the butt with their constant demands and funny little ways inevitably channelled through guys like me. So when I encounter a promoter who always goes out of his way to satisfy the whims of my 'boys' with a smile not a sigh, its pure heaven. His key people - Sebastian, Gabriel, Daniella Amrhein and of course Astrid are worth a mention and a huge thank you.

The site at Frauenfeld was immaculate. Wooden floors covered not only each dressing room, but all the walkways to and from the stage and the open area surrounded by the dressing rooms. (Don't forget this is in a field!) The dressing rooms were well rotated and cleaned for each band, spotlessly clean bathrooms that was almost a first, and a cleaned walkway to the stage just in case it rained thus avoiding the need for 'wellies'. I parked us all in the Swiss Hotel near by which, although part of a huge chain, was adequate for our needs although some non playing members of our entourage found it lacking in some luxury departments, no prizes for who?

The festival line-up was impressive although we missed most of them, specifically the Rolling Stones who appeared whilst we were getting nervous in Lebanon. We shared our day with Blues Traveller, Stroke, Richie Sambora, and Clawfinger with a guest appearance by Cheryl Crow. Iggy Pop and Björk played the day after followed by Bob Dylan and Joe Cocker the following day. A superb weekend for fans and great for us too as we were still managing to maintain a huge fan following at which, privately, I was increasingly becoming surprised. Purple had been a major force for over thirty years, not quite what they or I had envisaged back in 1972. Ten would have been a bonus back then, twenty quite unthinkable; thirty was in the realms of insanity, yet here we were, large as life. A few laughter lines around the face and the odd grey hair, I grant you. Okay, a lot of grey hair and some of that stayed on the pillow, but all in all we were all in reasonable shape.

With Frauenfeld over with and our fond farewells made with Andre, we went our separate ways before reconvening three weeks later in Western Canada for the Rocky Mountain Jamboree in High River, Alberta, about twenty miles due south of Calgary. It was a catastrophe compared to the efficiency of Switzerland. Everyone from the band to the crew arrived on separate flights. Airport immigration in Calgary was just a nightmare from start to finish. Everything was supposed to have been cleared prior to our arrival by the promoters, but for 'everything' read 'nothing'. It took me the best part of two days camped out at the airport awaiting each flight with Purple people, to ease them through the paperwork. Nazareth were not so lucky and spent the best part of a day the wrong side of the 'glass' awaiting clearance from an unconcerned immigration that almost seemed to take a sadistic delight in prolonging the process. Alas, although sympathetic, Nazareth weren't my problem. A fee was also supposed to have been paid up front by the promoters, but this had not materialised, neither had a detailed performance schedule. Bloody amateurs!

The festival ran for three days. The Friday had Molly Hatchet, my old sparring partners from Rainbow days - Blue Oyster Cult and fresh from immigration - Nazareth. Saturday saw, amongst others, Pat Travers, the obligatory (in Canada only) Bachman Turner Overdrive and the wonderful George Thorogood. On Sunday we appeared, which was a good job considering the hassle of actually getting into Canada, a fact some of you will seem odd as its not exactly third world or Eastern European where you take this type of problem as a given. Canada should be warm and friendly like your mum's kitchen. Maybe, it was just a bad weekend for somebody in charge who decided that those longhaired hippies needed a lesson. A throwback to the attitude of the mid sixties, not the so-called enlightened nineties.

Rick Derringer, Ratt and ELO shared our day, which was beset with Hammond organ problems in the form of a 220-volt feed to a 110-volt organ. Kinda exploded! The local radio came to the rescue with an announcement for anybody locally who could supply one Hammond organ. Some kid called up and the promoter duly dispatched a truck, saving the day. Sitting backstage after the show was a relief. To any outsider, it had gone well, much like a swan gliding over a placid lake: All peace and serenity on the surface whereas beneath, the legs are paddling furiously. I felt much like that swan.

The shows over, the next four months were taken up by the continuing recording of the album to be named 'Abandon' back in Altamonte Springs at Greg Rike Studios. The atmosphere at these recordings was much the same as at concerts. In short, they were fun, relaxed and creative. There were no issues, tantrums, or egos. A considerable change, yet had those very things given past albums their energy, excitement and edginess that had made them so successful? As I sat in the studio watching and listening to the meticulous construction of this next album, part of me sadly thought it a tad formulaic and predictable. With no disagreements and arguments, was the spark extinguished? Just a passing thought from an interested observer.

CHAPTER NINETEEN
FINGERS TO THE BONE

U nusually for Deep Purple, those rascals at Thames Talent decided to break with tradition and fill the run up to Christmas with nine shows in America all played pretty much exclusively in the House Of Blues chain of clubs that had recently sprung up. These were a marvellous change for the band as they were a return to the heady days of large clubs where there could be no hiding place, the audience being right in your face. The rig was cut down and the edge and energy were back. Photographs of the time show the sheer delight on the faces of the guys 'alive' in adrenalin city. We played Orlando on December 6th followed by shows in the clubs of Myrtle Beach, New Orleans (two shows), Chicago (three shows, one of which had the added attraction of Steve's wedding to Jacquie, live on stage, conducted by his father, the minister.) and finally Hollywood on Sunset Strip after Christmas, where we packed out four consecutive nights from the 28th. We finished with one show apiece in Mexico City at the National Auditorium and in San Jose, Costa Rica. Roger then whisked himself away to mix 'Abandon' at Platinum Post back in Orlando.

It was in Orlando, where I would meet and become great friends with Cliff and Kathy Massey. They had flown over just for this show and many others in various parts of the world, spending their entire savings on these trips. They were and are still, truly generous people, as Cliff would often slap down his credit card for a bar tab that included band and crew drinks, but he was there to have fun. They would subsequently come for a holiday to my house in Apopka.

As spring turned into early summer and the tourists began to clog up the freeways to Mickey Mouse Land, the rumblings from Thames Talent and dear Claire back in London were of a massive fifteen month world tour to promote 'Abandon'. There would be breaks between continents and to recharge, but this was to be a mammoth undertaking, not particularly in terms of organisation as that had become almost second nature especially as the crew were a stable, hard working bunch of mature guys who knew each other backwards and could second guess each others move. Rigging and the tear down had become a smooth efficient operation and the running of the show pretty much glitch free.

Long tours really presented problems of a more personal nature. Most of the crew were married with kids, so there were always problems of the 'absent father' nature to work out. You know, kids get into problems with school, other kids, illness and of course their mom, who doesn't have dad there to, well, do the dad things. It would and did bring problems, which inevitably knocked on, first Charlie's door, and then mine. Charlie had his wife Jan on the road with him as our wardrobe lady by this time, so he was a happy contented guy. She was essentially in charge of the bands clothing like cleaning washing and mending. Jan also prepared the dressing rooms to the bands personal liking, which she learned pretty quickly and did very successfully. In fact she was the best we ever had throughout my whole time, thirty years, with the band and that includes Rainbow.

Me, well my domestic situation was non-existent apart from the pub and soccer. I had long ago resigned myself to being 'married' to the band and frankly liked nothing better than to be 'out there' on the road. Being part of a road crew of a major iconic rock act is the closest thing to being the band itself. Yes, it's a massive ego trip, truth to tell. You can be free, young and have a ball even when you're touching fifty and that's a hard gig to give up especially if its all you've ever done since you actually were free and young. As I've said before, you really do not have to grow up, you're Peter Pan. Growing up and being an adult is when you come back off tour, then reality strikes and hard. Marriages are split asunder, relationships head down the gurgler and life gets a bit grim for some. Its cosy out on the road, a large comfort blanket awaits with everything taken care of, usually by me or those who work with me. That's why Jon Lord long ago had dubbed me 'Mother Hen". Could have been worse, I suppose.

During this brief lull, I bought a new house. I had owned my place in Connecticut, but when moving down to Florida I had lost a ton of money in the process. When I'd bought the Connecticut house, it backed onto to virgin woodland with all the accompanying wildlife as in raccoons, squirrels, deer and such like, a regular nature lover's heaven. That was until developers bought the whole shebang and my hideaway became a nightmare and the property value headed south. So I had been reluctant to venture once more into the property market until I found this great place in Apopka, north west of Orlando and close to Greg Rike Studios in Altamonte Springs. Detached with a high vaulted, open space lounge cum kitchen area with a study plus three bedrooms all en suite, it was superb. Massive TV to watch English soccer and I was made up. I also splashed out and bought myself my all time classic dream car - a Ford Thunderbird. Life was good at last. I had been staying in the interim at a rented apartment at Club Esprit in Altamonte Springs where the band also stayed whilst they recorded. This became a bad idea for me, as I was never 'off the clock'. Whilst recording, I was paid just my retainer with no 'per diem', but I was constantly called upon to fetch and carry around the clock. Charlie and I could never relax, especially Charlie as he was always on call to be at the studio no matter what time it was, or how many or few were actually there. Moving into the house improved my 'down time' considerably as I was not within touching distance, so to speak.

I spent most of April and May with Charlie, Diane Murphy and Lisa Ligouri from E.T. Travel in London who did all of our European hotels for us, except when covered by the promoter, fleshing out the itinerary with hotels, flights, freight, truck and coach costs, contracting caterers and all the ancillary backup in each location to keep this caravan a rollin'. Crew had to be mustered and lighting, sound and effects companies tendered. By the end of May in the year of our Lord 1998, we were good to go and flew to the sun kissed Mediterranean, to Turkey in fact, to play two nights at the open-air theatre in Istanbul. It had only been a four-month gap since we last played, so rehearsals were kept short if you can call four days short! The shows went really well, a blast in fact. The venue was comfortable and the crowd went wild, starved as they were of seeing major rock acts. The hotel was however a big surprise.

Although a Hyatt Regency, I usually don't expect much from the name if it's out in the 'boonies' so to speak. This was great, however, very luxurious, which should have set off alarm bells. I asked the hotel to make out separate bills for each room, which were guaranteed to my own American Express card, both room cost and incidentals. Normal practice, really. On departure $13,000 was charged to my account, which Thames would always cover, but thirty days later they ran my card through again with another $13,000 and I was of course long gone. No wonder the place was luxurious!

The office asked me why I hadn't paid the first bill on departure to which I showed them the copy of the original with a zeroed balance. The annoying postscript to this tale is that I had to sort out the problem with the help of American Express, not the office who were quite unconcerned. After all it wasn't their credit card. Had it been, all hell would have broken loose. Another big surprise, Cliff and Kathy showed up out of the blue; bless 'em, to see their favourite band in an unusual setting. What an expense that must have been for them, but Cliff just used to shrug and say, "It's all really worth it mate!" Of course by now, he no longer had to worry about buying any tickets, as anyone who would go to such expense in support of their heroes, deserved the star treatment themselves.

On then to Italy for five shows, with a side hop to the island of Malta. Great place, great hotel, great show, great people! The standout show in Italy was the Monsters of Rock show in Turin on 13th June. The cast included Uriah Heap, Status Quo and Suzi Quatro who did surprisingly well, as she was more pop than rock, but that's Italians for you. Suzie's pert arse in clinging leather flicked most of their switches, so I guess the term 'monster' had a slightly different connotation. Those Italians! Without pausing for breath we then launched ourselves into Europe doing seventeen shows in thirty days through Germany where we used, just for the change, personal Merc's for the band and crew. We then stormed like some marauding army into Poland, Austria, Hungary and France finally calling it a halt in Frauenfeld once again with Andre (had it been a year?) Christ, my life was in overdrive!

I returned to Apopka for a recharge, as the next leg would be stateside. Now usually American tours for Purple last four months, but unusually and pointedly there were only nineteen shows in three weeks, a sure indication that the bands star was waning in this part of the world. The shows kicked off at the PNC Art Center in Holmdel, New Jersey on a warm summer evening at the start of August and continued up and down the East Coast through Connecticut, Massachusetts, New York and Pennsylvania. We did three days in Canada before heading on down into the mid west through Ohio, Minnesota and Wisconsin. The US dates ended in Vegas where we played the Hard Rock Casino, prior to finally winding down at the Universal Amphitheatre in Los Angeles. A reformed Emerson, Lake and Palmer supported us on all the American dates. It was very pleasing to see the longevity of rock legends like ELP reaffirmed, the music almost eternally popular, the fans nicely ageing like a good wine right alongside the band.

Bruce obviously wanted to milk this tour for all it's worth. With a brief two-week gap to rearrange visas, get the washing done, pay personal bills at home and get replacements for some of the crew who had bailed out, I then had to sort out fresh itineraries with Diane and Lisa before we schlepped it back to Europe, to Madrid to be exact for five weeks of dates involving twenty-six shows. Three days in, we played the Coliseum in Lisbon, Portugal. Diane rang to say that she just could not fix a decent hotel and that she had booked us, with the help of the local promoter, onto a cruise ship berthed at the docks. Well, that was a first! The GIS Planet Conference was in full swing in the city, which jammed up all the hotels not only with attendees, but with an immense crowd of protesters from anti-whaling, anti-logging, anti-everything, environmentalists and just about anybody who had a beef about the destruction of Planet Earth.

It passed us by like so many other issues, cocooned as we have always been in our warm blanket of the rock business, never really peeping out at the world at large to see what ordinary folk were up too. Shameful really! The downside was that I got stiffed twice again with the accommodation bill. This was becoming a habit! The cruise line went bust afterward too, so the money could not be recovered directly although the nice folks at American Express did cover it. Once again, I got no help from you know where! They directly blamed Rick Taylor, who was far from blame. I was with him when he checked out at the purser's office, where he paid cash in local currency. He got a small, but signed and stamped receipt, but the cruise ship charged the whole thing to my American Express card as well, having used it for credit purposes at check in.

From Portugal we criss-crossed Europe with no particular logical geographical game plan other than chasing the next dollar. We finally ended up with four shows in England - Wembley Arena, Birmingham NEC, Glasgow Clyde Auditorium and Manchester MEN Arena. With eighteen days now to kill it was always a toss up whether to head for home in Florida or hang around in England. Yup, Florida won! Charlie and Jan, Steve Morse and I all lived in the same neck of the woods, literally, with Charlie no more than five minutes away from my place. Eighteen days was barely enough time to turn round, but it was still the preferred option. Nothing beats your own bed after all.

November would be the last set of dates in that year and inevitably they were back in Europe where the bands popularity just did not shrink. Sixteen shows in twenty-three days was not a bad stretch particularly for the band although its still fairly sleepless for the crew who pretty much hunkered down in the crew buses the whole time. These are in reality motels on wheels with bunks, a lounging area, kitchen and bathroom. It can get a bit ripe in there at times even though they are well appointed, but they ain't hotels, so when there's a day or two break, the nearest hotel with a proper bed becomes an oasis of soaking in a tub and hanging loose at the bar. We started with five shows in France, followed by Germany and then up into what was the old Soviet 'block' with shows in Prague, Moscow, St Petersburg, Bucharest, and Sofia, Bulgaria. A fantastic reception at all by fans that still see little of the rock icons such as Purple that they hear on radio.

****

By the first day of December I was home for Christmas and New Year with a lady in my life, Diana Love, (Yes, real name!) and her son by a previous marriage, Conrad. Well, I never said I had become a monk!

No shows until mid March when we were due to hit South America and then Australia, the whole deal set to last two months. South America is the sort of territory that you kinda look forward to going to, but once you get there you remember why you were keen to leave the last time. It was hot and steamy, and that was just the women! The shows were sell outs and as usual the band were oblivious to the constant stress of first getting the money and second hanging on to it. The first shows I'd done years before were, if you recall, ones where I got the cash and stuffed into my clothes.

Thankfully, by the late nineties, technology had eased the situation with money transfers and the like. There was still the problem of onsite merchandising which would always be a cash business, but thankfully box office receipts came in the form of bank drafts, not sacks full of money, much to the disappointment of many! We arrived in Via Funchal, Brazil on March 19th 1999 for three shows followed by four more shows including the Metropolitan in Rio. We then flew across the continent to Santiago, Chile for one show and then, you guessed it, back across that continent yet again to Buenos Aires, Argentina for the last three shows. Thankfully, I was aided once more by the ever loyal and brilliant Alfredo de Iluiis, who, although employed by the promoter, had all of my and the bands interests at heart.

Australia was twelve days away, but Ian Gillan fancied a bit of relaxation before the shows were due to start, so he, trusty tour accountant

Rick Taylor and myself flew into Coolum near Brisbane a few days ahead of the rest of the merry band to take in some golf, swimming and general 'gazing to the heavens doing jack all under a balmy sun' type things. The Hyatt Resort had agreed to provide free golf lessons and free accommodation providing they could have a small logo behind Ian or the band in any TV interviews. It was a fair swap, so Ian agreed. Drew Thompson who worked independently with Bruce on videos and Australian releases of CD's etc. had set up the whole thing.

Well, it rained for most of our planned four-day break, but golf was played, although Ian quickly got bored and stayed at the nineteenth most of the time. Rick and I rented a four-wheel drive truck and went for a drive up to Fraser Island along Fourteen Mile beach, which is what it says it is. We drove for miles without seeing a living soul, which was quite eerie. When you meet another vehicle coming the other way you must indicate which side you will drive to pass each other. It has been known for there to be 'head-ons' on this stretch with absolutely no one else around. We passed a truck doing sixty and us doing the same. A one hundred and twenty mile crash out there is not survivable, folks.

I loved it, the freedom, the absence of phones, the band, Bruce, especially Bruce. We came upon a shipwreck at the north end of the beach where an enterprising chap had set up a burger and hot dog bar. He was literally the only game in town for miles, except there was no town, and made a small fortune. He asked "Where yer headed? "Around the point and up to Fraser Island". He looked concerned and amused at the same time and tried to conceal a throaty chuckle at us dumb tourists. "Well if you take my advice, back track a couple of miles, cut into the bush to the main highway and head up to Fraser that way." "Why?" we asked so innocently. "Cos the fuckin' tides coming in and it's claimed way better outdoorsmen than the likes of yous two!" We smiled and said our goodbyes, feeling about two inches tall.

Later that day, having naturally taken his advice we stopped at a local bar which had a wall devoted to photos of the poor shmucks and their wrecked trucks, battered on the rocks at that point by the incoming tide who had, perhaps, not heeded the hamburger guy's advice (or maybe he hadn't given it) - there's a thought. Once back at The Hyatt, we packed, collected Ian and headed west to Perth to hook up with the rest of the party, ready to open at the Burswood Dome where we were supported by The Ian Kenny Band.

Peter McCrindle was working with me on behalf of Aldo Lennard, the promoter and Pete is the typical unshakeable Aussie. He sure made any tour a pleasure to work and could get anything, anytime, anywhere. It was never a bother (although it just must have been.) Perfect guy to be in the rock business. We moved on to Adelaide, supported by Freight Train and then Melbourne, supported by Smokin' Joker, where the proceedings were recorded for a 'live' album. Sydney, Brisbane and Newcastle followed, all supported by the great FOXC. I still chat to Colin from that band on occasion. By 27th we were done and headed for Kuala Lumpur to play a one-off at the Shah Alam Stadium. No big deal, almost a yawn really. We were like a well-oiled machine (as in efficient, not pissed, or there again...), it was business in every sense of the word and maybe that was the start of the problem at this point. The 'show' was efficient, loud, predictable and well received. Another day at the office, so to speak. We headed home for a four-week break.

Whilst in Australia, Jon Lord had expressed a desire to revisit his "Concerto". Bruce, I assume, thought it a reasonable idea and prompted him to develop the notion. The trouble was that Jon needed to get involved with a classical conductor with whom he could progress the thought. They mulled over some names but nothing concrete seemed to come up. It was later on, on a tour bus somewhere in Europe, that I suggested my nephew Paul who by now was conducting at a very high level with the London Symphony Orchestra and New York Ballet to name but two. Now that is high level in anyone's book, but I got a look of derision from Ian that I still remember to this day as if to say, "Fuck off, Harty. How can anyone from your family be anywhere close to being what we want"?

Jon, bless him, who had met my Paul many times over the last twenty odd years, had seen him growing up, watched his musical career develop, was keen and sent the manuscripts off to him. The original music had long been missing and had it not been for one Marco de Goeij, who had over the course of many, many months, taken the time to write the concerto, note for note from listening, yes, listening, to the original, all of this may never have happened! Thanks Marco. I had taken the precaution of phoning Paul to expect the package. Paul, a serious classical musician had always loved Purple and especially Jon, who, of course, is also classically trained. He jumped at this opportunity to try something fresh.

Whilst Paul and Jon kept in constant touch, we toured further and the plans where hatched for the concert with Paul and The London Symphony Orchestra. It gave me a huge buzz to think of what was to transpire. My nephew up there with Deep Purple. Respect, that's what it gave me. Eat your heart out, Ian who, it must be said, later revised his opinion about my nephew. Whatever misgivings he may have had about him initially soon went away and he couldn't have been more supportive. Shortly after the Albert Hall concerts, he even went with Jon to Bournemouth to see him conduct Elgar with the Bournemouth Symphony Orchestra.

CHAPTER TWENTY
OH LORD!

From June 4th, we started a thirty date European Tour which would take a sedate fifty-seven days. Quite pedestrian really compared with past dashes. Maybe it reflected the age of us all. Mid fifties and what you once rushed took a little longer and conversely what used to take a nice long time was now over in a flash. The perversity of life, eh! Save to say the tour went well. Pointless me mentioning everywhere we played, just think of past tours and you won't go far wrong. Except for one. Milan, Italy. Jörg Phillip, the owner of Beat The Street Bus Company, a fine man and the band driver, who helped me every which way he could on all our jaunts together, was behind the wheel as usual.

As we rolled into the car park of the hotel in Milan, I was riding in the shotgun seat of the coach ready to oversee check in. Jörg pulled around the back and I got out leaving him, as usual, safely behind the wheel, awaiting the bellmen for luggage. I alerted reception to the imminent big influx of guests. When I got back, Jörg was gone, distracted by a hotel employee who beckoned him to the door. My briefcase, which I had left behind his seat, was gone. It had my life in it - credit cards, contracts, and schedules, not to forget a considerable amount of my own and some of the band's money. My heart went into overdrive. I hurriedly looked all over the interior of the coach and even underneath it and then once more, slowly and carefully and in greater panic did it again. I saw Jörg and asked him, inwardly praying, if he had picked it up. No chance. He said an Italian guy from the hotel had summoned him to the front door. Whilst he did, his mates raided the front of the coach for what they seemed to know would be in that case.

We later learned that the hotel had the whole thing on surveillance cameras, but the police calmly pointed out that this was and still is a common crime in Italy with tour coaches and any chance of recovery was unlikely, even though we had these assholes on video. I started to get out of breath and panic set in. This was all I needed. Bruce was sympathetic on the surface, but I felt I had blotted my copybook big time with him. I got rip roaring blotto.

I spent hours on the phone cancelling bank accounts, calling credit card companies to arrange replacements. My ill-feeling and unease would not go away and I could feel myself getting worse, my heart seemingly wanting to burst out of my chest, as in the film 'Alien'. "Please God, not a heart attack, not now" I pleaded to the chap upstairs with the long white robe and flowing beard who I had rarely spoken to through out my entire life. Why would he take my call now? Trying to hide it from everyone compounded the feeling of being decidedly unwell. Charlie, I think, knew how bad I felt and bless him took the load. The next morning I had to get up really early and fly to London to get visas for our upcoming dates in South Korea, and was I suffering badly. Colin Claydon, of Traffic Control, my British Visa Company, met me. Thankfully, he didn't need me to accompany him, so I rested up in a Heathrow Hotel awaiting his return and flew back to rejoin the band in Rome. Thankfully, Jörg's insurance covered all the missing loot and the major loss was a ring that I had made to fit me, melted from the gold of both my mam and dad's wedding rings. That I miss to this day.

A third of our European shows were in Germany and, over many years we always got a welcome visitor back stage when we were close to Hamburg - Jürgen Richard Blackmore, Ritchie's son by his marriage to Margit, his first wife.* He had always lived and grown up in Germany with his mother apart from the first four years of his life. After the marriage broke up Margit returned to her native Germany with young Jürgen. For reasons unknown, Ritchie pretty much ignored him. Despite that, Jürgen would always be there at German shows through first early Purple days, then the Rainbow days, even though many times his father would not see him. Cozy, Roger and I would always make him welcome with his young mates and sometimes with Margit too and get them seats where they could see the old man strut his stuff. When Purple reformed he would always come around, growing now and playing impressive guitar too. He definitely has his father's talent and had a band in Germany called Iron Angel up to a few years ago.

Once Ritchie left the band, the friendship he had forged with us held firm and Jürgen now thirty-five would show up, hang out with us, and then

* Blackmore married Margit Volkmar on 18th March 1964. Jürgen Richard was born 7th October 1964.

disappear into the night until the next time the circus came to town. He was and is a happy, well-adjusted young man, one that any father would be proud of. I know the question that's on your lips, but I have no answer. Ritchie has, I guess. Jürgen pretty much considers he has no father now, but I believe that's just to cover the hurt of the old bastard's rejection.

It stems from a show we played with Purple in the last days of Ritchie's tenure. By that time I had been instructed by Ritchie not to let Jürgen into any venue, but I ain't that heartless and would always leave him an 'Access All Areas" pass at the door and sneak him into the backstage hospitality area to meet the rest of the band. Safest place really as that was the last place Ritchie would make an appearance! I believed Ritchie felt Jürgen and Margit only wanted his money, but in truth the lad only wanted to see his father. All Ritchie allegedly ever gave him were some amps, cabinets and a guitar. (For any aspiring guitar fan, that would be riches beyond measure, but we're talking father and son here!) On a couple of occasions I had to lie to Jürgen regarding his fathers whereabouts, which I was not comfortable with, but Ritchie was my employer in Rainbow days after all, so what choice did I have? On this particular occasion, Ritchie requested a different hotel to Purple, The Four Seasons, whilst we stayed at The Ramada Renaissance. Jürgen called as usual and I told him he would be on the guest list with his girlfriend and to come back stage after the show.

Ritchie sent his personal roadie, Rob Fodder down to the venue in the afternoon to scope the dressing room situation. Well, The Hamburg Sporthalle has only so many rooms and they were all assigned, but Rob was on a mission to find somewhere out of the way. There was a small gymnasium one floor down from the arena that we used to house the empty road cases during the show. Rob spent a couple of hours erecting a 'dressing room' from these road cases and gym floor mats. I fell about laughing when I saw it, but, hey, if that's what Ritchie wanted... so be it. Ritchie arrived at the venue just before showtime and virtually went straight onstage. After the show he was straight out the back door into a limo and back to The Four Seasons where he checked out and disappeared to who knew where. Jürgen was visibly upset at his father's thoughtlessness and for the first time in our company shed tears. The rest of the band did their best to console him and after a while he composed himself and said that from that day he 'had no father'. Since then Jürgen still came around when we were in the area and has struck up a close friendship with Steve Morse, the two of them chatting for hours about the guitar and music in general.* Boy, Ritchie what were you thinking, what the hell motivates you? Oh, well.

Our tour ended at the end of July and Jon went back to London to prepare for the "Concerto" concert scheduled for the 25th and 26th September at The Royal Albert Hall, London. Paicey, on the other hand, went to play with Paul McCartney! Not unlike a summons from God, really. He was flown to LA first class, naturally, for a one-off charity performance alongside such other luminaries as Dave Gilmour. Typically, our drummer boy traded in his ticket for cash and flew on his frequent flyer miles! Well, you would, wouldn't you? Later in the year, he played with Macca again at Liverpool's Cavern Club and on BBC TV, both times doing numbers from The 'Run, Devil, Run' album. Paicey, I know, was seriously chuffed to have been asked and to fulfil an impossible dream. Well, we all have our heroes!

The Albert Hall "Concerto" proved to be an absolute 'beast' to put together as there were so many musicians involved. We rehearsed at the Ritz Courtyard studios, in Putney, London with my nephew Paul Mann there the whole time. Getting the rotation right was problematic, the brass section, the backing singers, the guest musicians, all getting their bits right. It was a constant revolving door of getting people back and forth from the hotel with just Charlie and me as the 'sheep dogs'. Then we had extensive meetings at the very staid Royal Albert Hall to get them to open up extra dressing rooms for the huge cast we had assembled. They weren't keen especially as we were "rock n' roll".

Eventually we pulled all the strands together and it went off very well, despite the nightmare of getting all the 'guest' and normal musicians to and from the Albert Hall on time. Bruce did allow me to recruit Willie Fyffe, who was Ronnie James Dio's personal assistant, to help me out with the driving as even he could see it was a bit bigger than a normal Purple show. I also had much appreciated help from Alison Hussey, who was our English liaison person right from the concept of the project, and who did a great, yet thankless job throughout, even running to get music copied among the other mundane bits and pieces so necessary to the success of the overall concert. It was in two halves with the "Concerto" in the second half of the concert with all the solo stuff in the first. It was originally planned to put the concerto in the first half but this was changed

* Jürgen Blackmore actually performed on stage with Deep Purple in Hamburg on 27th November 2010 joining them for 'Smoke On The Water'.

during the rehearsal week and gave a better overall shape to the show.

The set list was as follows:-

Orchestra: Malcolm Arnold Four Scottish Dances (it was felt appropriate to include something by the man who had made it all possible first time round - the revised version of the concerto is dedicated to him - he was invited to the 1999 concerts but ill health made that impossible.)
Jon Lord: Pictured Within (with Miller Anderson) / Wait A While (with Sam Brown) (with orchestra)
Roger with Ronnie James Dio: Sitting In Dream / Love Is All (Butterfly Ball) (with orchestra)
Ian Gillan with Steve Morris: That's Why God Is Singing the Blues / Via Miami
Steve Morse Band: Take It Off the Top / Night Meets Light (with orchestra)
Paicey: Wring That Neck

INTERVAL

Concerto For Group And Orchestra
Purple Set: Ted The Mechanic (Purple alone), Watching The Sky, Sometimes I Feel Like Screaming, Pictures Of Home, Smoke On The Water (all with Orchestra, Ronnie and entire company.)

It might also be worth making the point that the first orchestra rehearsal on the concerto took place exactly thirty years to the day from the 1969 performance.

In addition to the special guests mentioned in the set list, we also had Miller Anderson along for the ride. Dave La Rue and Van Romaine also rounded out the Steve Morse Band. Ian Gillan did his individual pieces with Roger, Steve Morris, and the rest of the band and Paicey did a piece from his 'big band' stuff. My family, in the form of Carol and David were there of course to see me and most importantly, their son Paul conduct the orchestra and Deep Purple. Dick and Di were there too, just to make my family inner sanctum complete. George Harrison and his wife Olivia were the VIP guests of the evening and once again I got to chat with my hero. Nice sometimes, isn't it?

It was a great event, of that there was no doubt and then, of course, Bruce made plans to take it out on tour. My heart sank, not because it wasn't a great idea, one that would be very successful, but I just knew Bruce had no perception of the work it would entail and how that would impact on myself and Charlie to organise and take this whole enormous caravan on the road without a considerable back up of assistants.

Thankfully, in the meantime, we had a considerable break for three months on the lead up to Christmas followed by a further three months before we did six shows in Japan and then one in Seoul, Korea. It was the usual deal, Mr. Udo, full houses, great shows, nuff said. These were followed, for no particular reason other than a big cheque, with shows in Finland, Russia, Greece and Switzerland. This was to become the norm now. Purple would do shows so long as somebody waved sufficient money in their direction. Gone now were the days of a certain time off, then time to write and record the next album followed by a worldwide tour to promote said album. After all, the official 'Abandon' tour was long over.

Three months later in July, we returned to Switzerland to make an appearance at the Montreux Jazz Festival followed by a silly show in Vigo, Spain just to make the trip worth our while financially. Madness to get everything geared up for a one-off, after all. The return from Vigo was hell as the weather closed in and the incoming flight was diverted. We waited in departures. The English contingent managed to get a flight, but those New York bound chaps like me, kicked their heels for quite a while. Eventually we made it back to Florida totally knackered with our baggage who knew where? The joys of intercontinental travel.

****

Plans were now being finalised for the 'Concerto' tour or "The Albert Tour" as it became known. It was due to kick off in Buenos Aires, Argentina on September 1st. Not everyone agreed to, or indeed could, make the trek. Happily dear old Ronnie and sidekick Willie did come and, although it was agreed Willie would undertake the gig as assistant to me, he was never around right when I needed him, his duties for Ronnie always taking precedence. It was immensely stressful. Looking after my lads, Deep Purple, was a full time job. Add a full orchestra, singers and itinerant 'guests' plus of course a demanding manager and it began to tell on me. Not in any visible way, but the tiredness of any day was still there the next morning and it was dragging me down.

After much pleading Bruce eventually agreed for me to take on an assistant in the form of one Alfredo De Iuliis, who as mentioned before was Brazilian, and had always been a great help in South America where he had been our local tour manager. If I say so myself, Alfredo, Charlie and I made a very difficult job look easy. All Bruce cared about in truth was where he was staying and was the hotel good enough for him. These South American dates were made harder by the fact that it was a different orchestra in each country, which meant rehearsal days prior to concerts. We did two shows in Buenos Aires, three in Sao Paolo, Brazil ending with two in Mexico City. My Paul was terrific, taking to this business to the manner born, but then large orchestras were the norm for him, unlike me.

With a two-week gap, the tour moved to Europe, this time with an orchestra that would stay with us, the Cluj Philharmonic managed by George Enescu, from Romania, for the whole trip of twenty-two shows in thirty-five days. We enlisted a trio of ladies for backing vocals on this tour, led by Karen Melis, who were all from Belgium, which was handy, as the opening show was in Antwerp. We rehearsed there for a couple of days prior to the show and were joined by a new tour accountant, Tim Hook, who quickly became one of the gang, his mild outward persona disguising a chap who could 'hang with the best of 'em on days off or on overnight bus trips. Tim and I got along great and he was an enormous help in many ways throughout the tour.

Paicey, for some reason best known to himself, had got an agreement with Audi Cars for the all band to travel across Europe in courtesy cars - very grand. We were taken to the pick up point where a mad scramble took place for the best cars. Paicey, the dealmaker, naturally got the best - an Audi A5, which he hoped to have to himself. Then there were two A4's and a station wagon affair. Paicey whispered in my ear that I should take the latter as no one else would. "Why?" "Just do it," he said conspiratorially. I took the keys and attached my name to the tag. "Why" I asked him again as we started up beside each other. "Because it goes like hot shit off a wet shoveeeeeelllllllll…" he said, his voice, trailing away into the distance as he sped off.

I put pedal to metal and Jesus H, it whacked me back into the leather as it rocketed after the drummer. This was going to be fun. As always there was a downside to personal cars. At hotels, the band would merrily drive up to the front doors, jump out and saunter to the bar whilst the care worn tour manager, yours truly, in the absence of valets, had to park the buggers! Just took a slight edge off the driving from gig to gig bit, just ever so slightly. Lazy bastards! Of course when they wanted them again… don't ask! My vehicle naturally became the luggage car, which was fine by me as there would only be enough room for me (and the luggage)

- peaceful bliss.

The crew and orchestra, meanwhile, followed on in large tour coaches. The musicians seemed all at sea at first and took a little time to settle down. They complained a lot, especially about the travel arrangements as to who travelled with who. Feeding them too was a problem as they originally were left off the budget in that department, but happily our regional promoters dug a little deeper in to their coffers and nobody starved. From Antwerp we headed northeast to Hamburg. From there we left the cars in the care of the German promoters and we flew up via Denmark and Sweden to Hell in Norway for the first of three shows in, lets us say, Scandinavia, the other two being in Gothenburg and Stockholm, Sweden. Hell was great, actually. Lovely promoter, Knud Morten Johansen and his crew were superb. We then trekked back to Hamburg to grab the cars and headed to Berlin, Prague, Zwickau (Germany), Luxembourg, Strasbourg and into Germany. The hardworking Alfredo unfortunately left us in Prague to fly home to his seriously ill father and unsurprisingly was not replaced - more pressure. The rest of the crew played a blinder though from Louis Ball on lights, Moray McMillin with front of house sound and Rob Hodgkinson in particular, on monitors which was a tricky task at best as Ian always refused wedges, preferring them to be flown overhead which meant a tricky mix in the side fills. The whole crew pulled hard on this tour, bless 'em all.

On the run from Poland to Zwickau in Germany, I had to drop Alfredo at Prague airport, so I decided to use a remote little used border crossing which would entail back roads, but a shorter drive. I was tootling along at around 80mph on a two-way blacktop when I saw headlights fast approaching in my mirror. "Shit, it's the cops," I thought. The car flew past me, doing 110mph at least, with Paicey at the wheel, hair flowing free and one finger aloft. When I got to the border, he was long gone, but there stood the two orchestra coaches with the entire luggage out and musicians wandering around wishing they had taken another gig altogether. Bloody rock 'n' rollers! When they saw me, they waved frantically, the obvious savour to their plight on hand at last.

The border guards also saw me, but in a different light and my luggage was set upon with glee. The Romanian orchestra looked on in dismay. The sniffer dogs, well, sniffed and the x-ray machines scanned before the rather disappointed guards let us load up again. Seemed the cultural visas they had were not acceptable (probably never seen them before) but should have allowed them free passage. Impasse. Nothing for it, out came the T-shirts, baseball caps and any other visa waiver merchandising and, miraculously, we were free to go. On reflection, my back-road detour had saved the show in Zwickau. Had I not happened by, the orchestra would still be there to this day. Paicey apparently had just blasted straight through the checkpoint, as I had all the luggage… little bugger. One last note on the subject of our cuddly drummer concerning this cast of 'thousands' on the "Albert Tour". One sunny morning over brekky, Ian turned to Paul and said quite straight faced, "How do you keep 100 people together with that little white stick? I can't keep these four fuckers together with two". How true, how true.

****

Now, Brian Johnson of AC/DC fame was and is a great old pal, having first met up with him when we were jumped-up teenagers back in Newcastle and he was fronting the much-undervalued band 'Geordie' and I was still lugging amps for 'Toby Twirl'. Our paths have crossed many times, since those innocent days, as his fame has soared with those wild colonial boys of his. Mine has taken me around the globe countless times. He lived at this time in Sarasota, Florida, not far from me in Apopka and had still not lost his thick guttural Geordie accent and why should he.

Well, as this tour made it to Germany and the Schleyer Halle in Stuttgart, we stayed at the ever so posh Intercontinental Hotel and unbeknownst to me, AC/DC were due to play the city the day after us, 18th October. As I walked into the hotel lobby to reception, which, if you know the place, is a short walk with a piano bar way off to the right, dead classy, I heard the mating call of all Geordies the world over. "Hey yer fukka", very loud, very unmistakeably Johnson! "What the fuck are yoos deein heor?" at full volume. Such decorum, us Geordies are known for it. The lobby was stunned into silence. Teacups rattled, monocles fell from startled ageing Prussian eyes, small dogs shat themselves. A hundred or more German businessmen turned to look at these two specimens of English manhood. Brian just smiled at the mayhem he'd just caused and waved whilst I just shook my head with shock and pleasure at seeing the old git again.

I quickly checked in and got back to the bar ready to invite him to the show along with Angus Young who was grinning broadly beside him. Brian, a bit red faced I thought, enlightened me further also rather loudly, "Phwaor I'm a bit flushed - Newcastle just won - I just had to have a little wank". Geordie charm, nothing like it. Brian and Angus are both diminutive chaps next to my six feet three, but they have hearts as large as any NFL defensive linebackers. So, accompanied by their tour manager Mike Kidson and one or two others, they came to the show, where I had secured them their own dressing room, filled with white wine, as requested by Mike. They enjoyed and went on their merry way. They sure had come a long way to great success since the Rainbow days and hadn't changed a bit. Wonderful!

The tour slogged on to Zurich, Madrid and to Italy. We had dropped the cars and were once more flying in and out of the remaining cities, which were too far to drive, except for the poor crew, of course, who had to endure endless bus hours. I bade a fond farewell to the orchestra after the show in Katowice and said my private goodbyes to Paul, ever the proud uncle. He had vindicated me a million times over for recommending him to Jon and Bruce and for flying in the face of ridicule from Ian. I would mentally 'flip the bird' in Ian's direction many times after that despite his 'about face' in his opinion of my nephew. We carried on for two more shows in Minsk, Belarus and Riga, Latvia. The band and crew had decided to travel together by bus, as flying would have been a nightmare. However, the perceived nightmare followed us onto the bus, which had become very crowded now by adding band, Bruce and me to the full compliment of crew. The ride was long and bumpy, but we all made the best of this close encounter with each other, despite there being the odd muttering of "Harty's fault" to which by now I was quite immune. The border crossings were a hoot. Everyone wanted photos, T-shirts, and even a tour of the bus, much to the derision of the 'sweaty bodies' on board.

The tour of the outer limits of earth complete, I returned to Florida much relieved and quickly got my life back to some semblance of normality. The next tour dates would not be until March when we would hit Australia, Malaysia and China before doing some more orchestra dates in Japan.

CHAPTER TWENTY-ONE
INTO THE... FIRED!

My home had become everything to me and, once there, my social life picked up quite nicely too, thank you. (Diana, by now, had grown tired of my life on the road and we had split up; same old, same old!) I played football, now by choice, and hung out with Charlie and the guys. Golf, too, had been added to my repertoire of sports and every weekend I would head off with my chums, most of whom were not in the business, to a chosen course at the crack of dawn to merrily bash our way round in a semi-serious way. Yes, crack of dawn for those of you who reside in colder northern climes. You see, you have to try and get round before the sun gets high around noon - way too hot for white English boys. Florida courses have one overriding advantage over the more 'correct' ones elsewhere. Yes, the weathers great, that's a given.

However one neat difference that hasn't yet been adopted by The Royal and Ancient is that at every hole or so, a buggy will appear at the tee with a young blonde in appealing scant attire, blinding white even teeth and tan, dispensing liquid to the thirsty golfers. Yes, of course, alcoholic beverage would be amongst her cargo and by the time we made the eighteenth, some of us would be often, shall we say, more than a little happy rather than fatigued. Ah, golf in Florida! The doctor checked me out too. I was apparently fine, although a small, frightened voice murmured inside my head that that might well have been quite a different story had I been checked back in Milan. He just told me to not get stressed. Yeah, right!

Plans set and itinerary fixed, travel booked and equipment hired, we flew to Melbourne for some promotion work for the start of a run of seven shows in eleven days which would begin on March 5th 2001 in Perth at The Entertainment Centre. Aldo Lennard, as usual, promoted the tour, with the very able support of Pete McCrindle, his tour manager. This time the tour would include a brass section and backing vocalists. The brass section were, Greg Maundrell, trumpet. Charles MacInness, trombone and Paul Williamson on saxophone together with the trio of easy on the eye female backing vocalists, Billie Stapleton, Angela Stapleton and Natalie Miller, hence the rehearsals.

While in Melbourne, we were to perform at the Formula One Grand Prix motor race on qualifying day, to do two or three numbers. We did 'Highway Star', 'Black Night', 'Smoke On The Water' and appropriately (enthusiastically egged on by F1 boss Eddie Jordan), 'Speed King'. Eddie was an extremely nice chap and turned up again some weeks later at our gig in Malaysia. On this leg of the tour we took on a new tour accountant, one Ian 'Spider' Digance who very quickly got close to Bruce and would always be at his side ready to do anything that Bruce might demand. Australia is a huge country for those who haven't been, as wide as America with three time zones. Everybody lives around the edges, so doing shows entails an enormous amount of travelling mostly by air.

After Perth in Western Australia, we played Adelaide, Melbourne, Sydney, Wollongong, Newcastle and finally Brisbane on March 15th. Special mention here for Aussie rocker Jimmy Barnes who showed up in Wollongong and Newcastle and made brief appearances on stage at the end of the show. The crowd went nuts. Jimmy played in a band called Cold Chisel and really should have become a world star. Who knows, hopefully one day soon! He recently had a band called 'Living Loud' recording in Florida and London with Steve Morse, Bob Daisley, Don Airey and Lee Kerslake to name just a few. Almost family! Oh yeah, I was there too. Anyway, I'm getting ahead of myself.

It was in Wollongong that I had the first real confirmation that Bruce and I, after thirty years together, were no longer friends, but just business associates. We were staying in Sydney at The Stamford Plaza Hotel in Double Bay and would commute to the shows in Wollongong and Newcastle from there. It was a few hours drive to Wollongong and we were travelling in vans with the band, brass section, backing vocalists, Aldo Lennard, Bruce and myself. Space was tight, so I had to split everyone up in order to get every arse a seat. There was one spare seat out of all four vans, but Bruce showed up at departure time with a young lady he had acquired that afternoon while shopping. Incredible what you can get browsing in a store! Ah, the tough life of a rock manager.

Well, with a slight reshuffle, I managed to get everyone in and settled, bearing in mind I had to try and avoid having Steve with Ian, Jon or Bruce in the same vehicle as the American boy and his constant guitar practice always annoyed the crap out of the afore mentioned. A tough call this trip but I managed it. The fun really started on the return journey. To be sure I got everyone out when they wanted, I had two of the vans ready right after the encores. However on this night nobody seemed to want to leave except Ian Paice and Jon Lord. I asked them to wait a little, while I mustered other travellers.

Finally I was left with the last two vans for Aldo, Spider, the remaining three band members, Bruce and myself, not forgetting his lady friend who by now was paying him no attention whatsoever. I asked Bruce to be ready to leave when I needed him and he suddenly got really pissed off. Odd, but not unknown. He had probably realised he would be alone that night! I got everyone else to the van and then went back to Bruce and asked him gently if he was now ready as the van was about to leave and that he had to come now or there would not be enough seats for the arses. He reeled around like a wild man and yelled at the top of his voice "The last time I checked, I was the manager of this band and I'll go when I fucking say so". Well, I guess he wasn't going to get laid that night, but I was shaken by his reaction, nevertheless.

He stared at me and I stared at him feeling myself colour up, but praying I wouldn't in front of everyone, crew, band and promoter. "You prick," I muttered under my breath. McCrindle hurriedly pulled me aside, fearing I think, that I was about to do something I might regret. "Does he always treat you like that?" he whispered. "Not really" I truthfully murmured with a deep sigh. "If I'd had been in your position, I would have knocked his fucking head off. There was absolutely no need for that at all". I wandered away and knew that something had inexorably changed for the worse in my life. In hindsight now, McCrindle was probably right, but then, at that moment, I was a different guy. Purple and, yes Bruce, were my family. I had long ago happily foregone any other relationship that could or would damage or threaten my relationship to them. They came first, last and anywhere in the middle. For the first time in thirty years, I felt vulnerable and alone.

Apart from McCrindle, nobody said a word. The atmosphere was oppressive, heavy with my public humiliation. The band and crew shuffled, got in the van and got lost in their thoughts, feigning sleep or giving the old thousand yard stare out of the window as we sped back to the hotel. Over the next few days, I got many words of kind sympathy from those who had witnessed the outburst and from some who'd inevitably been told about it, but no apology from Bruce, then or since.

We left Australia for Kuala Lumpur in Malaysia, where I actually played golf with Charlie and Bruce, but would not have gone had Charlie not been there. I was not really comfortable around Bruce anymore, wondering if the ugly side would make an appearance again. Then to Hong Kong for a one off show at the Coliseum. From there, we flew to Tokyo for three days of rehearsal with nephew Paul, the Shin Nihon Philharmonic and not forgetting Ronnie James Dio. Jon's "Concerto" would be reprised for Japan at the International Forum. The hectic nature of the show in terms of numbers of musicians did not abate. Backwards and forwards, hither and thither, from hotel to rehearsals and back again through the unending Tokyo traffic. Drove me nuts! Paul as ever was in control and as I watched from the wings as my flesh and blood took the band and orchestra through their sweet moves, I could feel the presence of my mam and dad. Proud as punch, each and everyone. After Japan, we flew, for a large cheque no doubt, to Bangalore, India for a meaningless one-off at the Palace Grounds. As we flew home to Florida, I had no idea that I had done my last show with the band.

****

I got home to Apopka late on April 3rd. The next day I contacted the office for the American dates that were due to start on June 2nd. No point in hanging around. If the dates were firm I could start setting up the schedule with Diane Murphy and the 'technicals' with Charlie. All was going well, when, about three weeks into June in the middle of the night at about 3am, I woke up out of a deep dream feeling like Charlie was jumping on my chest. Now Charles is a big lad and this hurt! I was alone in the house and was frankly scared shitless when I realised that Charlie wasn't around, but the pain was. It was just horrible, gasping for breath with this monumental pain in my chest. I just knew what was happening. Instead of calling 911, as I should've, I called my friends Ron and Cindy Strickland who lived about five minutes away. I knew I was in no fit state to drive to them or anywhere. I dragged some clothes on and tried all manner of things to ease the pain, which, by now, was immense. I was sweating like a bull too. I stumbled to the door, yelping in pain and fear; unlocked it and lay slumped against the wall.

Within minutes Ron arrived, took one look, hustled me into his car and broke all speed limits getting me to Emergency. The medical folks in ER took one look at my tortured self and admitted me into intensive care. I stayed there the rest of the night stressed to hell, although whatever they had given me eased the pain. The next morning I got transferred to The Florida Hospital in Altamonte Springs where they had a cardiac unit. My worst fears were realised - this wasn't indigestion! I'd had the big one. They put me on medication and gave me what seemed a million tests. The cause? No question, it was stress. They decided to have a look inside and told me they would insert a probe in my femoral artery and go up into the heart and look around through the magic of chemicals and video. I asked if I could be awake when they did it. Well, how many chances do you get to look inside yourself? The doc thought I was joking and explained that whilst there would be no pain inside as there are no nerve endings there, there would be pain as he cut into the artery. He gave me some really nice stuff that just kept me on the woozy side of unconscious, just enough to know what was what, but not enough to feel any pain. Cool stuff! They injected this dye and I was hooked up to the ying yang, wires everywhere. A hot sensation in the chest and the TV screen lit up showing all my arteries, an awesome roadmap. He pointed out the tiny serration on my heart and said it was really small and with care I would make a full recovery. Certainly there were no blockages and no sign of booze abuse.

The comforting part was that, with a good dose of 'r and r', I would recover fully or so the good doctors said, but I had to avoid the stressful situations that had put me there. Now that was going to be a tad harder to avoid. I knew the band and Bruce had been told of my situation by Doree, who was my everything during that time, visiting every day and bringing me anything I needed, she was and is a true angel. Yet it was three days before Bruce called and disappointingly not one member of the band got in touch. 'Dr' Bruce Payne, true to his inimitable style, diagnosed drink as the root cause of my heart attack, totally trashing the prognosis of my medical team. I was dumbfounded and angry with him. Jesus, the guy allegedly put away twice as much as me sometimes!

His call, to be frank was not to enquire after the health of somebody he had worked very closely with for over thirty years, more a call of discovery as to the immediate, medium and long term prognosis of my ability to carry out my duties. This was business. My stress level went through the roof. He bade farewell assuring me that the band would call "now they knew where I was." Pardon me, they did know, as Charlie had rung them all and no, they didn't call.

I laid there running over and over in my mind what Bruce would do. Plainly, I was fucked in the short term, but I was determined to regain my health in double quick time and get back on the case. Doree was a rock and got me whatever I needed, which really was just a bit of sympathy and plain old fashioned TLC. From the first moment I met her, she had always got stuff sorted, whether it was for me professionally, personally or for anything I needed for the band from apartments, restaurant bookings, limousines right down to Band-Aid and throat lozenges. You needed it; Doree got it, no problem. Ron and Cindy, my neighbours and saviours checked in too on a regular basis. Charlie poked his head round the door one day and seemed nervous and eager to get away. Maybe, he was on a scouting mission for Bruce to see, first hand, how I was or perhaps I was getting paranoid? Maybe Bruce had already given me the Emperor's thumbs down and this particular gladiator was toast. I never asked, perhaps fearful of the reply. We did some innocuous chitchat for about ten minutes then Charlie fled. I'm probably doing him a grave injustice as some folk just hate hospitals and have to get away. I like to think Charlie was one such person.

The hospital decided to give me the ultimate stress test on my heart to be sure I would be fit enough to go home - they told me Ritchie was rejoining the band! No, kidding! I got hooked up to loads of wires and did the old treadmill thingy. Well, I passed with flying colours. Dave Duckworth, my friend and golf buddy came to get me and took me home and for the first time I think in my entire life, I felt dreadfully alone. Well, the cure was to throw myself right back into the fray and get working on plans for the forthcoming US leg of the tour. I beavered away in my office setting up the whole shebang with Charlie and Diane Murphy. I began to feel better and better each day, back in the old swing of things, although I was sleeping badly. Just couldn't get the 'attack' out of my mind, just kept listening to my body like you would listen to the creaking of an old house, imagining that every slight sound out of character was flagging up impending doom.

The tour dates were due to start on June 2nd at the Tweeter Centre, Tinley Park, Illinois and run for a month up to July 8th, finishing in Houston, Texas. We would be accompanied by Ted Nugent and Lynyrd Sknyrd, which sounded like a lot of fun. Then Bruce phoned (once I'd pretty much set it all up) and told me that, in his opinion, I should stay home for this tour and get fully back to health and work on the European tour set to start in August and rejoin the band then. He explained that some guy called Jake would take over my duties temporarily for the US dates. I asked him if everything was okay and he replied that, yes, it was, just carry on as normal. So I did.

As mid summer rolled through Florida, I worked steadily on the European dates with hotels with Lisa at E.T. Travel and the intricacies of the itineraries. The tour would start on August 9th at a festival in Skanderborg, Denmark and run just over a month finishing in Greece. One bright morning my world blew apart when I received this curt email from Bruce:

"IT SEEMS YOU ARE UNDER THE IMPRESSION THAT YOU WILL BE DOING THE EUROPEAN TOUR THAT IS NOT THE CASE AS THE BAND FEEL IT WOULD NOT BE FAIR TO THEM OR YOU TO RISK IT AT THIS TIME"

Very cold, badly written, no punctuation, all in capital letters for emphasis, I guess. Could he not pick up the phone? What was the problem? Had I suddenly become unapproachable? I immediately replied that I had been declared fit to resume work by a proper bona fide medical type doctor, so what was the real reason? His responses were weak, short and very vague. He said maybe next year would be the better option. Maybe? What fucking answer is that? He appeared to be somewhat economical with the truth. I had known him far too long, knew his style of working. So he'd kept me on through the summer to set up the US and European tours and then kissed my arse goodbye. He has just ripped my heart out as surely as any heart attack. The phone calls and emails stopped pretty much overnight from the office.

My world came to an abrupt stop. My nephew, Paul, was my one contact with the band and specifically with Jon Lord who wouldn't say that much other than he was very sorry the way things had worked out and that he would try to get me back. Charlie kept in touch too and said that things were not that brilliant from an organisational point of view and that the crew were not happy. He was very sympathetic and did his best to cheer me up. Then Roger's wife Les called to ask how I was, which was nice and she asked if I'd spoken to her husband. I said, no, he hadn't called. Some months later, however he did, once the European tour had finished and he was back in Connecticut. He apologised on behalf of the band saying they were 'embarrassed' to call me. What the fuck for? I'd been ill, I'd recovered, I was ready and more than able to resume the job I thought I did very well. What was embarrassing about that? How could they not call a close friend, which I was, simply to shoot the breeze, commiserate, and express a desire for me to get back with them? No, another agenda was at work here.

I got more and more depressed and sort solace in the old booze. Now I was miserable and hung-over! That was not fun. Charlie would ring from time to time as did some of the crew who were still around as there was now a culling of 'my lads'. New crew were being brought in and the atmosphere, I was told, not good although the band I'm sure would have been unaware of the growing discontent. I felt a certain irony in that, though why, I couldn't say. I went on binges of the alcohol kind and frankly got sick pretty quick. I was in the depths of despair. Sister Carol like all good sisters flew from England to my aid. That was a huge call as she and David were having health problems of their own which weren't self inflicted like mine. Selfish bastard, me! Basically she gave me a good bollocking! What was done was done. Fine, but what was I to do? I knew absolutely nothing else, yet a voice in my head, probably Eddie, told me to get a grip.

Dick and Di were my next visitors who I was so pleased to see. They were very kind, telling me, what I knew in my heart, that this maybe was meant to be and that I should look forward, not back. Most importantly, I should get back on the wagon, sort out my blood disorder, which had now invaded me caused by, curiously, the heparin that I'd been given to thin my blood. I knew I had to get a job, any job, to regain my self-esteem and of course pay my escalating medical bills, which had hit the giddy height of $250 per month on pills alone. Dick insisted I get back in touch with Thames and work out some sort of severance settlement. After thirty years, he felt, I was due something. I began a dialogue with the office. Eventually, I got a cheque for my last months salary together with a "the final goodbye" payment. It didn't even amount to a thousand dollars for every year I'd put in for them. In the front line of the rock business, there are no contracts of employment, no unions for tour managers. What insurance you have, you find and fund yourself, except for the few years when I got coverage instead of a raise! There's plenty who will queue for your shoes, work cheaper and longer too, just to be 'in the business', just to step out of the mundane into the heady drug that is rock 'n' roll. I should know.

January 2002, Altamonte Springs, Florida. It was the evening around 7pm and I was having a very enjoyable fish supper with Dick and Diane. I had been off the road for seven months. My blood was more or less back to normal and I was more or less off the booze, and drank lots of iced tea. Not quite the same but not quite the same consequences either. Checks and balances. I was cool. We were reminiscing. The crazy days with Vanity Fare, my thirty years with Purple and Ritchie, Dick's crazy times as an agent and promoter and lately in sports television as an event director. Seems sportsmen are just as crazy as rock stars! Di listened. I hope she didn't feel out of it. "Write the book", he said. "Well… only if I remember and you write it down," said I. Deal!

CHAPTER TWENTY-TWO
EPILOGUE

It's now 2007: The book's taken way longer than we thought. Well, hell, so much happened and to be frank it took a lot of remembering. Let me bring you up to date with the various folk who've weaved their way through my life and me through theirs. Charlie is out of the band as is Jan, his wife, who went first, falling out with, err, Bruce and Ian G. Who else. To this day she says no one has given her or Charlie an explanation. Charlie missed one leg of a tour because he needed knee surgery caused by humping too many flight cases too far for too long, probably, but finally aggravated to the extreme by a fall through a hole in a stage. So he too, fell to the axe of Payne. I had knee surgery years ago too - a football injury, which in retrospect, the band should have paid for, as many times I had tried to call off my playing, as the pain really was that bad, but nobody listened. Insurance paid for most of it, insurance that took me years to get from Thames. I remember, prior to the surgery, ringing Bruce more than once and telling him that I couldn't turn out for Ritchie's soccer game because of it. Bruce replied; " It's a good idea that you play and I mean that". A phrase that was repeated to individuals on the crew many times, too. I played, knee went, I paid! Charlie is out now, out again on that rock n' roll road with Heaven And Hell. He has the production managers seat.

Jon Lord left the band in the late summer of 2001 with first a knee injury, but later with, I believe, permanent boredom. Jon still has other musical goals to pursue away from Purple and it would be pointless for him to put them off. No one has a guarantee that there is a tomorrow after all. Don Airey replaced him.

Crew-wise, long servers Rob Hodgkinson and Moray McMillin had left, Mickey Lee Soule had retired, Skoots too. However, at the time of writing, I hear Rob is back. Mickey Lee is now Roger Glover's bass tech. Go figure! I saw Skoots out on a Steve Morse / Dixie Dregs tour a few months back and he swore that was his last one... again!

The band is still touring, round and around and around. The album

'Bananas' and another one, 'Rapture Of The Deep' was released to reasonable acclaim. Dick and his best pal Roger Wilkinson saw them at Plymouth Pavilion in England in the fall of 2004. He said the sound was off, but it was a sell out, so Bruce would be happy. Ian looked odd in a white kaftan affair and bare feet. Ritchie wouldn't have thought that very 'rock 'n' roll'. Dick and Roger left half way through confused why support band Thunder had a great sound, but Purple didn't to the point that it physically hurt.

In hindsight, which is a wonderful thing, I was too nice, too considerate throughout my thirty years at the helm. Should have been way more aggressive as I'd seen other tour managers be, but you are what you are at the end of the day and Bruce would probably have revolted at someone who threatened his position in any way. Will I ever get back with Deep Purple? Not a chance all the while Bruce is there. I don't think he'd have me back if his life depended on it and certainly not now after this little tome.

Ritchie rings me now and again, usually on his birthday, so I can wish him all the best. Love that guy! Jon updates through Paul by email and Paicey keeps in touch spasmodically. Roger, too, keeps a tenuous link open. I never hear from Ian or Bruce.

I flew to Long Beach, California in January 2006 to a convention with my "on again" lady Marlene, and I was reading the local paper to see who was in town and was astonished to see Mr. Blackmore was billed to appear at the Grove in Anaheim doing his "Blackmore's Night" show. We were due to meet Diane Murphy that day too just to say hi and swap 'war stories'. Like me, she's left the business - just too much hassle and Bruce drove her nuts, especially towards the end. At least she had the satisfaction of quitting, like Artie many years before.

We decided that seeing Ritchie was a must do. So the four of us hooked up, Diane, her friend Rita, Marlene and me. I went round the back feeling very much like the fans of old must have felt taking a shot at getting hold of the old me to wangle a back stage pass. It was very surreal! I asked for Jim Manngard, who was Ritchie's guitar and now mandolin / guitar tech. I was told that as it was so close to show time, Jim could not be disturbed having some fifteen assorted stringed instruments to tune prior to our boy hitting the stage. My next shot was Carole, Ritchie and Candy's manager and, of course, mother of Candy. She remembered me! "Was it that long ago" I thought wistfully. She shot out the stage door like

I was royalty and hugged me saying I was often the subject of conversation, in a good way, of course. Really? I asked what the chances were of saying hi to the guy before he went on. "I'm not allowed to go in their dressing room before shows, let alone anyone else" came the reply. "Here's some tickets for the show and come back afterwards and who knows?"

I took that as a less than maybe, but it was worth a try. It was a fair sized venue and he had drawn a really good crowd of which about a third were dressed in renaissance costumes, a requirement for the best seats, I was told. 8:00pm came and went and no Mr. B. "Nothing changes," I whispered. Then came an announcement, "due to the lack of Scotch backstage, there will be a short delay". I nearly wet myself with laughter. Possibly a joke, but one never knows with The Man In Black! Some poor schmuck was now running to the nearest liquor store for some Johnnie Walker Black and wondering if he's got a job on his return. Though knowing the history, it did seem a reasonable request! I had no idea what to expect when he eventually hit the stand, but in all honesty, I was pleasantly surprised.

There were, as I expected, flashes of sheer brilliance, no matter if it was on mandolin or on whatever else he played during a long set. He surprised the hell out of me too when he played 'Child In Time'. His band was good, solid and very definitely 'led' by the man. It consisted of drums, keyboards, bass, violin and two backing vocalists with Candy and Ritchie as the front 'men'. A few desperate fans shouted, "rock 'n' roll". They were totally ignored, not even a glance in their direction. The one thing that struck me immediately was that he was a changed man up there; far removed from the last time I'd seen him back in Helsinki. He looked totally happy and enjoying every note and every positive reaction from the crowd. Before the first encore and, yes, he did them and with a smile, we decided to head out to the parking lot. We couldn't hear the many encores, but were told he did Rainbow and Deep Purple numbers. "Quelle Surprise". We had now hooked up with yet another couple, Iain Hersey and his friend Claudia who worked with Wendy Dio, Ronnie's manager. Iain, as it happens, is a rather talented guitarist and songwriter himself, and great fan of Ritchie's and was very keen to meet the man himself, so I decided a trip to the stage door was in order and was met once again by Carole.

Eventually, and after the customary cooling off period, she led us back stage where we were the only guests! After twelve years, I looked at him and he at me in silence, not knowing quite what to do. His faced cracked into a broad grin and he extended his hand. I grabbed it, and much to his and my surprise I hugged the old bugger and he hugged me tight. Now this ain't the Ritchie I had known. That boy just was not 'huggy feely' whatsoever. This was a new Ritchie, a wonderful Ritchie. "Long time, huh," he said stupidly.

He seemed genuinely pleased to see us all. We talked about all sorts - football, Deep Purple, music in general, old times and new. He told stories just like he used to in the old days after a blinding show, glass of red wine in hand. We had a damn good laugh. He asked Diane if she would come back and do his travel. She pointed out that she'd had quite enough and was done with the music business, but thanks all the same. We eventually said our goodbyes, vowing to keep in touch. I hope so. The next day I flew back home to Florida.

Diane did return to do some hotels for a U.S. run for Purple and then did some hotels for the Heaven And Hell tour, but I think that was enough to remind her of why she'd quit in the first place!

As I sit now on my balcony overlooking Altamonte Springs on a balmy night, the ghosts of the past visit me. Ah, Cozy, dear sweet Cozy. The only musician to stand up to Ritchie and for whom there was a great respect and love. Thanks for scaring the crap out of me on German autobahns! Of course, Ian stood up to Ritchie as well, but no respect then or since. Calling His Blackness a bloody banjo player can't have helped.

And Ian - fighter of everyone's battles and his own demons. Ian is a charismatic leader of men, but only if no one else in the immediate vicinity has a will as strong as his. Then it's war. A bon viveur, lover of life and one who will hopefully never grow up to be a grumpy old man. Rock 'n' roll was just made for him.

Roger - what's not to like, too nice for his own good at times. Just a smashing bloke. I hope all his wives appreciated him and those who did not - shame on you.

Jon - gentleman Jon in every sense. No trouble at any time that I can remember and I cannot recall us ever having a crossword. A superb musician and diamond geezer.

Paicey - asking for the rent, getting his damn satellite receiver fixed in hotel rooms like his life depended on it. Oh yeah, and just the best drummer in the world alongside Cozy.

Ritchie - The madness, the mayhem, the perfection of his skill and the imperfection of his self. That's genius, I guess. Well, he appears totally happy now for probably the first time in his life, so let him be. Those who crave his past, and let him pursue his future - he owes you nothing.

Steve - What can I say? A superbly talented guitarist, pilot extraordinaire and pizza lover. It was a pleasure to have worked with you.

Joe Satriani - Another ace of a man. Sincere, honest and one hell of a guitarist, too.

Paul Mann, my talented nephew - still working with Jon on projects and currently conducting several large well-known symphony orchestras across the globe. I'm immensely smug, yes I am!

Sister Carol and David - retired now and living quietly in Cornwall, England. Thanks for being there.

Nephew Stephen and wife Marianne, Mara and wee Angus Mann, My Mam and Dad - Still watching over me, I know. I owe them everything.

David Coverdale - A colossal talent, although we did not know it at the time. Surprised me, surprised you and probably surprised himself too.

And so to Bruce - No slagging, really. It wasn't personal, I know - just business. A great manager and without whom you fans would not have had thirty years of Deep Purple and Rainbow. Be very grateful. Tough? Sure he is. An asshole? No more than any other good rock 'n' roll manager - goes with the territory. If you're not, the business will crush ya! Do I bear a grudge? Actually no, not really, not now. Leaving may well have saved my life as Dick often points out. The manner of my leaving could have been better and the guys could have placed a call to the hospital, or even right after the split, but you cannot have everything you want in life.

I have my health back and a little, but not enough, put away. I am happy. The itch to hit the road again comes and goes and comes again. I suppose it could happen if the right thing came along now. I often wonder where I would be now, had I taken any of the many offers that were made to me along the way to jump ship, but I thought that loyalty would be the way to go, but we can all make mistakes!

The fans - Through out my life as a tour manager, to what I consider were two of the greatest rock bands ever, I did go to great lengths to make everybody comfortable backstage including band member's families and people from fan clubs. I prided myself on being able to coordinate the backstage areas, get all the shit together, and make it as comfortable for the band as well as everybody else. I always tried to accommodate as many people as possible without it getting totally out of control. People who I thought deserved to be backstage, who I'd seen at hundreds of shows, who paid a fortune for tickets over the years, I would treat to back stage soirees. I'd see them waiting outside for autographs and I would bring them in; they deserved it for their loyalty. These would be fans that would drive hundreds of miles and sleep in their cars outside venues. I don't think the two bands under my care ever appreciated how complicated it was pulling all that together. I always took care of fan clubs, which I believed was very important. The Swedish club, the German fan clubs and of course, Perfect Strangers of Finland with dear, sweet Sirpa Hammar. They were all so great, so polite and so kind in return for just the simplest things like an autograph. Then there was the U.S fan club, who all came together once at Hartford, Connecticut, as well as a few other venues, where I had to make room for these loyal, long time warriors, including my friends Dana McDermott, and Michael Oakman.

As previously mentioned, Cliff and Kathy Massey and their great friends, including Axel Dauer from Germany, who spent almost all of their life savings following Deep Purple around the world and Cliff was a Jaguar mechanic, but also a terrific drummer who needs to catch a break! They planned their vacation each year around the bands itinerary. Quite naturally I wouldn't let them buy a ticket for the show as they had taken all that trouble to come and see the band. He had a big heart and was unbelievably kind and I know overstepped his finances in following his band.

He even showed up in Montreux at the Jazz Festival staying at the crew hotel. That was not cheap. He knew how to handle himself backstage, never straying into the wrong areas and he wasn't alone. Fans are so important. Mind you there are some who do overstep the mark, but I'll not mention names here. To all those hundreds I haven't mentioned, please forgive me, but you all know who you are and how important you are.

Fans of Deep Purple and Rainbow - I salute you.

ACKNOWLEDGMENTS

T hanks and to those… etc. Dick, Di, Malcolm and the gang for the constant support and push to do this project.

First and foremost, to every crew member who I ever worked with, all of whom worked their asses off and often thanklessly for less than just rewards.

Raymond D'Addario, Charlie and Jan Lewis. Mickey Lee Soule. Scoots Lyndon. Scott Porterfield. Moray McMillin. Rob Hodgkinson. Matt Schieferstein. Louis Ball. Willie Fyffe and all those who came and went. To Ian Broad and Heather.

To every fan who ever came along, some who lived out of their cars and spent their entire vacation time following the bands across several countries to catch as many shows as possible. Especially, Cliff, Kathy and Axel.

To all the fan clubs, often overlooked, yet so important, and particularly, PSOF, The Perfect Strangers of Finland, who, with their lovely Sirpa Hammar, were the most polite and comfortable of all to work with.

Tony Mazzucchi. "Sarge" to those close, who anchored the lighting crew for most of the Rainbow years. "There we were, surrounded" preceded his every story.

To all the studios and recording units, especially Greg Rike Productions, Greg, my inspiration when I ever felt sorry for myself, Wally, Brian and of course Doree and Greg Rice and their kids. Le Mobile and Guy Charboneau; The Rolling Stones Mobile, Jethro Tull's Mobile.

The chateaus, castles, private homes we abused and to all their owners who trusted them to our care. To Diane Murphy, our never sleeping travel manager who pulled off the most amazing feats. E.T. Travel and Lisa Ligouri. My dear friends Alfredo De Iluiis, Christer Lorichs and Nathalie. John Gould and Trish… never give up with "Rusty."

John Murphy, Artie Hoar, Rob Fodder, Jim Manngard, Cookie

Crawford, Doogie White, Rick Taylor, Nick Cua, Chris Patterson, Tim Hook, Neil Warnock and Claire Stone at The Agency; Perri Entertainment for all our tour passes, and to Tina at Knowhere for our itineraries. Anthill Trading, George Grater.

Our record companies and their reps; Our promoters, especially, Mr. Udo and his staff at Udo Artists, Tack Takahashi. Aldo Lennard, Australia. MAMA Concerts, Germany.

Our trucking and bus companies across the globe, Trans Am, Rock-It Cargo, Florida Coach Company, Jörg Phillip and Beat The Street, Wharfdale, LSD. Electrotec.

Our Caterers, who kept us alive: Eat To The Beat. Special thanks to the following people: David, Carol, Paul and Stephen, Geoff Tate, Billy Borthwick, Laurence Sinclair and my pals from school.

Drew Thompson and Nikki, Jimmy and Jane Barnes and his lovely kids, Bob Daisley, Lee Kerslake, and very special thanks to Mick Box for his help over the years. Joe Satriani and BGM. Mick Brigden and Mike Manning.

Bruce Payne, Denise, Barbara Fucigna, Angela Malizia, Betty Hance and Thames Talent, Frank Solomon, Phil Banfield, Lois James, Wendy Dio and of course, Ronnie Dio. Cozy Powell, Bobby Rondinelli, Jimmy Bain, Tony Carey, Don Airey, David Stone, David Rosenthal. George and Olivia Harrison, Les Glover, Jackie Paice, Vicky Lord, Sara Lord, Joe Brown, Sam Brown, Pam Darlak and Tracy. Michael Oakman, Storck Petersen and Pat and their kids for amazing support through the years.
John Harrell and Koh from Burrn Magazine.

To St. Andrews Tavern, John, Dot, Nick, Tom and Jackie and of course, previous owners Sue and Bob Zeng. All the soccer teams and players that allowed me to make a fool of myself among such excellent talent. Ron, Cindy, Peter, Stella and "The Sunday Club." Dave Duckworth and Neil McCormick and lately, Rick Vincent and all those involved for their thankless efforts getting our weekly golf sessions together for the BAGS Tour.

The list could go on forever, but I have to stop somewhere. My sincere apologies to those whom I may have overlooked or who I simply forgot to mention.

I thank you all.

ABOUT THE AUTHORS

Colin Hart was born 5th March 1947 in South Shields, County Durham.   After leaving school he enrolled at the Marine & Technical College studying architectural drawing and then secured a job in the Engineers Department at the Town Hall: "A proper civil servant in a proper nice suit" is how he describes it. In the evenings he helped bands by doing a spot of "gear-humping" and soon became roadie for local band Toby Twirl. He then roadied for Vanity Fare, and by 1971 got a "temporary" crew job with Matthew's Southern Comfort, which is where his fortunes were soon to change when he joined the payroll of Deep Purple.

By 1973 he had become the band's tour manager but left two years later following Ritchie Blackmore's departure. He continued in his role of tour manager for Blackmore's band Rainbow.   In 1984, with Blackmore (and then fellow Rainbow member, Roger Glover) joining the reformed Deep Purple Colin was once again Purple's tour manager until his departure in 2001.

Colin moved to America in the mid seventies, initially with Rainbow; firstly to California, and then Florida where he currently resides.

Dick Allix, is Hart's long-standing friend and former drummer with Vanity Fare who had two top ten hits in 1969 with 'Early In The Morning' and 'Hitchin' A Ride'. Both achieved Gold status in America where the band had its greatest success. After his stint with the band Dick became a trainee publisher working alongside Sir George Martin, then became a booking agent running tours for the likes of Marvin Gaye before tour managing Heatwave and AC/DC. He currently works in TV production and lives in East Yorkshire with his wife Diane.

Also available from Wymer Publishing

WP
WYMER
PUBLISHING

MAGAZINES

More Black than Purple
Established in 1996 this is the leading Ritchie Blackmore magazine, documenting the Man In Black's exploits with Rainbow, Deep Purple & Blackmore's Night.
ISSN 1478-2499 More info at: www.moreblackthanpurple.co.uk

Autumn Leaves
The official magazine of Mostly Autumn, established in 2000. This A4 magazine published twice a year is the official spokespiece for York's finest band, and arguably one of the greatest British bands to have emerged over the past decade.
*I*SSN: 1473-7817 More info at: www.autumn-leaves.co.uk

BOOKS

Rock Landmark's: Rainbow's Long Live Rock 'n' Roll (Jerry Bloom)
This book, the first in a series on landmark albums is an in-depth look at the classic Rainbow album 'Long Live Rock 'n' Roll'. The full story behind the making of the album; track by track analysis, recollections by the band and crew, all combined in a full colour CD size book designed to sit on your CD shelf alongside the album as its perfect companion.
ISBN 978-0-9557542-2-7
Paperback 125x140mm, 64pp (8 x colour). **£7.99**

Sketches Of Hackett - The authorised Steve Hackett biography (Alan Hewitt)
The first full and authorised biography of former Genesis *guitarist Steve Hackett. Written by Alan Hewitt, a recognised authority on* Genesis, *whose previous writings include the critically acclaimed* Genesis Revisited. *Hewitt is also editor of the* Genesis *web fanzine* The Waiting Room.
ISBN: 978-0-9557542-3-4 plus 90 minute DVD
Hardback, 234 x 156 mm, 320pp (16 colour). **£24.95**

Zappa The Hard Way (Andrew Greenaway)
Documenting Zappa's last tour. If you think touring can be fun, think again! Yes there were groupies and the usual paraphernalia associated with rock 'n' roll, but there was also bitterness and skulduggery on a scale that no one could imagine. Greenaway has interviewed the surviving band members and others associated with the tour to unravel the goings on behind the scenes that drove Zappa to call a halt to proceedings, despite the huge personal financial losses.
Foreword by Candy Zappa.
ISBN: 978-0-9557542-4-1 Deluxe slipcase
Hardback, 234 x 156 mm, 224pp, (32 colour (74 images). **£40**

Rock Landmark's: Judas Priest's British Steel (Neil Daniels)
The second in our series of landmark albums looks at the sixth album by the British heavy metal band Judas Priest, recorded at Tittenhurst Park, home of former Beatle John Lennon. It is arguably the album that really defined heavy metal and is regarded as the band's seminal recording.
Written and researched by respected Judas Priest authority Neil Daniels, author of the first full Judas Priest biography, Defenders Of The Faith.
Foreword by Ron "Bumblefoot" Thal
ISBN 978-0-9557542-6-5
Paperback, 125x140mm, 72pp, including 17 x b/w images. **£4.99**

Zermattitis: A Musician's Guide To Going Downhill Fast (Tony Ashton)
Written in 1991, Tony Ashton's incredible tales of his career with Ashton Gardner & Dyke, Paice Ashton & Lord, bankruptcy, skiing in Zermatt, Switzerland and many other adventures within the heady world of the music business are documented in this hilarious roller coaster of a ride. His writings have laid unpublished for twenty years, but in conjunction with Tony's wife this wonderful and unbelievably amusing story will now finally see the light of day. With a delightful and moving foreword from his dear friend Jon Lord, this is truly the last word from a man who sadly died in 2001, but whose life enriched so many. Although Tony wasn't a household name, within the entertainment world his numerous friends read like a who's who, including Dave Gilmour, John Entwistle and Ewan McGregor .
Foreword by Jon Lord
ISBN: 978-0-9557542-9-6
Hardback, 234 x 156 mm, 208pp (Limited edition with DVD)*
*The DVD contains previously unreleased Ashton Gardner & Dyke material including a live performance from the Gala Rose of Montreux in 1970; a rare promo film, and a performance of their biggest hit 'The Resurrection Shuffle'. The DVD also includes Tony's song 'Big Freedom Dance' written about John Lennon and filmed at Air Studios by TV presenter Chris Evans.

Forthcoming:

Norfolk Rebels: Fire In The Veins (Joanna Lehmann-Hackett)
Stories of Norfolk's rebels, from Boudicea to modern day rebels. Many of them linked and weaved into the vibrant tapestry of rebellion that is our inheritance. With a foreword by one of Norfolk's most well-known modern day rebels Keith Skipper, and another, beautifully written by Joanna's husband, former Genesis guitarist Steve Hackett, *this book depicts the many fine men and women of Norfolk who through the centuries have defended their ways, as only Norfolk people can.*

Turn it On Again: Genesis Live Guide 1976-2007 (Alan Hewitt)
From the Trick Of The Tail *Tour through to the 2007 reunion. Recognised* Genesis *authority Alan Hewitt details the hundreds of rare recordings the document* Genesis *in it's natural environment- the stage. Fully illustrated throughout this is an essential guide to* Genesis *live recordings from their most commercially successful period.*

All titles can be ordered online at our webstore- www.wymeruk.co.uk/Store
or from any decent retailer by quoting the relevant ISBN.

The Good Old Boys - Live At The Deep Purple Convention

Catalogue No: TSA1001. Released 13th July 2009

The Good Old Boys is: Nick Simper (Deep Purple); Richard Hudson (The Strawbs); Pete Parks (Warhorse); Simon Bishop (Renaissance) & Alan Barratt (Jo Jo Gunne).

Recorded live 3rd May 2008 at the Deep Purple Convention to celebrate the 40th Anniversary of the formation of Deep Purple. A unique performance that showcases their rock 'n' roll roots and musicianship. This 13-track CD includes a blistering version of Hush, the song that launched Deep Purple all those years ago. It also comes with a 12-page booklet with full band history, behind the scenes stories and previously unpublished photos from the actual performance and soundcheck.

Tracks: I'm Ready / A Fool For Your Stockings / My Way / Shakey Ground / Sleepwalk / Twenty Flight Rock / Somebody To Love / Don't Worry Baby / C'mon Everybody / Shakin' All Over / Oh Well / Hush / All My Rowdy Friends Are Comin' Over Tonight //

Nick Simper & Nasty Habits - The Deep Purple MKI Songbook

Catalogue No: TSA1002. Released: 16th August 2010

The Deep Purple MKI Songbook is up to date re-workings of Deep Purple songs from the first three albums performed by original Purple bassist Nick Simper with Austrian band, Nasty Habits. Powerful and hard-hitting arrangements of Deep Purple songs that have largely been over-looked since Deep Purple first had success in America with these songs. This initial release is a special limited edition (1,000 copies only) enhanced CD with bonus video footage including a Nick Simper interview.

Reissued as standard CD without video, September 19, 2011 (TSA1004)

Tracks: And The Address / The Painter / Mandrake Root / Emmaretta / Chasing Shadows / Lalena / Wring That Neck / The Bird Has Flown / Why Didn't Rosemary / Kentucky Woman / Hush //

Liam Davison - A Treasure Of Well-Set Jewels

Catalogue No: TSA1003. Released: 21st March 2011

The debut solo album by Mostly Autumn guitarist Liam Davison is a cornucopia of aural delights. Guests include fellow Mostly Autumn band mates, Heather Findlay, Anne-Marie Helder, Iain Jennings and Gavin Griffiths plus Paul Teasdale (Breathing Space) and Simon Waggott. The first edition strictly limited to 1,000 copies, is an enhanced CD with bonus tracks and video footage.

Tracks: Ride The Seventh Wave / The Way We Were / Emerald Eternity / Eternally Yours / In To The Setting Sun / Once In A Lifetime / Heading Home / Picture Postcard / Bonus tracks: A Moment Of Silence / Immortalized // Bonus video: Liam's Treasure //

Amy Leeder - Fisticuffs With Cupid

Catalogue No: TSA1005. To be released: Late 2011

With this album we have broken with our own policy of only releasing works by established artists. Just 18, Amy has been writing songs since she was 14 and we believe she is destined for stardom. The maturity in her songs belie her age. Songs such as Chavs Of 2023 and Rough Around The Edges will resonate with people of all ages.

All titles can be ordered online at our webstore- www.wymeruk.co.uk/Store or from any decent retailer. Also visit Wymer Records at http://records.wymeruk.co.uk